A POLITICAL SOCIOLOGY OF EDUCATION POLICY

Helen M. Gunter

P

First published in Great Britain in 2024 by

Policy Press, an imprint of
Bristol University Press
University of Bristol
1-9 Old Park Hill
Bristol
BS2 8BB
UK
t: +44 (0)117 374 6645
e: bup-info@bristol.ac.uk

Details of international sales and distribution partners are available at
policy.bristoluniversitypress.co.uk

© Bristol University Press 2024

British Library Cataloguing in Publication Data
A catalogue record for this book is available from the British Library

ISBN 978-1-4473-6333-0 hardcover
ISBN 978-1-4473-6334-7 paperback
ISBN 978-1-4473-6335-4 ePub
ISBN 978-1-4473-6336-1 ePdf

The right of Helen M. Gunter to be identified as author of this work has been asserted by her in accordance with the Copyright, Designs and Patents Act 1988.

All rights reserved: no part of this publication may be reproduced, stored in a retrieval system, or transmitted in any form or by any means, electronic, mechanical, photocopying, recording, or otherwise without the prior permission of Bristol University Press.

Every reasonable effort has been made to obtain permission to reproduce copyrighted material. If, however, anyone knows of an oversight, please contact the publisher.

The statements and opinions contained within this publication are solely those of the author and not of the University of Bristol or Bristol University Press. The University of Bristol and Bristol University Press disclaim responsibility for any injury to persons or property resulting from any material published in this publication.

Bristol University Press and Policy Press work to counter discrimination on
grounds of gender, race, disability, age and sexuality.

Cover design: Hayes Design and Advertising
Front cover image: Alamy/vectorjuice

Contents

List of tables and boxes iv
List of abbreviations v
About the author vii
Preface viii

1 Introduction: Education reform claimocracy 1

PART I A political sociology of education policy
2 Modernising education 19
3 Governing by knowledge production 35
4 Policy mortality 51

PART II A political sociology of education policy in action
5 Vantage points 69
6 Viewpoints 82
7 Regimes of practice 97
8 Exchange relationships 113
9 Critical education policy studies 128

10 Conclusion: Intellectual activism 145

Appendix 162
References 165
Index 200

List of tables and boxes

Tables

2.1	Modernisation trends	24
2.2	Modernisation trends in education policy	30
6.1	Knowledge production and viewpoints	84
7.1	Knowledge production and regimes of practice	98
8.1	Knowledge production and contractual exchange relationships	115
8.2	Change and UK education policy for schools in England	120
9.1	Criticality in education policy research	130

Box

1.1	Extract from *Teachers: meeting the challenge of change*	4

List of abbreviations

BA	British Academy
BECTA	British Educational Communications and Technology Agency
BERA	British Educational Research Association
BTEC	Business and Technology Education Council
CEO	Chief Executive Officer
CEPS	Critical Education Policy Studies
CfBT	Centre for British Teachers
CMT	Change Management Team
CoE	Church of England
CPR	Conservative Privatisation Regime
CST	Confederation of School Trusts
CTC	City Technology College
DCSF	Department for Children Schools and Families
DfE	Department for Education
DfEE	Department for Education and Employment
DfES	Department for Education and Skills
EA	Educational Administration
EEIR	Educational Effectiveness and Improvement Research
EERA	European Educational Research Association
EMAL	Educational Management, Administration, and Leadership
EPKP	Education Policy Knowledgeable Polity
ERA	Education Reform Act (1988)
ERC	Education Reform Claimocracy
ESRC	Economic and Social Research Council
EU	European Union
EWB	Electronic Whiteboard
FE	Further Education
GCSE	General Certificate in Secondary Education
GMS	Grant Maintained Status
HR	Human Resources
ICT	Information and Communications Technology
IQ	Intelligence Quotient
KHS	Kingswood High School
KPEL	Knowledge Production in Educational Leadership Project
LA	Local Authority
LEA	Local Education Authority
LE	Life Expectancy
LMS	Local Management of Schools
MBA	Master in Business Administration
MAT	Multi-Academy Trust

MCA	Metropolitan City Academy
MP	Member of Parliament
NCLSCS	National College for Leadership of Schools and Children's Services
NCSL	National College for School Leadership
NCTL	National College for Teaching and Leadership
NDPB	Non-Departmental Public Body
NHS	National Health Service
NLPR	New Labour Performance Regime
NPQH	National Professional Qualification for Headship
NRT	National Remodelling Team
NUT	National Union of Teachers
OBON	One Britain One Nation
OECD	Organisation for Economic Co-operation and Development
Ofsted	Office for Standards in Education
PEP	Policy Entrepreneurs and Popularisers
PM	Prime Minister
PRR	Policy Research Regime
PS	Policy Sociology
PwC	PricewaterhouseCoopers
RC	Roman Catholic
REF	Research Excellence Framework
RSC	Regional Schools Commissioner
SEF	Self-Evaluation Framework
SES	Socio-Economic Status
SEU	Standards and Effectiveness Unit
SIP	School Improvement Plan/Partner
SLSR	School Leadership Satellite Regime
SPSO	Distributed Leadership and the Social Practices of School Organisation in England Project
SRP	Students as Researchers Project
SSAT	Specialist Schools and Academies Trust
TA	Teacher/Teaching Assistant
TDA	Training and Development Agency for Schools
TF	Teach First
TINA	There Is No Alternative
TMCC	teachers: meeting the challenge of change
TPSF	Thinking Politically-Sociologically Framework
TSWPP	Transforming the School Workforce Pathfinder Project
TTA	Teacher Training Agency
UK	United Kingdom
US	United States
UTC	University Technical Colleges
WAMG	Workforce Agreement Monitoring Group

About the author

Helen M. Gunter is Professor Emerita in The Manchester Institute of Education, University of Manchester, UK. She is a Fellow of the Academy of Social Sciences, and recipient of the BELMAS Distinguished Service Award 2016. Her research focuses on the political sociology of education policy and knowledge production in the field of school leadership. Her most recent books are: *Consultants and Consultancy: The Case of Education*, coauthored with C. Mills, 2017, published by Springer; *The Politics of Public Education: Reform Ideas and Issues*, 2018, published by Policy Press; *Policy Consultancy in Comparative Perspective: Patterns, Nuances and Implications for the Contractor State*, coauthored with C. van den Berg, M. Howlett, M. Howard, A. Migone, and F. Pemer, 2020, published by Cambridge University Press; and *Hannah Arendt on Educational Thinking and Practice in Dark Times: Education for a World in Crisis*, co-edited with W. Veck, 2020, published by Bloomsbury.

Preface

Cemeteries across England are full of people who have died of cancer, but what goes unrecognised are the many graves of those who never had the chance to find a cure for cancer. I can say this with confidence because my generation experienced both the denial of aspirations and capability to make a difference, but also benefitted from the common school that enabled investment in all children as worthy of an education. And yet I am now witnessing the intensification of segregation in education services, knowing that if I were of school age I would not have the opportunities that the abolition of the 11+ and the creation of comprehensive education provided. Having failed the 11+, and so officially categorised as incapable of benefitting from an academic education, I have just retired as a professor where my world was and remains within academia. This is why when I visit my parent's grave, I look at the names on the other gravestones and realise that there are those who have not been fortunate to live at the time that I have, and there are those who would recognise how the stereotyping of bodies that disadvantaged them remains integral to unfolding education policy. There is an irony in these observations that goes beyond the matter of those who did not get the opportunities that I have had. Segregated services based on eugenics not only impacts negatively on those who are rendered inferior and unworthy of an education, but also on those who seemingly gain from being identified as having superior bodies. Cemeteries across England are full of people who may not have died of cancer if only they had allowed other people's children to have the same educational opportunities as their own.

This book is the third instalment in a trilogy of critical education policy books where I have pioneered political and sociological thinking for the field (Gunter 2012, 2018). In 2012 I used Bourdieu's thinking tools to generate understandings and explanations of how and why leaders, leading and leadership came to dominate UK government policy for reforms to educational services; and in 2018 I used Arendtian scholarship to investigate the meaning and practices of the politics of education policy in the dismantling of public education services. This third book makes an empirical and conceptual contribution to critical education policy studies through interplaying insights from both Arendt and Bourdieu's thinking in order to examine the endurance and impact of eugenics and segregated education services. I have re-examined evidence from EPKP projects undertaken over a number of decades (Appendix), where I have taken inspiration from Roscoe's (2020) analysis of the importance of researcher thoughtfulness and reflexivity not only in regard to data, but also in relation to the contextual issues in which a researcher is located. He goes on to say that Arendt and Bourdieu 'saw teaching everyone how to think, not just what to think, as the key to improving society and promoting justice' and so I adopt intellectual activism as a key research strategy. In addition, he poses an issue for all researchers who set out to think with Arendt and Bourdieu: 'what are the issues their lines of thinking bring to light as most important today?' (NP) This book sets out to address this question in education policy by identifying the core issue of the survival and revival of segregated education services in England.

I have been able to engage with such thoughtfulness and reflexivity through completing a Doctorate in Social Science at the University of Manchester, and material in Chapters 9 and 10 in particular are connected to the thesis (Gunter 2020a). I am deeply indebted to a range of people who supported me, particularly to Professor Erica Burman who has acted as my advisor, and her insights and support have been invaluable. I would also like to thank Professor Steve Courtney, Professor Steve Jones, and Professor Tanya Fitzgerald for providing excellent feedback on the doctoral draft. Thank you to Professor Carlo Raffo for acting as Independent Chair and to my two external examiners.

I have been sustained over the years by a range of colleagues and doctoral students, and those who have visited us at Manchester. Thank you to all past and current members of the Critical Education Policy research group at Manchester. Huge thanks for personal and professional friendship and collegiality to Professor Tanya Fitzgerald at University of Western Australia, to Professor Jorunn Møller and colleagues at the University of Oslo, and to members of the European Leading Democratic and Democratic Schools (LE@DS) network.

Thank you to Colin Mills who read and provided excellent feedback on the full draft of the book. I take full responsibility for the text.

I have much to be thankful for, and without Barry nothing would be worthwhile or make sense. We have been married for 40 years, and I look forward to another 40 years…

1
Introduction: Education reform claimocracy

Introduction

In 2019, the UK media reported the case of a housing development in London where a communal recreational area had been provided but the children living in rented social housing were prevented from accessing it and playing with the children of homeowners (Grant and Michael 2019). This is one of an accumulation of cases of proactive segregation and speaks to 'poor doors' architecture, whereby housing developers in London construct different entrances into an apartment building for those who rent and those who own, along with different postal delivery and waste disposal services (Osborne 2014, Wall and Osborne 2018). Permission to build currently requires plans for affordable housing, but it seems that housing developers operate on the basis that purchasers of high value properties in the same complex do not want to mix with such people. This is one example of how property rights are used to inscribe entitlements to certain bodies, and how sectarian divides are constructed and secured based on notions of superiority of one type of human over another inferior type. While communal mixing with the sharing of common services has increased in the UK, a worrying feature is that 'segregation is increasing in a number of very particular respects in the UK, especially the growing isolation of the White majority from minorities in urban zones' (Kaufmann and Cantle 2016: NP).

The segregation that is experienced by children who are enabled or prevented from living and playing together is also evident in how they access and benefit from education services. Proactive legal separation is a sustained education policy strategy of successive UK governments in England and across the globe. For example, children are divided on the basis of school place provider and parental choice into fee charging and taxpayer provided schools, and/or boys' and girls' schools, and/or faith or secular schools, and/or academic and vocational schools (Gunter 2020b). In addition, segregation is co-produced through how structural advantage and disadvantage operate in everyday decisions, practices, and market exchanges (van Zanten et al 2015), and while it may be unlawful to discriminate on the basis of race, evidence shows it is a resilient feature (Coughlan 2015; Meatto 2019). Certain bodies are, in Galton's (1874) terms, identified as 'undesirables' (Kevles 1999), and thus in Gramscian (1971) terms, rendered 'subaltern'.

While education debates and policy goals are inflected with notions of aspiration and achievement, it is the case that education reforms actually set out to waste the economic, political and cultural potential of citizens through exclusionary policies where in order for the few to succeed, the majority of children, families, and communities, are required to experience either the fear or actuality of failure. A historically located *claimocracy* of views and practices proclaims the vitality of private freedoms to provide and gain access to a 'good school place', where parental consumer choice operates in the interests of oligarchic occupiers of the state who exercise sovereign power through public policy. Governing is used to legitimise and authorise approved-of intelligent knowledge production where the language of new and aspirational change is used to mask the visceral reality of segregation based on *eugenicist populism*. Parents and children are enabled to know and accept their place in the natural order of things, where the educability of a child is decided before birth and is evident in ordinary categories regarding who is 'bright' and 'deserving' of the best education, and who is not.

The core issue that this book confronts is how to describe, understand and explain the endurance of segregated education through undertaking a political sociology of the location and exercise of power in education policy scoping, decision-making, and enactment. I do this by presenting data and analysis from the *Education Policy Knowledgeable Polity* (EPKP) projects as a novel approach to restoring government and governing to the study of education policy. I think about the data using both Arendtian and Bourdieusian scholarship, where the examination of power as both political and sociological is vital for investigating *oligarchic club sovereignty* by policy actors who use the occupation of the state to variously produce, package, publicise, practice, and perform an *Education Reform Claimocracy* (ERC). I conceptualise the ERC as a form of *policy violence*, as an absence of relational political and social power, where I examine who was and is involved, and why, and how they have used and benefited from knowledge production as a means of codifying and delivering an unmodern modernised education system. While I draw primarily on data from UK government education policy for the school sector in England, I present a framework of analysis that has relatability to other policy areas in the UK, and globally.

Claimocracy

Claimocracy, or rule by assertion, continues to be constructed and enacted for, about, and within education policy. An education reform claimocracy demands change based on a crisis framed according to a particular version of history that makes targeted accusations (failing teachers, failing schools), and supplies credible solutions (autonomous schools, corporate leadership) that are a complex confection of nostalgia and visions of 'better' and 'new' types of private provision and access to that provision. The transformation imperative and what it means for schools as organisations and for the profession is imagined, codified, and communicated in speeches, manifestos, tweets, and government documentation (for example, Legislation; White Papers that lead to legislation; and Green Papers that outline a policy consultation), and supported and developed through traditional and social media, commissioned evaluation projects, and by training programmes and advocacy consultancy. A set of pessimistic narratives are constructed to justify a 'what needs to be done' agenda with optimistic solutions brimming with certainties, where the way out of the crisis cannot be found within the what is regarded as the 'monolithic' public system provided for the majority of families.

A number of thematic proclamations made in oral and written texts and associated practices can be identified in the ERC for education in England over the past 50 years: first, that public service education is failing because it is public (owned, funded, and based on open access by, for, and about the public), where the involvement of the state gives unaccountable power to local politicians, professionals and bureaucrats who conspire to use public processes and funds for their own gain; second, that education is a private good and so the provision of school places in a diverse market and the exercise of consumer choice will efficiently and effectively meet parental requirements for their children; and third, the shift from parents dependent on the state to active traders and deal-makers in the market will revitalise educational services to improve and be more effective, and so those who are employed to provide educational services will be incentivised to supply what is demanded rather than teaching children what parents do not want them to know and what employers and the economy do not require. The significant achievement of the ERC is to proclaim a focus on education but actually shift attention towards the organisational conditions in which education is provided and accessed. The talk may be about children, but in reality, the focus is on the protection, enhancement, and legitimacy of hierarchy through organisational and systemic arrangements.

For example, the 1988 Education Reform Act (ERA) saw the introduction of Local Management of Schools (LMS) based on delegating financial decision-making to the school as a business, and this required the profession to adopt 'a positive attitude from the head, staff, and governing body' to the idea and reality of management (Coopers and Lybrand 1988: 6). In 1997 New Labour took office and built on this legacy by setting out the requirements for 'the highest qualities of leadership and management from headteachers' because 'good heads can transform a school; poor heads can block progress and achievement' (DfEE 1997: 46). New Labour adjusted the ERC to accept both public and private sectors as the source of potential solutions to the crisis, where the exercise of private choice based on outcome data in a diverse market would improve quality (PM and Minister for the Cabinet

> **Box 1.1 Extract from *Teachers: meeting the challenge of change***
> All the evidence shows that heads are the key to a school's success. All schools need a leader who creates a sense of purpose and direction, sets high expectations of staff and pupils, focuses on improving teaching and learning, monitors performance and motivates the staff to give of their best. The best heads are as good at leadership as the best leaders in any other sector, including business. The challenge is to create the rewards, training and support to attract, retain and develop many more heads of this calibre.
>
> (DfEE 1998: 22)

Office 1999; Barber 2007b). Educational professionals had to become more responsive to users, and so the Green Paper, *teachers: meeting the challenge of change* (TMCC) (DfEE 1998), articulated how and why headteachers had to convert into certificated school leaders. The ERC is illustrated by Box 1.1.

The extract in Box 1.1 shows, first, the headteacher as leader is separated from and then elevated above 'staff and pupils'; second, a causal relationship is established between the person as head, their leadership and outcome indicators of success; third, the headteacher as leader is defined in regard to organisational unity and performance, with the adoption of transformational forms of leading and leadership; fourth, school leader status is awarded equivalence to stratified notions of the corporate best; and fifth, the problem for policy to resolve is talent spotting, training, and accreditation. These declarations are justified in regard to the school being able to secure and demonstrate 'success', based on evidence that validates how everyone knows what this 'success' looks and feels like. The meaning of 'success' is recognition and acclaim through the objective measurement of student outcome data, and when interplayed with other reforms such as the privatised provision and governing of diversified and specialist school places, then school leaders lead schools where the focus is on marketised inclusion and exclusion.

This leader centric and hierarchical approach stressed by the ERC was and remains empirically dubious, but it illustrates how rationality and coherence are used within a 'language of consensus' (Fairclough 2000: 160) in order to build a commitment to a 'hegemonic' truth in ways that are designed to prevent debate (Gramsci 1971). Policy texts often show that private opinions and experiences are presented in public as facts, where urgent practicalities determine how those facts are made legible and convincing. While reality may not live up to the actual proclamations this does not seem to matter, it is the use and recognition of articulate reasoning that make change mythologies attractive: first, the manipulative use of state *simplifications* (Scott 1998) (often called spin and soundbites) in order to generate acceptance of major public policy by bullet points and domesticated analogies (for example, the case for austerity from 2010 equated the national debt to a 'maxed out credit card', Wren-Lewis 2018: 2); second, the promotion of *fictions* that create aspirations for everyone for the good life while denying access to the resources necessary to achieve this (for example, social mobility and meritocracy are used to support parental aspirations while maintaining eugenicist stereotyping that prevents their realisation); third, the employment of *mimicry* whereby families without resources to compete in the market place are incentivised to impersonate those who can choose, not least by adopting make-overs and ventriloquising the simplifications and fictions (for example, exercising choice for domestic services such as gas and electricity as a simulation of liberty that can be transferred to choosing a school place).

Simplifications, fictions, and mimicry work together to produce a language for attitudinal certainties, whereby selecting children and selective schools are talked about but segregation is not (see de Waal 2015). The realities of everyday routines in schools are subjected to plausible causality for and within hierarchy, that not only generates cognitive and affective engagement with 'one way' as 'the only way', but also closes down the options for even thinking that there might be alternatives. This is what has been characterised in the US as 'big lies' or 'conscious, intentional, popular deceptions' (Gorski and Zenkov 2014: 2), as a 'hoax' (Ravitch 2014), or even 'measured lies' through the production of 'scientific proof' (Kincheloe et al 1996). As Frankfurt (1986) argues, lying is premised on knowing the truth and preventing knowledge of the truth, whereas other forms of trickery are identified as 'bullshit', and this is about disguising intentions of what is said: 'that in a certain way he misrepresents what he is up to' (16). Fabricated lies or falsity, and bullshit or fakery have produced truths that have perpetrated a deception on the profession and wider community in order to lie about public education and to mislead the intention to remove universal and shared access to educational services through privatisation.

The ERC manufactures the technology of language and processes (for example, performance, targets) and valufactures the ideals and emotions (for example, aspirations, success) as both individualised and corporatised fabrications (Courtney and Gunter 2020). Duplicity with the self and others is premised on knowing the self and to associate with 'others like me' through predetermined categorisations of the body in ways that are evocative of anti-democratic cultures and practices (see Gunter 2018). It is not so much that people are gullible or even give their formal consent, but as Havel (2018) explains, it is about ordinary coping:

> Individuals need not believe all these mystifications, but they must behave as though they did, or they must at least tolerate them in silence, or get along well with those who work with them. For this reason, however, *they must live within a lie.* They need not accept the lie. It is

enough for them to have accepted their life within it and in it. For by this very fact, individuals confirm the system, fulfil the system, make the system, *are* the system. (21, original emphasis)

This connects the provision of and access to educational services to those who occupy government roles, where the use of fabricated knowledge is a malfeasant tactic that is not only about the veracity of what is said, but is designed to spread confusion about reality, and in potentially seductive and entertaining ways (Kakutani 2018; Oborne 2021). Not only are human beings injured but also trust within public lives and institutions (see Dittert 2021), where what is happening in education policy in the US resonates in England. Notably, there 'are bold, dishonest attempts at shifting the very assumptions upon which our nation's notions of "public" and "public education" are founded' (Gorski and Zenkov 2014: 2).

Modernised segregation

ERC fabrications are used in order to construct the meaning of the modern as an inclusive and vital process where functionally deliverable normative statements for a world class education (for example, Morris 2002; DfE 2014a) and standards (for example, Joseph 1984; Miliband 2004) can be spoken by those in distinctive ideological positions as the means of providing exciting froth, but also conviction and comfort that the disruption caused by the proposed reforms is worth it. Blair, in the spirit of other prime ministers, proclaimed that: 'the status quo is not an option' (DfEE 1998: 4), but in spite of the relentless policy churn it seems that the segregated provision of and access to school places remains secure. As such modernisation is a useful ERC camouflage tactic to disguise the big lie of *eugenicist populism* in order to legitimise proactive exclusion based on reasoned friend–enemy distinctions.

Modernisation may be rhetorically vacuous, but it facilitates ordinary brutality, where UK education policy for schools in England has extended and intensified the conditions in which schools can both enable and block entry to identified categories of children. Recognition that human beings have different talents and dispositions is vitally important, but the problem is how and why rank ordering (with the deployment of praise or stigma) determines very different lives (and deaths), where power is located, exercised, and disappeared in order to award/deny binarised entitlements. Beliefs are used to reify and measure the worthiness of bodies that behave genetically (boy–girl; academic–vocational; secular–faith; abled–disabled; wealth–poverty). In spite of the persuasive oratory about parental choice, it is schools that choose children, not only to fit their brand but also to provide the outcome data that demonstrates the pre-eminence of that brand, and so schools position parents and children in regard to the offer of a school place. Parents respond to the resulting dilemmas through how they handle identifying and exercising a preference, where socio-economic class and faith can intersect (Allen and West 2011; Butler and Hamnett 2012). Scarce public resources are invested in keeping children out of schools, and requiring parents to choose to engage in litigation or to secede if they do not like the product. Once in a school, a student experiences capability setting, streaming, and banding, special needs units, and distinctive lessons for boys or girls, where professional resources are used to sort and resort children into manageable but stereotyped classes or groupings that impact negatively on inclusion (Fabes et al 2013; Hallam and Parsons 2013). Beyond the organisational efficiencies of how best to manage large groups of humans regarding service provision, the main rationale for segregation is based on socio-political biological distinctiveness: certain bodies matter more than othered bodies. Bodies are rendered a security issue, and so segregated education has carceral features to the design, processes, and outcomes of pupil internment.

Research shows how segregation operates in a range of systems (for example, Baki 2004; Amnesty International 2010; Prieto-Latorre et al 2021), and while the OECD (2012) argues for the better management of choice in order to mitigate segregation, it is clear from Bonal and Bellei (2020a, b) that moderating practice will not work because there has been a growth in segregation that connects local conditions, traditions, and elite projects with the impact of globalisation on the geographies of residence, employment, and the impact of migration (into and within a nation state). Notably research has identified the impact of and interaction between what Rothstein (2017) identifies as *de facto* and *de jure* segregation. Where people live and the effects of wealth/poverty on the neighbourhood, and how markets work in the provision of and access to educational services, all generate *de facto* segregation as an aggregation of choices. For example, race (Street 2005) and intersectionality with the economy (Rooks 2017), dominate in the US, where Donnor (2016) identifies the use of 'lies, myths, stock stories and other rhetorical tropes' (344) to perpetuate folklore. People decide to live and work here or there, and to depend on services that enable separate groupings to be normalised (for example, estate agents, banks and the funding of mortgages, builders and developers regarding the land, houses and amenities). This can be used to explain away class, race, sex, and gender divisions as a 'de facto segregation myth' (xii), but such explanations are, according to Rothstein (2017) based on the failure to understand *de jure* segregation. Government policies and laws create, sustain, and enable the economy, politics, society, and culture to be divided, where the Holocaust was legal in Nazi occupied Europe and apartheid was legal in South Africa. As such, the idea and reality of separation is not only shaped by private decisions in homes and offices, but is dynamically created by private interests in government who construct and maintain exclusionary barriers within civil society, and hence between and within schools. Bonal and Bellei (2020b) give attention to 'the direct role of education policies regarding admissions systems and compensatory policies' and what they identify as the 'institutional characteristics of education systems' (5–6). For example, the tracking of children generates within-school segregation according to ability, and 'early allocation' into a set or band 'inhibits the development of learning potentialities among many students' (7). Specifically, children with measured abilities have access to different qualities of teaching, learning resources, classroom conditions, and overall opportunities, where some children are worth less or more than others in regard to public investment (Levačić and Marsh 2007).

Oligarchic sovereignty

Segregationist policy projects for and within educational services are secured through how sovereign power is exercised by the oligarchic occupation of the state. Consequently, the EPKP projects are located within established debates about elite studies (for example, Miliband 1973; Parry 1976; Wright Mills 1977), where the focus of enquiry is distinctive through an emphasis on how and why occupiers present and use the state as *knowledgeable* in regard to what is said and done about and for the public interest. In the Westphalian tradition, the state is a 'unit' that requires allegiance and secures consent for the rule of law from members, and so exercises sovereignty over people and territory, and is legitimately independent (King and Le Galès 2016). The UK state inter-relates with civil society in the four home nations of England, Northern Ireland, Scotland, and Wales, where the notion of 'unit' may mislead because the state is not a unified and settled 'it' but is historically located and dynamic through rupture and resilience (Chernilo 2006). The uncodified UK constitution is dependent on conduct and conventions by state occupiers of the executive, legislature, judiciary, and military/security as 'good chaps' (Blick and Hennessy 2019), that is in tension with democratic notions of public sovereignty, inclusion and participation. The emergence of an 'elective dictatorship' (Hailsham 1976) through the executive control of Parliament means that elections are about ensuring the capture and retention of state institutions (Kavanagh 1987). Oligarchic rule by the few ensures that authority, legitimacy, and intelligence regarding the relationship between knowledge and public policy are safeguarded, and so includes the monarchical and aristocratic birthright to hold and exercise sovereign power, theocratic rights to public office through the integration of Church and State, and wealth and property rights through trade and corporate representation and public appointments. For example, Tett (2021) identifies the importance of Goldman Sachs alumni in government institutions (for example, Sunak, ex-UK Chancellor; Pill, Chief Economist at the Bank of England; Draghi, ex-European Central Bank, and now Italian PM; Carney, ex-Bank of England Governor; Rubin, ex-US Treasury Secretary), and shows how 'the symbols, rituals and social bonds of this professional tribe – like those of any tribe – matter' (9). Such oligarchic occupiers hold dominion by spanning and interconnecting state and civil society through: first, *private oligarchies*, that are often characterised as 'the establishment', including: 'politicians who make laws; media barons who set the terms of the debate; businesses and financiers who run the economy; police forces that enforce a law which is rigged in favour of the powerful' (Jones 2014: 5); and second, *globalised oligarchies*, that are active beyond the nation state in families, think tanks, and supra-national organisations (Gunter et al 2017). Importantly, while private and globalised oligarchies need not actually occupy the state, they do provide a pool of potential occupiers, and they hold current occupiers in their thrall through shared interests and how fear works (not least by media owners).

While oligarchic occupiers are not homogeneous, and elite interests within and external to state institutions may vary or even conflict, it is the case that elite security is premised on segregationist fabrications:

> It is only because the majority of people in many affluent societies have come to be taught (and to believe) that a few are especially able, and others particularly undeserving, that current inequalities can be maintained. Inequalities cannot be reduced while enough people (falsely) believe that inequalities are natural, and a few even that inequalities are beneficial. (Dorling 2011: 103)

Oligarchic occupiers use the ERC to deny plurality by teaching I/us who I am/we are before birth, particularly by investing in modernising feudal hierarchies and superstitions, and creating the illusion that 'the rich are scarce and precious members of a superior race of more intelligent beings on whom the rest of us depend' (Wilkinson and Pickett 2009: 262). Oligarchic sovereignty is a form of 'government by a club, or rather by a nexus of clubs' whereby they might not know everyone in their own or other clubs, but 'they have known and trusted the other members of their own; and they have assumed, on the whole rightly, that the members of the others could be trusted also' (Marquand 1981: 36). Hence *oligarchic club sovereignty* means that what is known and is worth knowing is known by those in the club, it is learned in families, schools, and boardrooms, and buttressed by residence, neighbourhood, and the control of relational networks.

Clubs form within clubs, where Harris (2021) shows that prestige for the very few and worthlessness of the rest is learned at private schools. Taylor (2021) shows how student–teacher relationships in elite schools are sites of approved-of challenge, where the hidden curriculum is about learning how to navigate hierarchy through 'the ability to feel comfortable making challenges in the first place'. What matters is how this demonstrates 'the embodied sense of ease or confidence that students feel in the company of those in positions of authority … [because this] … is valued by elite institutions and recruiters as a form of "polish" that sets them apart from others who do not embody such ease' (13). Such embodied club-ness is enabled through everyday life, where Harris (2021) notes how those who seek club approval actually foster a kind of nonchalance where being seen to work hard is frowned upon, and importantly standing aloof from but still within the club is vital. In talking about Boris Johnson's two terms as London Mayor (2008–2016) and UK Prime Minister (2019-2022) the argument is made that 'the trick is not to be clubbable, but to achieve power and influence as a means of then acquiring friends and admirers' where the power base of a club as the club means that 'rules and conventions – along with consistency – can be casually pushed aside' (NP). When confronted with a different truth to that with which he is working, Johnson pushes back through a 'sod this' rejection followed by an attitude that illustrates how privatised beliefs, positions, and requirements underpinned by entitlement matter the most (Rawnsley 2021).

Such analysis allows recognition of what Davidson and Rees-Mogg (2020) identify as the 'sovereign individual' who is biologically as well as economically and culturally predetermined to thrive as a liberated, resourceful, talented, and adroit individual who is ready for a new technological age. The ERC is what enables such oligarchic position-taking to be made appealing to those who are actually denied access to oligarchic club sovereignty. Notably what is claimed are shared notions of individual choice for all within neoliberal practices, where oligarchic club occupiers continue to stage an anti-state insurgence but actually use the state to defend and extend their interests, particularly by presenting modernisation as apolitical – the issues apply to all and so are neutral, and as anti-political – practical sense means there is nothing to talk about, and so alternative ideas, evidence, and spaces for debate are marginalised or closed down.

Ongoing threats to the club and the cultures of club-ability remain (Moran 2003), where club members are concerned about concessions to democratic cultures, practices, and rights with the need to retain dominion (see: Raab 2009; Kwarteng et al 2012). Oligarchic club sovereignty continues to be both sustained and redesigned through the resolution of what Mann (1986) calls novel 'non-traditional' problems. Such crises require the state to operate at intersections with civil society in ways that are 'interstitial' or in-between what is in the public domain and what is rendered private. Public policy (along with agendas, agreements, disputes) creates borders between the legitimate authority of the state and the private in civil society, and is the prime focus of activity at this intersection (for example, debates about and for problem identification, options, and solutions). Public services such as education are problematic for oligarchic positioning projects and have created an 'interstitial crisis' (Mann 1986: 32) due to campaigns for more inclusion and participation. The notion and reality of public education threatens the ERC by legitimising universal access, where investment produces outcomes for working class and ethnic minority families that not only challenge bodily distinctiveness, hereditary bloodlines, and superior achievements of those who are deemed to be the majority's betters, but also exposes how those who are set up as better are unable to meet the economic, political, and cultural demands that an educated population have been promised (Ranson 1984). Oligarchic policy actors within and external to the state have set out to deal with this by turning to and using particular knowledge claims to provide the tools, language and symbols for the ERC regarding notions of opportunity, talent, and social mobility to intensify segregation that is underpinned by what is declared to work best for improvement and effectiveness. Importantly, while oligarchic occupiers aim to be and practice as sovereign individuals, they need the state because it has authoritative reach that is intensive and coercive, and in Mann's (1986) terms can outflank civil society through the 'institutionalization' of preferred people and networks. While the composition of the few has stable features (elite families, corporate alumni), and operates with some permeability to borders (processes of inclusion, exclusion, co-option), the actual rule by the few is buttressed and expanded.

Political sociology and the EPKP projects

Generating understandings and explanations of the ERC and its role in creating, securing, and nurturing segregated education through oligarchic club sovereignty requires a *political sociology* of education policy. Power can be studied politically through focusing on legitimate authority to control the processes and outcomes of debate and decision-making (Bachrach and Baratz 1962; Lukes 1974). Hence there is a need to examine the state as a polity regarding government institutions, formal roles (ministers, civil service), constitutional rules, and electoral mandates. Power can be studied sociologically when it is exercised by the occupiers of the state, who protect and defend their interests as being in the public interest by utilising the relationality of networked connections with private oligarchies in order to variously coerce and influence, and manage disputation both within state institutions and at the interface with civil society (for example, business, faith, unions, friendships, families) (Clemens 2016).

Consequently, a political sociology of education policy requires 'the examination of the links between politics and society, between social structures and political structures, and between social behaviour and political behaviour' (Rush and Althoff 1971: 3). I have developed knowledgeable polities in order to examine these links, where the EPKP projects demonstrate the primacy of the knowledgeable state as an investor in and user of the ERC (see Gunter 2018). The focus is on the authority, legitimacy, and intelligence of sovereignty that is held and used by occupiers in order to access and commission knowledge, promote particular ways of knowing, contract selected knowers, and use particular ideas, languages and claims to demonstrate preferred knowledgeabilities. What makes a polity knowledgeable about and for educational services is through how and why particular ontological and epistemological positions interplay with personal beliefs and experiences, and with ideological values, convictions, and normative aspirations of those who occupy state roles, and those who they associate with and formally contract to provide knowledge that secures the occupation.

EPKP projects are located in political sociology, where I take inspiration from the work of Kennelly (2018) and Topper (2011), and debates about theory by Walsh (2016), in order to shift from my separate deployment of Bourdieusian (Gunter 2012) and Arendtian (Gunter 2018, 2020c) understandings and explanations by thinking about data using both. This means that like other Arendtian and Bourdieusian scholars I 'encounter' (Benhabib 2010) them separately and together as people and thinkers, and like other researchers I put my data 'in conversation' (Nixon 2001; Kennelly 2018) with their insights. Importantly, while each has been subject to important critique (for example, Benhabib 2010; Walsh 2016), I argue that engagement with Bourdieu's 'thinking tools' (Wacquant 1989: 50) and Arendt's 'network of concepts' (Bernstein 2013: 82) has provoked new understandings because they are: 'people you can ask to give you a hand in difficult situations' (Bourdieu 1994: 28). However, I take the warning from both that doing such work is not always welcome and may provoke attacks from those who have a stake in silence (Bourdieu 1988; Arendt 2003). I also need to take care with intellectualism, where such unthinking can 'put to sleep our common sense' (Arendt 1970: 8), not least through the 'ritual embalming' of 'canonical texts' (Bourdieu 2000: 48). Importantly, how power is located and exercised in research cultures and practices matters, where both Arendt (2013) and Bourdieu (1994) have challenged how they have been subject to powerful yet meaningless categorisations (are they Marxists, or not?), where methodological matters feature in how they examine and question the social sciences as a power structure (Arendt 1970; Bourdieu 1999). With this in mind, I frame my contribution based on Bourdieu's (1994) position that: 'I think that enlightenment is on the side of those who turn their spotlight on our blinkers' (16), where the metaphor of light and dark features in Arendt's (1993) work as well. Hence in the dark times of the ERC, my contribution is about presenting some 'illumination' as an 'uncertain, flickering, and (perhaps) weak light' that has the potential to enable the field of education policy research and practice to generate knowledges that shine as a 'blazing sun' (Arendt 1993: ix–x).

Taking this forward can be illuminated through a question asked by Jenkins (2002) that speaks to eugenicist populism: 'how does a social system in which a substantial section of the population are obviously disadvantaged and exploited survive without its rulers having to depend on physical coercion for the maintenance of order?' (119). Arendt and Bourdieu (like others) do not set out to provide a definitive answer to this, but their thinking has been used to engage with marginalised communities who demonstrate the impact of and challenges to claimocracies (for example, Topper 2011; Kennelly 2018). This is evident in how both Arendt and Bourdieu are concerned with what it means to participate in the public realm, where freedom is not a personal individual property but is relational: 'freedom is not something given: it is something you conquer – collectively' (Bourdieu 1994: 15). Importantly, Topper (2011) argues that Arendt makes visible what happens when people do participate, while Bourdieu helps to see the barriers to participation: 'while Arendt extols the way that words and public speech bond and constitute political communities, Bourdieu explores the ways in which they quietly wound and dissolve them' (Topper 2011: 358). Both present incomplete theorisations of the meaning and practice of power, but it is the case that 'when viewed in tandem Bourdieu's and Arendt's accounts supplement and emend one another, providing a defensible conception of democratic discourse and its limits' (Topper 2011: 356).

For Arendt (2005) the political is what happens 'in-between' people and hence it is a process of relational exchange based on action, plurality, and natality in the public realm. A person may think in private, but in public there is an opportunity to understand the views of others 'in the space of appearances' (Arendt 1958), and while change may be spontaneous, unpredictable, and irreversible, there are political processes that enable promising and forgiveness as the means of resolving disputes. Kennelly (2018) argues that 'it is among others with whom we reveal our *whoness* through actions and speech' (199, original emphasis), and following Kennelly (2018), the ERC requires '*whatness*' (198), where the uniqueness of the plural individual perishes, where people are required to labour for survival with work used to produce approved-of artefacts; and the fact of birth enabling the capacity to do new things is rendered a privilege for the few. Importantly work as a form of making means that Arendt (1977) gives recognition to the endurance of not only artefacts that outlive the maker, but also to 'the "web" of human relationships and narratives that pre-exists every individual, sets the context for their activities, and shapes the way actors are understood, responded to and remembered' (Bowring 2011: 18). People may be active but work is not the same as action, and hence while things may be produced as a product of busyness they do not enable political relationality; instead, industrious crafting is used to replace the idea and reality of taking action (Arendt 1958). Consequently, and following Walsh (2016), it seems that the primacy of eugenics with a gloss of scientific expertise is being generated for and by the ERC is not only using work to make things work better but to demonstrate how political action, plurality, and natality are unnecessarily disruptive. Hence the 'whatness' of parental consumer choice works best for relating requirements to provision, and so is rarely questioned regarding the impact of a myriad of aggregated choices on other people's children. This is because the alternative exercise of parental citizenship choice is based on the 'whoness' for all in a shared and relational service that is negotiated in the public realm. In other words, consumerism is based on the immediate satiation of the private, whereas citizenship is replete with potential private and public satisfactions and disappointments, whereby what we say and do, who we vote for, and how we present ourselves, all require a commitment to notions of trusting people in private and in public to both problem-pose and solve over time where settlements may not be visible or secure.

Bourdieu is helpful with understanding the ascendency of Kennelly's (2018) 'whatness', whereby the ERC is a *doxa* or 'an uncontested experience of the daily lifeworld' (Bourdieu and Wacquant 1992: 73), that is a self-evident reality in relational exchanges. The ERC doxa is integral to the game of inclusion–exclusion, where the breaching of the field of education by the fields of power, economy, and the media (Thomson 2005) means that the content, language, and processes of the ERC is produced by 'constitutive *naming*' (Bourdieu 1994: 55, original emphasis), as a codification of the truth. Categories are made by 'imposing a vision of divisions' (Bourdieu 1989: 17), where it seems that bright and dim children are fabricated because: 'each member helps to impose this on all the others, willy-nilly, the same constraint that they impose on him' (Bourdieu 1992: 110). Importantly, 'truth is at stake in a series of struggles in every field' (Bourdieu 1994: 32), where domination is enabled by *illusio* or the game as worth investing in, and through the staking of *social, cultural*, and *symbolic capitals* to demonstrate you are a recognised and acclaimed player who displays sanctioned credentials (Bourdieu 1996). Dispositions or *habitus* are revealed through the playing, where the 'structured structures' of eugenicist populism enables distinction to be recognised, and where the game enables 'structuring structures' to legitimise distinctiveness (Bourdieu 1992). The language of ritual, position, and postures enables three types of fallacy in the game: 'the universalizing of a particular case'; 'the vision of the world that is favoured and authorised by a particular social condition', and 'the forgetting of repression of these social conditions of possibility' (Bourdieu 2000: 50). Such forgetting is about misrecognising how, where, and when Kennelly's (2018) 'whoness' becomes 'whatness' through how we are 'fish in water' who do not recognise the situation we are swimming in (Bourdieu and Wacquant 1992: 127).

Arendt (1972) makes such speedy and urgent processes visible through her engagement with how: 'a fact is safely removed from the world if only enough people believe in its nonexistence' (Arendt 1972: 13). She examines this in two ways: first, the consequences of lying in the US Republic regarding how the Pentagon Papers demonstrated a 'quicksand of lying statements of all sorts, deceptions as well as self-deceptions' (Arendt 1972: 4) about the conduct of the Vietnam War. Lies were developed and used by 'public-relations managers' and 'professional "problem-solvers"' as image management about the game in play (Arendt 1972: 7–10). Second, a total breakdown in Nazi Germany and Stalinist Russia 'through the invasion of the political processes by sheer criminality' (Arendt 2009: 265), where exclusion is based on totalising disposability (Arendt 1963): 'the point is reached when the audience to which the lies are addressed is forced to disregard altogether the distinguishing line between truth and falsehood in order to survive' (Arendt 1972: 7).

Thinking with Arendtian and Bourdieusian scholarship has generated an understanding and explanation of *policy violence* based on a range of EPKP projects that I have undertaken over the past 40 years (see Appendix). I continue to address the question: what is the relationship between the state, public policy, and knowledge? If a segregationist ERC is being intelligently designed, authorised, legitimised, and funded by public institutions based on consent, then what knowledge is being used, and why? What ways of knowing are considered to be valid and why? What forms of knowledgeability are used and why? And, who are acclaimed as knowers and why? I investigate this in Part I where I present three chapters that provide a political sociology of policy violence as the annihilation of power within political and sociological relationality: first, *eugenicist populism* and the ERC, whereby hierarchy is normalised and conceals biological determinism through notions of meritocracy and social mobility as forms of *legitimised violence* (Chapter 2); second, *depoliticised governing by knowledge production* and the ERC, whereby identifying and understanding the *private* is vital for *authorised violence* within and for problem solving (Chapter 3); and third, *policy mortality* and the ERC, where failure is the core objective of *intelligent violence* – the gains made by public service in-common education and professionals are pro-actively characterised as failing, and must actually fail in order to both deal with the fear of the other and so secure the conceits of the few (Chapter 4).

I go on to explain the development and dynamics of the ERC as a form of policy violence in Part II. I use a *Thinking Politically-Sociologically Framework* (TPSF) of, within, and about Critical Education Policy Studies (CEPS) through investigating *vantage points, viewpoints, regimes of practice*, and *exchange relationships*. Specifically, I use strategic themes and illustrative data from EPKP projects to examine the UK government education policy interventions in school education in England from the 1980s onwards: first, I focus on academisation in order to examine how and why diverse policy actors operate from different vantage points where I reveal the dominance of the *core vantage point* (Chapter 5). I then use data about workforce remodelling to examine how and why policy actors locate (and relocate) in knowledge production through deploying viewpoints where I reveal the dominance of *normative-functional viewpoints* (Chapter 6). I examine the investment in school leadership by policy actors who form regimes of practice where I reveal the dominance of *state regimes* (Chapter 7), and I focus on local policymaking in schools by engaging in exchange relationships, where I reveal the dominance of *personal-cultural contractualism* (Chapter 8). I then move onto examining the intellectual histories that support and sustain the development of identifiable and prevailing vantage points, viewpoints, regimes of practice, and exchange relationships (Chapter 9). I focus specifically on the approaches taken by CEPS researchers to thinking and doing criticality in order to present an explanation of the relationship between the state, public policy, and knowledge, where I identify the ascendency of *entrepreneurialism*. In conclusion, I summarise the gains made through deploying the TPSF (Chapter 10) and this raises questions about the need to undertake a political sociology for and by CEPS regarding the place of thinking in knowledge production.

PART I

A political sociology of education policy

2

Modernising education

Introduction

The 2020–2021 COVID-19 lockdowns in England have revealed much about the disparities in wealth and the impact of poverty on children's learning: 'a mother wakes at dawn to copy out worksheets for her children onto pieces of paper. Secondary school pupils attempt to write essays on their mobile phones, while younger children queue to wait their turn on the one computer in the house' (Wakefield 2021: NP).

While the UK government and charity have provided assistance through the distribution of hardware into homes, it has not eradicated structured resource deprivation:

> It is estimated that 2.6 million school children live below the poverty line in England alone, and Ofcom estimates that about 9% of children in the UK – between 1.1 million and 1.8 million – do not have access to a laptop, desktop or tablet at home. More than 800,000 children live in a household with only a mobile internet connection. (Wakefield 2021: NP)

Even in an affluent country it remains the case that gaps in educational achievement are still related to significant disparities in parental income and involvement: 'children do better if their parents have higher incomes and more education themselves, and they do better if they come from homes where they have a place to study, where there are reference books and newspapers, and where education is valued' (Wilkinson and Pickett 2009: 105). While much is claimed about social mobility, it remains the case that the ERC is based on *eugenicist populism* that constructs and legitimises poverty through superior–inferior calculations about the natural educability of children (as either aspirational winners or unambitious losers). Research shows this to be historically embedded (Chitty 2007), and the COVID-19 lockdowns have intensively exposed the visceral inequity of being a child and growing up in England (Longfield 2020).

This chapter examines evidence from the EPKP projects regarding how public education services have been modernised through and for the education reform claimocracy as a 'new and improved brand', but where the endurance of the 'unmodern' remains crucial to the purposes of education. I focus on how political sociology reveals deeply entrenched eugenicist populism and highly protected segregation of the provision of and access to educational services. Notably I demonstrate the endurance of oligarchic club sovereignty within the UK nation state as a private but globalising process, and I use thinking by Arendt and Bourdieu to expose claims for social mobility as a form of *legitimised violence*.

Unmodern modern

The proactive creation and protection of advantage and disadvantage is evident in a range of data in the UK: first, The Equality Trust (2021) reports that for the richest fifth of households, the average income has risen by 4.7 per cent, whereas for the poorest fifth it has fallen by 1.6 per cent, and 'the richest fifth had an income more than 12 times the amount earned by the poorest fifth' (NP); second, the Women's Equality Party (2021) reports that while women are 51 per cent of the population, 'there are only 29 per cent of MPs, 25 per cent of judges and 24 per cent of FTSE 100 directors' who are women, and 'women still occupy the lowest-paid jobs – three-quarters of the people who've done minimum wage jobs in the last 10 years are women' and 'around 1.2 million women suffer domestic abuse a year and – every day – there are 250 rapes or attempted rapes. Conviction rates are low' (NP); third, the Equality and Human Rights Commission (2021) reports that 'unemployment rates were significantly higher for ethnic minorities at 12.9 per cent compared with 6.3 per cent for White people' and 'rates of prosecution and sentencing for Black people were three times higher than for White people, 18 per thousand population compared with six per thousand population for White people' and, 'Pakistani or Bangladeshi and Black adults are more likely to live in substandard accommodation than White people' (NP); and fourth, Scope (2021) reports that 'disabled people are more than twice as likely to be unemployed as non-disabled people' and 'the proportion of working age disabled people living in poverty (26 per cent) is higher than the proportion of working age non-disabled people (20 per cent)' (NP).

While there are legal rights (for example, vote, equal pay) and identified types of discrimination are illegal (for example, on the basis of race and sex), it remains the case that exceptions are made – for example, single sex schools, faith schools (DfE 2014b), and many rights are assumed rather than codified, and so there are deeply embedded structural discriminations that create complex forms of intersectional advantage and disadvantage. Notably diet and air pollution all interplay with home, income and life expectancy that construct parallel but separate and shorter or longer lives, whereby the Office for National Statistics (2021) reports that 'in England, the gap in life expectancy (LE) at birth between the least and most deprived areas was 9.4 years for males and 7.4 years for females in 2015–2017' and importantly 'since 2012–2014, there have been statistically significant increases in the inequality in LE in England for males and females at birth and at age 65 years; the inequality in female LE at birth had the largest growth, rising by 0.5 years' (NP). Indeed, the Windrush and Grenfell Tower scandals, and COVID-19 death rate data, visibly demonstrate that Black lives do not matter (Editorial 2020).

Underpinning such public policy are beliefs and espoused attitudes that I describe as *eugenicist populism* whereby reasoning, categorisation, and labelling are used to identify and distinguish approved-of bodies from dangerous bodies in ways that are normalised:

> Populism is not a doctrine. It is a disposition, an approach, a *style*. For populists, wisdom and virtue, an intuitive unschooled wisdom all the more profound for being unschooled, and an instinctive, innocent virtue uncorrupted by excessive ratiocination, reside in the people, and not in any elite or institution. … Values are not in tension with each other, and there is no need for the negotiation and debate which were fundamental to the civic ideal. The people decide which values are to prevail. (Marquand 2004: 100–101, original emphasis)

Hence populism is about speaking for the people in ways that speak to people against those who do not accept what the people believe and want. Populist mantras are presented as anti-elite and inclusive while remaining an elite project that connects certainties to 'an exclusionary form of identity politics' (Müller 2017: 3). Visible traits and constructed differences between bodies are made obvious through what is witnessed and experienced in everyday lives, and weaponised when talent and ability are harnessed to power structures of superior and inferior lives. The validation of eugenics by Galton (1874), and the 'eugenic movement' (Field 1911: 2) it created, made it possible to causally connect the 'feebleminded' to the unemployed, poor, homeless, drunk, immoral, and ill (see Rutherford 2022). Hence 'some human life was of more value – to the state, the nation, the race, future generations – than other human life' (Levine and Bashford 2010: 3–4). Consequently, public policy as a form of 'cultural eugenics' (Wilson 2018: 38) was devised to manage the population, through direct interventions to control breeding (for example, sterilisation), and by influential lobbyists (including scientists, media owners, politicians, philanthropists, educators) who argued that investment in housing, sanitation, education, and justice would not improve the 'quality' of the population (Lowe 1979). While eugenics has been discredited, not least due to the Holocaust (see Kevles 1999), it is the case that it is not 'a regrettable past' (Wilson 2018: 11) but is evident in public policy where science is making claims about genetic predetermination or 'naturally occurring individual differences in ability and development' (Asbury and Plomin 2014: 12) that restore the legitimacy of biological heritability as vital to the human condition (for example, Herrnstein and Murray 1994 Murray 2020). While research challenges the methodologies and analytical declarations of such projects (for example, Richardson 2017), and eradicates the nature–nurture binary through the examination of epigenetics (for example, Meloni 2019), it remains the case that biological determinism remains seductively alive and well (see Chapter 10).

Eugenicist thinking prevails, is modernised through 'newgenics' (Wilson 2018: 25), and is popularly normalised through how claims are made in appealing ways where there is nothing to discuss because 'we all know it to be true'. Anyone who thinks otherwise is an unwelcome expert, and is rebutted as irrelevant through the characterisation of 'political correctness gone mad'. For example, former PM Johnson has made public his contributions to eugenicist populism through espoused misogyny, homophobia, and racism. As a journalist in 1996 he attended the Labour Party conference, and wrote about 'the hot totty' present; when he was leaving a job, he provided advice to his successor 'just pat her on the bottom and send her on her way'; and when campaigning for election in 2015 he declared that 'voting Tory will cause your wife to have bigger breasts'. He wrote in 1998 about 'tank-topped bumboys'; in 2002 about 'flag waving piccaninnies' in the Commonwealth, and described African people as having 'watermelon smiles'; and in August 2019 he compared women wearing burqas and niqabs to letter boxes (Bienkov 2020). Importantly, Johnson does not engage in incidental or serial *faux pas* in what he writes or says, there is an identifiable and sustained position visible in a pro-Thatcherite speech as London Mayor in 2013 where he espoused eugenicist claims: 'I don't believe that economic equality is possible; indeed, some measure of inequality is essential for the spirit of envy and keeping up with the Joneses that is, like greed, a valuable spur to economic activity'. He justifies inequality on the basis of IQ where he derided the 16 per cent 'of our species' with a below 85 IQ and lauded the 2 per cent above 130 IQ, concluding that 'the harder you shake the pack the easier it will be for some cornflakes to get to the top' (Watt 2013: NP). Eugenics was at the core of the Johnson government (Mason 2020), in the House of Commons (for example, Ben Bradley MP, Asthana and Mason 2018), and in support of government policies (for example, Young 2015), where certain bodies are regarded as naturally deficient, and so public money should not be wasted on services that will not make a difference. While Wedge and Prosser (1973) asked the question: 'do we care that so many are born to fail?' (61), it seems that there is no need to care because failure is to be expected of those who are predestined to fail at what their betters are proclaimed to be better at.

Research shows how such eugenicist thinking is prevalent in discriminatory practices based on deeply embedded categories such as class (Jones 2014; Gilbert 2018), disability (Kliewer and Drake 1998; Wilson 2018), race (Bhopal 2018; Saini 2019) and gender (Fine 2010; Saini 2017). As Rutherford argues, the myths are spoken and sustained:

> by well-intentioned people whose experience and cultural history steer them towards views that are not supported by the modern study of human genetics – the misattribution of athletic success to ancestry rather than training, the continued assumptions that East Asian students are inherently better at maths, that black people have some kind of 'natural rhythm' or that Jews are good with money. (Rutherford, 2020: 4)

That bodies are different is a given, but eugenicist populism sustains stereotypical human variation (Wilson 2018), and so 'in the pursuit of power and wealth, the fetishisation of these differences has been the source of the cruellest acts in our short history' (Rutherford 2020: 4). Visible indicators such as skin colour, facial features, and genitals along with family blood inheritance are used to categorise bodies, and are causally related to wealth, status, and intelligence, and imbued with entitlements, privilege, and notions of civilised lives (language, accent, deportment, and good taste). Discrimination enables these categories to persist within practice, whereby I am the person I am assumed to be, and the temporal and spatial as well as relational worlds are structured through responses to requirements. The writing of the history of the UK is deeply implicated, where symbols of eugenicist power are evident in the everyday world from the names of streets through to museum exhibits, and are animated by shared forgetting about eugenicist positions taken by populist icons (Olusoga 2016). Such positioning is espoused through attributing status, not least by liking someone in public life who we have never met and never will meet, and by denying respect through the use of put-downs in order to stop certain types of people from getting above their station (for example, statements such as, "she's no better than she ought to be", are used to show disapproval of women, often by women, regarding the morality of conduct, language, dress).

Unmodern modernising

The adoption of unmodern eugenicist populism is evident in the urgent conviction to break with the past but at the same time to preserve the past. Hence successive UK governments from the 1960s onwards have set out to modernise the UK based on planned public policy outcomes as 'new' or 'up-to-date' or 'leading edge' or 'world beating' or 'will make a difference', but at the same time appealing to what are called traditional values regarding what people are expected to believe, hold dear, and regard as decent. Notions of individualism are simplified as an entitlement of the natural human condition, and therefore any encounters with other individuals are based on responsibility for the self and freedom as a property of the distinctive individual. Eugenicist populism is energised on the basis of the preservation of this natural order but with opportunities for those with preferred talents and a commitment to work hard in allowed occupations (for example, sport, music, drama). The practices involved are exhausting and corrosive but also vitally necessary for the legibility of the individual not as a person (whoness) but as 'one of us' or 'not one of us' (whatness), and so as being deserving or not deserving of a particular place in the pecking order (Gunter 2021).

The lexicon is about the validity and rituals of choice that speak to the inviolability of the private, and this is evident in five main modernising trends: *medieval, enlightenment, trade, corporate,* and *civic,* outlined in Table 2.1.

The *medieval* 'right to rule' is historically embedded and enabled through bodily and biological individualism (hereditary principle of the sovereign and legitimate bloodline) and socio-economic power (family, primogeniture, inherited wealth, military, faith). State ritual as a benign but coercive spectacle means that there is an accepted order to the location and exercise of power, where challenges are deemed heresy and possibly treason. Nevertheless, the potential sovereignty of the 'people' or 'masses' is strategically important in regard to controlling the potential threat of talented individuals outside of the bloodline, or the sheer power of the 'mob'. Hence myths and mysteries are used to buttress the entitled, and are combined with 'knowing your place' structures for 'others', where property rights interplayed with race, gender, and sexuality endure as discriminators of who is and who is not worthy of inclusion (for example, marriage). This is evident not only in

Table 2.1: Modernisation trends

Modernisation	Sovereignty
Medieval	Hierarchical control as 'divine right' through established family, blood inheritance, faith, and cultures of privilege.
Enlightenment	Expert control through observation, questioning, methods, evidence, and reason, evidenced in professional credentials and codes of practice.
Trade	Financial control through product design and manufacture, marketing and exchange.
Corporate	Company control through ownership (private and shareholding), profit and dividends, deals and contracts.
Civic	Citizen control through constitutional rights and duties, procedures and transparency, voting and representative democracy.

Source: Based on Gunter 2018

the privilege and prerogatives of those who occupy state institutions and associated organisations within civil society (for example, media), but also through how oligarchic domination is maintained through the constitutional legitimacy for the executive domination of governing (for example, the use of Henry VIII powers regarding Brexit, Gunter 2018).

Following Finlayson (1998) it seems that: 'by not having a "proper" revolution Britain failed to eradicate the feudal legacy, leading to a compromise arrangement where new structures of capital co-existed with an archaic "superstructure" encompassing aristocratic traditionalism and unable to embrace the necessary processes of "rationalization" to develop a fully modern state' (20). Bargains and concessions involved are located in the various contextual settlements reached with enduring medieval forms of legitimacy: first, *trade* claims for the right to rule through free markets and profit that defy feudal entrenchment in state institutions; and second, the *corporate* focus establishes the company as the rival elite structure to the medieval family or mercantile trade association. The intersectionality of the medieval, trade, and corporate claims to sovereignty is around the notion of worthiness as vital for the acceptance of hierarchy, the purity of the family name, bloodline and property rights, and exclusionary purposes and practices against the 'masses'. However, challenges to oligarchic club sovereignty are located in *enlightenment* claims for the modern, whereby power is located and exercised according to reason, and is evidence-based as professional expert knowledge, for example, lawyers and the rule of law, economists and sound money, and doctors and public health. Oligarchic occupants of the state have variously compromised with enlightenment forms of modernisation (for example, introduction of accredited/appointed civil service; removal of nepotism and corruption; establishment of transparent rules for governing), but continue to demonstrate that the protection of assets, entitlements, and segregated privileges is an essential freedom of what it means to be English.

Oligarchic club sovereignty locates security in the medieval interplayed with trade, corporate, and enlightenment forms of pragmatic conciliation. Risk of breakdowns in this settlement is endemic, and the challenges against state occupiers are evident in everyday resistance (for example, comedic satire) through to rebellions (for example, poll tax in 1381 and 1990), where campaigns for inclusion are located in *civic* forms of modernisation. This has been a key feature of public policy in the post-Second World War era, where who governs is determined through free and fair elections, the peaceful transfer of power based on the mandate to govern (Stoker 2006), with an emphasis on the politicisation of public services with universal access and shared investment in regard to health, education, and welfare. Civic forms of sovereignty are located in the public as the self-governing 'commons' (Ostrom 2015), where agentic and plural forms of local sovereignty are evident in subversion and co-production that demonstrate different sites of decision-making and enactment (Barnes and Prior 2009). Such civic trends are rooted in local and regional democratic traditions from the Anglo-Saxons onwards, with reformist upsurges such as the Levellers, Chartists, Suffragettes, and Climate Change Activists (for example, see Hill 2020), and have depended on aspects of enlightenment rationality. Leader-centric social democracy has developed as a compromise that has largely left the bargaining between medieval entitlements, trade, and corporate demands in place. Notably, civic gains have been utilised to defend and protect oligarchic club sovereignty whereby the extension of the franchise has enabled elite individual and group occupation to be legitimised through elections. Segregated health, wealth, property, and education is accepted, and this is based on views such as, 'this is how it is,' with opportunities generated for the cooption of the selectively talented, and where problem-posing is deflected away from elite tax avoidance towards welfare free-riders.

The success of oligarchic sovereignty is premised on the stability of club interests and the dynamics of handling risks, where Marquand (1981) argues that the strategy has been to maintain the status quo but give the appearance of having made a difference through visible modernised changes. While trade, corporate, enlightenment, and civic claims to sovereignty have allowed access to state institutions, it is the case that the club has attempted 'to practice oligarchy under conditions of formal democracy' (Moran 2003: 4). Moran (2003) argues that the club has tended to operate on the basis of self-regulation whereby the shift back to private services from the 1970s not only enabled trade and corporate interests to marketise state services, and replace public provision with commodified hospitals, prisons, and schools, but also to restore the notions of autonomy for individuals and organisations (Gunter 2019). Shifting decisions from public agendas and relocating them to private arenas (homes, offices, media platforms) was vital for:

> insulating interests from democratic control, for easily the most effective form of protection was to organize an activity out of politics altogether, by defining it as belonging to the domain of self-regulation. But this was a strange, historically fragile settlement: oligarchy designed to provide protection against democracy. (Moran 2003: 66)

For Moran (2003), by the 1970s the club was in ruins, whereby public professionals had to succumb to the 'new regulatory state' (7) of public audits and accountability. However, this did not invalidate the idea of the club as oligarchic occupiers, rather what the new regulations allowed was a 'spring cleaning' of club membership and practices. Thatcherism challenged enlightenment rationalities provided by professional experts with an espoused public ethos, and began to deprivilege actual and potential club members – from civil servants to teachers to coal miners. Oligarchic club sovereignty remained intact but was redesigned and repositioned regarding the endurance of medieval control buttressed by trade and corporate interests that became emboldened through the intensified entry of privatised ideas and privatising strategies for public policy. This is evident in the entry of individuals with private but oligarchically shared agendas, for example, Sir Derek Rayner from Marks and Spencer headed up the Efficiency Unit (1979–1983) and intensified corporate methods and cultures (Gunter 2020b).

Unmodern modernising in education

The relationship between eugenics and the provision of education is deeply rooted (see Allen 2014), and each new UK government that takes office inherits segregated education provision in England, and when they leave office they pass on a largely intact segregated system. The school workforce experiences segregation that is classed (Gunter and Courtney 2021), raced (McNamara et al 2009), gendered (McNamara et al 2010), and based on faith (Milliken et al 2021), with impacts on career aspirations and structures. The segregation of children has been researched internationally (for example, Wiseman 2008; Benito et al 2014; Council of Europe 2017; Sahoo and Klasen 2018; Adamson and Galloway 2019; Boterman 2019; Kornhall and Bender 2019; Gutiérrez et al 2020) with research into the provision and access to school places in England (Gorard and Smith 2004; Jenkins et al 2006; Weeks-Bernard 2007; Kulz 2011; West 2014; Bhimani 2020).

It is estimated that just over 60,000 children in England are proactively separated from other children by being educated at home, with a steep rise in some localities even before the COVID-19 lockdowns (Hazell 2020). Those who do access a school place are characterised and categorised in order to detach and divide according to 'needs', where such 'needs' are met by educational services that create and legitimise groups and the process of grouping between and within a school (see Sumroy 2022). Segregation is premised on formal entry requirements that are not held in common (biology, wealth, faith, capability), and marketised choice and personal beliefs enable distinction to operate within local geographies of homes and work (see Burgess and Wilson 2005; Gorard and Siddiqui 2018). Of the 24,360 schools in England there are those that provide a place on the basis of family resources and identities, including: wealth, with about 2,331 fee paying schools; faith, with 6,822 schools including 4,593 CoE, 1,985 RC, 26 Methodist, 152 other Christian, 43 Jewish, 14 Muslim, four Sikh, and five other faiths (Fair Admissions Campaign 2021: NP); capability, with 1,051 special schools, 349 pupil referral units, 163 grammar and 117 secondary modern schools (DfE 2021a); and biological sex, where the number of boy and girl schools has declined but it remains the case that of the 3,260 secondary comprehensive schools, 3 per cent are for boys and 5 per cent for girls, and it is higher in secondary selective schools, where 34 per cent of grammar schools are for boys and 37 per cent for girls (Peck 2020: NP). According to the Fair Admissions Campaign (2021) faith selection dominates with 16 per cent of children subject to religious criteria, compared to 5 per cent who pass the 11+ and go to grammar schools, 5 per cent in single sex schools, and 7 per cent in fee paying schools.

Gorard (2016) concludes that 'in England, around 30% of students would have to exchange their schools if SES segregation between schools were to be eliminated' and he goes on to say that 'it is associated with greater unfairness in practice, worse opportunities for the most disadvantaged, lowered aspirations, and lower participation rates in later education. And all of these risks are run for no clear gain' (143). However, while discrimination is unwarranted, 'the drivers of segregated schooling are in the fundamental wish of individuals and families to optimise their social position given the resources at their disposal' (Coldron et al 2010: 32). This includes decision-making based on what school places are on offer, and where the local can be shaped by national discriminatory discourses, for example, Shain (2011) shows how and why stereotyping works in regard to Muslim boys and education in England, where there has been a shift from a marginalised passive position to that of being 'firmly recast in the public imagination as a threat to the social order' (ix). Such labelling also operates in how children separate themselves by not attending school each day where 'the average pupil missed 8.4 of the 195 scheduled days in the 2018/19 academic year ... with 10.9% of pupils absent for more than 10 days' (Sims 2020: 2). In addition, an average of 2,307 children are suspended each day, and 41 children are permanently excluded from school each day (Express and Star 2020). The dynamics of how this works is evident in decisions about higher education, and where the choice of a place to study is raced, classed and gendered regarding how 'people like me fit in' (Reay et al 2005).

Eugenicist populism is evident in the ERC. Policy actors speak confidently about basing policy strategy on inherent capabilities, for example, Keith Joseph (1974) (Secretary of State for Education, 1981–1986) claimed that 'the balance of our population, our human stock is threatened' and he goes on to say that the causes are girls who 'are producing problem children, the future unmarried mothers, delinquents, denizens of our borstals, sub-normal educational establishments, prisons, hostels for drifters' (11). Such ideas endure where Boris Johnson argued in 2006 that the children of working class mothers are more likely to 'mug you on the street corner' (Stewart 2019: NP). However, according to Johnson it seems that middle class graduates are different because they 'pool their advantages' through 'assortative mating' (Stewart 2019: NP). Indeed, Chris Woodhead, former chief inspector of schools in England (1994–2000), argued that middle class parents have 'better genes'. In addressing the question 'why do we think that we can make him brighter than God made him?', Woodhead argues that 'children who are "not very bright" should be taken out of the classroom and given practical educational courses' (Shepherd and Curtis 2009: NP). More recently government advisors have espoused eugenicist claims (see Cummings 2013), as do those contracted to deliver policy where Toby Young (Director of New Schools Network and co-founder of four free schools, 2015) has talked about the 'poisonous heirlooms' of 'teenage pregnancy, criminality, drug abuse, ill health' (NP).

Other policy actors are more circumspect in how these ideas are expressed. Tony Blair (PM 1997–2007), talked in 2005 about how all children should 'get the chance to make the most of their God given potential' (quoted by Ball 2008a: 12). Notably as Chitty (2007) shows, the 2005 White Paper *Higher Standards, Better Schools for All* divided 'children into three main categories: "the gifted and talented, the struggling and the just average"' (121). This identification of and provision for 'needs' within policy tends to have the fizzy imperative of the modern, but it remains unmodern through a combination of personalised and shared technologies (settings, data) and cultural imperatives (the deserving and undeserving child, Gunter 2021). Such thinking is also extended to the profession, whereby the EPKP data show that a senior Cabinet member talked about the quality of headteachers in England, and argued that leadership training was necessary because "we don't have enough of the 24,000 (headteachers) who have the natural skills, so we need to nurture other people to be able to develop their innate leadership skills and to develop proper management skills" (Project 15).

Eugenicist populism in education policy is historically embedded and enabled by the five modernisation trends as illustrated in Table 2.2.

Civic modernisation as a challenge to eugenicist populism is deeply rooted but is primarily a feature of post-1945 reconstruction and development of public education services. For example, while Leader of the Opposition, the future PM Harold Wilson (1963) argued for the modernisation of the UK through the 'white heat' of a scientific revolution that required an end to 'educational apartheid' because 'as a nation we cannot afford to force segregation on our children at the 11-plus stage' (3). Historically, the evidence of class-based advantage–disadvantage and the debunking of myths about social mobility (for example, Jackson and Marsden 1962) and the gains of the common school (for example, Simon 1955) meant that Wilson's governments (1964–1966; 1966–1970) continued to work on desegregation through the reorganisation of post-11 education provision into common schools (Benn and Chitty 1997) where 'all children have ability, not potential, capacity or capability' (Dorling 2011: 89). While selection at 11 years of age remains a salient issue with assertions about talent and aspiration in the state system as a means of buttressing private provision, the rejection of the majority of children, and certainly for the middle classes, is unpopular (see de Waal 2015).

Table 2.2: Modernisation trends in education policy

Modernisation	Education policy claims are...
Medieval	Embedded and immutable. Entitled access and status on the basis of position and inheritance. For example, private/faith schools.
Enlightenment	Measured and data determined. Scientific methods used to provide evidence and recommendations. For example, effective teaching and learning.
Trade	Designed/packaged and sold. Private goods are traded based on needs. For example, parental consumer choice.
Corporate	Globalised and branded. Competitive expansive trade to secure profit and trademark dominance. For example, testing and software packages.
Civic	Provided and inclusive. Public goods are shared and all-encompassing. For example, common school.

Source: Based on Gunter 2018

Civic forms of modernisation identified and deployed values and evidence-based claims to eradicate segregation but in the longer term it merely interrupted exclusionist policies. Attacks on civic forms of comprehensive education came from both the political right (Cox and Dyson 1968, 1969) and left (Adonis 2012), where the commodification of educational services meant that new providers could operate 'independently' outside of local democratic control (CTCs from 1988; GMS from 1988; Academies from 2000; Free Schools from 2010; Studio Schools and UTCs from 2011; DfE 2015). Importantly, while private education may have been rendered obsolete in the post-war period, it revived itself in the market as 'engines of privilege' (Green and Kynaston 2019), where Gamsu's (2021) research shows that 'in 2017–18, on average the private schools in this sample had a mean per pupil income 3.7 times higher than their local state-funded schools' (1). However, while parental consumer choice clearly operated in favour of a minority, it seems that 'parents, provided their own children got better chances in life, didn't care about the toffs who gripped the commanding heights of politics and the professions. On the contrary, they continued to vote for them' (Wilby 2021: 51). For example, Rachel Johnson (journalist and sister of Boris Johnson) recognises how class advantage works, and she argues for the abolition of private schools and in favour of all children going to the same school, but notes that it is unlikely because of how freedom is a selfish property (Jones 2012). It seems that eugenicist populism is protected by a distorted notion of liberty, and operates on the basis of ongoing retention of entitlements (see DfE 2018).

Medieval hierarchy and eugenics remain robust, and claims from *trade*, *corporate*, and *enlightenment* interests have been simultaneously and dynamically accommodated and resisted. The restoration of the private through the dismantling of the civic is evident in how the public system has become a site for profit that is both financial and personal (as philanthropic acclaim). The vitality of business experiential knowledge is lauded as essential for educational services, where business people operate in what is colloquially called the 'university of life,' and so have a validity that educational professionals do not have, and so should not be subject to democratic accountability. This conflation of the medieval with trade and corporate interests is evident in the deregulation of the provision of school places, where Mansell (2021a) has shown how the Harris Federation, a Multi-Academy Trust (MAT), has adopted the hereditary principle in order to secure corporate control of '48 state funded academy schools that educate 32,500 pupils and with an income from the government in 2017–2018 of £173m' (NP). Lord Harris of Peckham, a Conservative Peer and carpet manufacturer, is actively involved in the sponsorship of academies:

> Lord Harris of Peckham, sponsor of seven Academies plus other specialist schools, keeps a very close eye on his schools. He does not interfere with the professionals on a day-to-day basis, but he does judge quality and ask searching questions. His own success has permeated the culture of his schools and he will visit them, keeping his finger on the pulse. He makes a particular point of speaking to the students, who are aware of him and his role as sponsor. (SSAT 2007: 90)

The special characteristics of the sponsor are imbued in the Harris family, where Mansell (2021a) shows that the Articles of Association for the Harris Federation state that Lord Harris has the right 'to appoint fellow members and trustees', and on his death the role of Principal Sponsor will pass to a family member (his wife with legal provision to pass to his sons). A MAT is a 'publicly-funded, but privately controlled, organization' (NP) that is a medieval and corporatised private monarchy.

A political sociology of unmodern modernisation

Social mobility is a UK public policy strategy that is focused on enabling individuals and families to move upwards and prevent movement downwards regarding class status, income, and recognition. In Arendtian terms, social mobility has the potential to recognise the plurality of humans, and the capacity for natality:

> what makes man a political being is his faculty of action; it enables him to get together with his peers, to act in concert, and to reach out for goals and enterprises that would never enter his mind, let alone

the desires of his heart, had he not been given this gift – to embark on something new. (Arendt 1970: 82)

Indeed, the UK Government website states that the Social Mobility Commission 'exists to create a United Kingdom where the circumstances of birth do not determine outcomes in life' (Gov.UK 2021: NP). However, research evidence continues to show that social mobility is a myth:

> Social mobility has not created a fairer society – instead it has helped those at the top to justify their position. By allowing a tiny minority to ascend to the highest rungs, the wealthy and powerful elite have claimed that Britain is a place where merit is rewarded. But because they are the ones who determine membership of these prized perches, they are able to specify what skills and personal qualities are required. Competitiveness, selfishness and the acquisition of personal wealth at the expense of everyone else have been lauded. These practices have impoverished millions of people – most conspicuously by causing the financial crashes of 1929 and 2007–08 and the recessions that followed – and denied opportunities to many more. The myth of social mobility has resulted in most of us having very limited access to advanced education or fulfilling work, and few chances to exercise political and economic power in ways that might reshape society and our own lives. (Todd 2021: 3–4)

One solution put forward by the Social Mobility Commission (2020) focuses on: 'creating a better social mix in schools' because 'children gain from the broad range of backgrounds of their peers, and this diversity particularly helps the academic achievement of less advantaged groups' (11). However, as long as social mobility is nested in eugenicist populism and segregated services, the ERC will remain impervious to the Social Mobility Commission recommendation. Importantly, while New Labour governments (1997–2010) focused on aspirations and 'stuckness' in the matter of mobility, the issue tended to be articulated as functional. For example, the EPKP data show that one minister said that the government had: '"a belief that disadvantage and deprivation are not a block on achievement, they're a hurdle to be overcome, they're an extra blockage in achieving it. But they're not going to be allowed to get in the way of bringing out the talent, the ability, the self-fulfillment of students" (Project 15). Tackling those barriers was by focusing on the school as an organisation, where a different minister stated: "we had that notion of a school improvement crusade" based on "policy which was a combination of what was educationally sound with what was politically possible" (Project 15). Successive UK governments from the 1980s onwards have dealt with underachievement as an obstacle issue rather than as an inclusion matter, and so social mobility was and remains an individualised and corporatised fabrication as legitimised violence, where research shows that children learn how inequity operates (Lucey and Reay 2002; Horgan 2009), and their role in making 'demonized schools' work in ways that are cruel to them (Lucey and Reay 2002: 254). Violence as physical and mental harm to humans is integral to the ERC where intention is veiled in consensus language and imaginings, but for competition to work there has to be real and visible failure, and for failure to be acceptable it has to be causally linked to biopolitical conditions that both denies and amplifies agency.

Bourdieu (1994) focuses on symbolism where in objective power relations there are credentials, experiences, and positions that are forms of capital which 'give one a right to share in the profits of recognition' (135). When former PM Theresa May (2016) argued that 'I want Britain to be the world's great meritocracy – a country where everyone has a fair chance to go as far as their talent and their hard work will allow' (NP), she then proposed to intensify segregation by removing restrictions on the opening of more faith and grammar schools, and protecting fee paying schools. In Arendtian terms this renders the measured and displayed 'untalented' and 'lazy' to labour for survival, and to possibly work and produce artefacts, but never to be able to take action in the public realm, and as such it is an example of what Bourdieu identifies as 'ordinary violences which are neither simply consented to nor simply imposed' (Topper 2011: 361). Bourdieu characterises such 'symbolic violence' as a form of indirect control of what people think, say, and do, and as such it prevents the possibility of thinking otherwise:

> giving an action or a discourse the form which is recognized as suitable, legitimate, approved, that is, a form of a kind that allows the open production, in public view of a wish or a practice that, if presented in any other way, would be unacceptable (this is the function of the euphemism). (Bourdieu 1994: 85)

May (2016) had accrued sufficient capital through ongoing political struggles and in her role as PM to enact such policy violence. Eventually her credit ran out and she left office in 2019, but she had demonstrated in Bourdieu's (1992) terms a 'logic of practice' that is integral to how oligarchic club sovereignty sustains the ERC. The extension of parental consumer choice may be a fabrication, but it outlasts the current fabricator, where 'of all forms of "hidden persuasion", the most implacable is the one exerted, quite simply, by the *order of things*' (Bourdieu and Wacquant 1992: 168, original emphasis). The ERC relies on misrecognition, where listening to May's claims about grammar schools is based on 'disguising from themselves and from others the truth of their practice' (Bourdieu 1992: 106), and this is 'the fact of recognizing a violence which is wielded precisely inasmuch as one does not perceive it as such' (Bourdieu and Wacquant 1992: 168).

Arendt and Bourdieu develop their concerns about the violent exclusion of people from participation in the public realm, where Bourdieu (1999) argues that the violence inflicted by external social causes can be recognised by those who may think they are the cause of their own suffering. Arendt goes further than this where in her study of totalitarianism she shows that 'violence appears where power is in jeopardy, but left to its own course it ends in power's disappearance' (Arendt 1970: 56). In other words, the dismantling of constitutional procedures and rights for a safe public realm means that policy violence is based on whatever oligarchic club members say the situation is. For example, PM May set out to expand grammar schools, and is reported as saying: 'you could have "all the evidence in the world" but … headteachers told her "grammar schools are good for disadvantaged pupils"' (Pells 2017: NP). The ERC logic of practice is in play in this statement, where the huge volume of independent evidence from research is ignored (for example, Gorard and Siddiqui 2018), and is sustained by unsubstantiated beliefs about what this means for children from families who are deemed to lack the Bourdieusian capitals to invest. Such banality is recognised in public discourses where forms of 'civil disobedience' (Arendt 1972) by the public, including experts, 'fire back' (Bourdieu 2003) at the individual and corporatised fabrications that create and sustain such thoughtlessness. This therefore requires a political sociology of governing, and so I now turn to the idea of authorisation within policy violence.

3

Governing by knowledge production

Introduction

In August 2020 the examination results for 16- and 18-year-olds in England were released. The COVID-19 pandemic lockdown meant that assessment was undertaken by teachers who provided an estimated grade for each student and a comparative ranking to allow for standardisation. An algorithm was used to adjust the grades based on the school's performance in each subject over the previous 3 years. When the A-level results were published, '36% of entries had a lower grade than teachers recommended and 3% were down two grades' (BBC 2020a: NP). It became clear that students who attended fee-paying schools had their estimated grades protected through a combination of selective entry into school, smaller classes, and better funding, because 'an algorithm based on past performance will put students from these schools at an advantage compared with their state-educated equivalents' (BBC 2020a: NP). Smaller classes in private schools meant that the standardisation process could not operate and so teacher estimates were used, but a student in a larger class in a school or FE college would have their grade adjusted according to past performance. The design and deployment of a 'neutral' algorithm enables the segregated education system to be preserved through the supportive use of narratives that enable and sustain the wasting of talent: first, students in a state school cannot be awarded the highest grades and so the reality of 'bright' and 'able' students outside of the private sector is disavowed; and second, the exercise of professional judgement in a state school is distrusted because larger classes and limited resources incentivise grade manipulation by teachers. This example illustrates how the ERC requires authorisation through governing by knowledge production whereby what is known, how it is known, what is worth knowing, and who the knowers are is integral to how structures operate in regard to strategic and tactical public policy design and enactment. Policy is infused with eugenicist populism where the ERC is replete with justifications of exceptionality:

> Somehow the idea of the 1 per cent of the population being particularly clever has become mixed up with the idea of there always being 1 per cent at the top. It is in the interests of those who have the most to promote the idea that they deserve their riches because they are very special. (Dorling 2014: 51)

The 99 per cent of individual students and families are therefore made responsible for surviving within and dealing with the consequences of a rigged system. Much is left unrecorded and seemingly without significance, but it seems that a pragmatic concession was secured in 2020 for students in state schools where policy was changed so that estimated grades would be used, but this is not a permanent settlement.

This chapter presents analysis from the EPKP projects regarding how this governing by knowledge production operates as a form of policy violence, where I deploy Arendtian and Bourdieusian thinking to examine *authorised violence*, and attention is given to how isolated disposability operates through a process of depoliticisation.

Governing by knowledge production

The occupiers of state institutions are known as the government, and are deemed to have the legitimacy to govern as a form of authoritative control, and engage in governance over and with the governed through the display of intelligent knowledge. Governing by knowledge production is concerned with the relationship between government policy and the identification, access, and use of types of knowledge and ways of knowing, and the knowledgeabilities of those who are recognised as trustworthy knowers. Importantly, the private beliefs, experiences, evidence, and practices of those who are *in* the government is vitally important to understanding the scoping, design, and engagement with policy. The EPKP data show that a minister in the 1997–2010 New Labour governments said: "so you come to government with anecdotal evidence that heads make a difference, and if you look at Ofsted information … I don't think we made a decision that we'd concentrate on leadership, there was a point when that decision was made, it was obvious" (Project 15). Hence the power and veracity of the assertions that constitute the ERC is located in oligarchic governing where know-how and know-why is shared, understood, and accepted by 'people like me'. Knowing is enabled through what Marquand (2004) identifies as the anti-public and pro-individual cultural struggle or 'kulturkampf' that has been globalised through the promotion of markets and libertarian freedoms as a means of both limiting and extending state control. The state is a contradictory site for the security of oligarchic club sovereignty because while the occupation of government institutions provides opportunities for strengthening and developing elite authority and legitimacy, the occupiers depend on anti-government and anti-public ideologies to retain access to the state. Occupiers need the state, but at the same time eschew the state.

Oligarchic governing operates within and against government institutions of the state. The location and exercise of sovereign power enables governing as a form of authority that is located within and exercised through the public institutions of government. Notably those who occupy roles as *the* government actually govern through the law involving finances, sanctions, and rewards, and use electoral mandates and consent, together with interpretations of the UK uncodified constitution, in order to justify agendas and outcomes. The border between the state and civil society is dynamic, and in the 19th and 20th centuries the remit and extent of governing expanded through the politicisation of major social, economic, and political issues. Civic forms of modernisation have sought to politicise issues by making them the responsibility of the public through dependency on the government as the site for accountable decision-making and provision. This involves the funding and enactment of policy by public institutions, based on agreed rules, transparent processes, and accredited staffing, and where bureaucracy was pro-actively and productively developed into 'a many-sided, evolving, diversified organizational device' (du Gay 2005: 3). This is evident in regard to common services from roads, to employment, to health and education, and this politicisation means that government ministers have data and policy options about cancer or motorway congestion or air pollution or pupil testing on their desks, and so are publicly accountable for policy in ways that impact publicly on lives, businesses, and culture, as well as on election results. The government provides solutions through the development of a public sector staffed by professional experts, a public service ethos based on universal access, with services owned and funded by the public, and through regulatory legislation and inspection.

Public sector politicisation has faced attack with allegations of 'bloated' and 'self-serving' red tape, where 'pen pushers' demand more and more from the taxpayer but cannot be removed from office. Ideological work undertaken by Friedman (2002) and Hayek (2001) has characterised politicisation as a form of state overload, where the argument is made that:

> government is essential both as a forum for determining the 'rules of the game' and as an umpire to interpret and enforce the rules decided on. What the market does is to reduce greatly the range of issues that must be decided through political means, and thereby to minimize the extent to which government need participate directly in the game. (Friedman 2002: 15)

Such restricted-state, pro-market, and low-tax influential texts have global influence (for example, Bobbitt 2002), where brutal change can take place either in the form of a coup such as Pinochet in Chile, or through elections where the UK Thatcher government from 1979 focused on what they labelled as 'rolling back the state,' with the shift from service provision to contractual commissioning and regulation (Carrasco and Gunter 2019). This attrition of democratic norms is evident in UK culture and practices, whereby oligarchic club members have acted as 'democracies assassins' who continue to 'use the very institutions of democracy – gradually, subtly, and even legally – to kill it' (Levitsky and Ziblatt 2019: 8).

In England, public assets were sold off by UK governments from the 1980s and new service providers encouraged to enter the market with claims for 'unchaining' (Kwarteng et al 2012) in order to create 'the genuine privatization of sovereignty' (Davidson and Rees-Mogg 2020: 321). Anti-state texts present the logic of humans as customers of state services (law, residence, security), and so the self-governing 'sovereign individual' in a globalised band-width economy 'will bargain for whatever minimal government they need and pay for it according to contract' (Davidson and Rees-Mogg 2020: 29). State membership is part of the goods and services that individuals can purchase, where the potential and actual decision to remain or exit (for example, taxation, regulation) is an exercise of marketised power that makes demands on how those in government actually govern. For example, this is evident in how the relationship between territory and space are being reworked into 'charter cities' in order to remove politics from the reform agenda (Charter Cities Institute 2022), and 'free' zones/ports where large scale projects require formal state-like structures that operate outside of the state as private oligarchic polities or 'extrastatecraft', where 'the zone typically provides premium utilities and a set of incentives – tax exemptions, foreign ownership of property, streamlined customs, cheap labor, and deregulation of labor or environmental laws – to entice business' (Easterling 2014: 15).

The idea and reality of 'governing without government' (Rhodes 1996) has been influential, with the argument that the UK unitary state has undergone a process of 'hollowing out' (Rhodes 1994), with a shift from 'government' (for example, Moran 2003) towards the dynamics of 'governance' (for example, Bevir and Rhodes 2003), 'markets' (for example, Hodge 2006), and 'networks' (for example, Kickert et al 1997). Importantly, Rhodes (1996) argues that governance as '*self-organising, inter-organisational networks*' (660, original emphasis) is the best descriptor of the provision of services, with 'no sovereign actor able to steer or regulate' (666). A de-centred research approach exposes how those in government work within networked rather than top-down structures, where 'game-playing, joint action, mutual adjustment and networking are the new skills of the public manager' (666). In addition, theorising using Foucault's concept of 'governmentality' has enabled explanations of 'power without a centre' that required investigations into 'a type of regulated freedom that encouraged or required individuals to compare what they did, what they achieved, and what they were with what they could or should be' (Miller and Rose 2008: 9). The impact means a shift in the canon, with a reorientation in research focus and methodologies (Bevir and Rhodes 2003), including within-state investigations into decentralisation

(Cheema and Rondinelli 2007) and beyond-state examinations into globalised digitisation (Dunleavy et al 2006).

These new orthodoxies have been challenged, where the continued dominance of hierarchy has been charted, with a focus on the legitimacy and authority of legality, coercion, and resources in public policy making (for example, Scott 1998; Davies 2002, 2011; Capano et al 2015). Consequently, it is argued that 'governments may depend on a variety of state and non-state actors to deliver policy but at the same time the centre retains a unique set of powers and resources that are not available to those actors beyond the centre' (Marinetto 2003: 606). While the restructuring and re-culturing of state institutions is in progress, this is more about the relocation decisions from public gaze than the residualisation of government (Burnham 2001). Put another way, a restoration of government as a 'unified and autonomous institution' may not be underway (Marinetto 2003: 605), but the 'hollowing out' thesis has been overstated because: 'although government has been subject to restructuring, these reforms have tended to reinforce the ability of the central core to exert control' (Marinetto 2003: 606).

What the focus on networks has actually achieved is the exposure of the club as *private* and *globalised oligarchies* (Chapter 1), whereby the oligarchic occupation of the state is used to enable oligarchic dominance in the economy and wider civil society. Rather than the state reduced to 'steering at a distance' (Kickert 1995), those who occupy both the state and private institutions actually co-steer and control, not least because it is in the interests of oligarchic sovereignty to retain a dominant position within and external to government in order to resist demands for further democratisation (Moran 2003). Such control also serves to extend and integrate shared identities and dependencies through inviting private oligarchic interests in civil society into government to advise on and run public services for private gain in the public interest. Notably the endurance of hierarchy is recognised, not only in the location and exercise of power within and by public institutions, but also within business, professions, and civil society (for example, Davies 2011). Institutions are 'an organized fiduciary, organized trust, organized belief, a collective fiction recognized as real by belief and thereby becoming real' (Bourdieu 2014: 37). That reality is useful in regard to the control and denial of plural-relational power locations and processes, whereby governing by the government against the idea of big government in order to strengthen the oligarchic occupation of government is actually a 'governing strategy' (Bache 2003). Importantly, state institutions, roles, titles, and processes can be understood through Bourdieu's metaphor of the state as:

> this 'central bank of symbolic capital', this kind of site where all the fiduciary currency circulating in the social world is produced and guaranteed, as well as all the realities we can designate as fetishes,

whether an educational qualification, a legitimate culture, the nation, the notion of state border, or spelling. (Bourdieu 2014: 122)

The primacy of government within, through, and by the state is maintained, but also the oligarchic occupation of organisations within civil society (faith, business, media) is strengthened and expanded.

The security of oligarchic club sovereignty is based on a complex process of including, disposing of, and disciplining, rival privileged interests who at various times have either become club members and/or have thwarted oligarchic control. Inclusion is premised on actual or assumed benefaction where exchange relationships facilitate deals through cultures of trust by like-minded people, with a dependency on what Blick and Hennessy (2019) characterise as 'good chaps'. However, events show that conduct in public life is in decline where Blick and Hennessy (2019) argue that the question that needs to be asked is whether those who hold public office are: 'Good chaps no more?' Such a question is valid due to the disposability of people, rules, and values, through identifying, isolating, and then discrediting based on personal dislikes and threats, where public service professionals (lawyers, teachers, social workers, doctors, nurses) within or outside of the UK (for example, exiting from the EU) are constructed as a protected elite ('job for life' contracts, salaries, and pensions) within a rules-bound bureaucracy that prevents change. For example, the civil service has been re-cultured to deliver privatisation and those who remain or join are disciplined through performance contractual control (Gunter 2020b). Integral to this are forms of employment vulnerability through what Pollitt (2007) describes as a permanent form of 're-disorganization' regarding structures and processes.

The reality and threat of isolated individual and group disposability is vital to knowledge production for the retention of segregationist structures, cultures, and practices. This is related to what Wood and Flinders (2014) have identified as the proactive de-politicised relocation of decision-making from government to agencies, to social networks in the form of families and individuals, and to nowhere by the removal of shared issues from public discursive and practice agendas. Depoliticisation has three forms: first, *depoliticised privatism* is the relocation of decision-making to private interests that is not only in regard to selling off public assets and the entry of private providers, but also in relocating what has been public and political into a non-political private matter for individuals and families; second, *depoliticised corporatisation* is the construction of a shared identity as privatised decision-makers, whereby oligarchic interests are presented as inclusive and democratising for all, and so while individuals may not have the same family resources as each other, they do have the same libertarian opportunities to make choices about whatever resources they do have;

third, *depoliticised populism* is about giving consent to policies (or at least not opposing) what may not be directly in your interests but because 'they know better' then it is in your interests to know your place. Depoliticisation means that individuals and families are denied plural-relational power-dependency with strangers (taxpayers, the public, the community, or neighbourhood), but can experience forms of effervescent belonging where associative separation is handled through accepting 'one of us' group identities, or what O'Brien (2020) characterises as 'the accelerating "footballification" of public discourse' (2). Consequently, public policy is limited regarding necessity and design, where the private is the prime authorisation for what is deemed to be a problem and what is necessary to resolve it. Philanthropy can be used to publicly symbolise resolve for change, where acclaim is used to applaud 'the gift of giving' (Saltman 2010) rather than anonymously paying tax.

Governing by knowledge production in education policy

Governing by knowledge production in education policy is located in an ERC of biopolitical distinctiveness (Gunter 2018). The individual is expected to assert the worth of their bodies in the public realm, and their bodies are categorised and assessed, and then acclaimed or disposed of according to eugenicist populism. Post-war civic modernisation challenged such claims, and not only demonstrated the problems generated for all children, but also how the common school based on educability and public investment enabled gains in outcomes – an educated working class was producing high achieving professional outcomes in spite of the barriers constructed to prevent this (Todd 2021). The politicisation of public education and the relationship with democratisation meant that oligarchic club sovereignty was threatened, and so as already stated the club was redesigned through the construction of a crisis in public services education where the root cause of the problem was identified as unaccountable education professionals and feral families.

The ambivalent relationship between the profession and the club meant that those who found the club congenial embraced the changes, and those who did not took early retirement or experienced redundancy. Notably, modernising processes such as performance management enabled a scientific gloss of data, targets, and value-added calculations to be used to cover judgements about appointments, promotions and contract renewal regarding whether a person is 'worth it' or 'deserves it'. The design, provision, and access to educational services are therefore premised on the anti-public and pro-individual kulturkampf, and is evident in the use of state occupation to halt the gains in the civic project and to restore oligarchic advantages. For example, Sir Keith Joseph (Secretary of State for Education, 1981–1986) in an interview with Stephen Ball stated:

When I started the job in September 1981, I was anxious to free up the system – to free it from unnecessary bureaucratic controls. I'd already questioned the whole nature of the relationship between the state and education provision. And I wanted to see if there was a way, a practical way, of delivering more parental choice of schools – particularly at the secondary stage. I've always been attracted to the idea of the education voucher and I've always been worried about the state's involvement in education. … We have a bloody state system; I wish we hadn't got one. I wish we'd taken a different route in 1870. We got the ruddy state involved. I don't want it. I don't think we know how to do it. I certainly don't think Secretaries of State know anything about it. But we are landed with it. If we could move back to 1870, I would take a different route. We've got compulsory education, which is a responsibility of hideous importance, and we tyrannize children to do that which they don't want, and we don't produce results. … (Chitty 1997: 80)

Such a position is rooted in his own espoused eugenics (Joseph 1974, see Chapter 2) and the pro-Hayek and Friedman economics that underpinned major education policy changes from the 1980s onwards (Joseph 1984; Baker 1987). The purposes of education were re-framed around oligarchic preservation through isolating and discarding professionals, particularly by extending the idea of parental consumer choice to parents who did not have the resources to exercise a choice, and by facilitating capital accumulation for the few through enabling public services to be opened to the market.

While some of Joseph's ideas have yet to be fully delivered (for example, vouchers have been used in nursery provision but not yet introduced across the school sector in England), his anti-state pro-oligarchic reforms to public services education from the 1980s onwards have impacted through how both right- and left-wing governments have embraced what can be strategically characterised as the 6Rs:

- first, *remodelling* of existing staff through the construction of the preferred type of educational worker as corporate visionary leader/follower and entrepreneurial deal maker/deliverer using a combination of national standards and comparability with the City, and the identification of role model heads/teachers as archetypes to symbolise success and fear of failure;
- second, *replacement* of education professionals by staff who have been trained (not necessarily as teachers) into remodelled professionality as the norm, and the appointment of non-educational staff as managers, HR services, and marketing to run the education service as a business;
- third, *responsibilisation* of practice through remodelling and replacement based on the collection and use of data (attendance, punctuality,

examination results) to construct high-stakes accountability resulting in liberation rewards (performance related pay) and name and shame punishments (contract termination; school closure);
- fourth, *redesigning* professional identities, priorities, and practices through remodelling, replacement, and responsibilisation in order to secure policy delivery with accountability;
- fifth, *restructuring* through the dismantling of the Local Authority (LA) democratic system and the creation of schools as the local firm with a brand, where head office is the new middle level structures with CEOs and MATs, and the introduction of Regional Schools Commissioners (RSC); and
- sixth, *reculturing* where a combination of the five Rs enabled a speedy reform imperative that was framed as There Is No Alternative (TINA), and so one best way generated and sustained what was imagined, said, and done regarding problem identification and solutions.

The intellectual work necessary to authorise these changes is located in a complex and dynamic associative community including those who hold (or have held) public office (for example, Thatcher, Gillard 2018); advisors (for example, Sexton 1994); researchers in universities (for example, Tooley 2000); researchers in think tanks (for example, Lawlor 1988); education professionals (for example, Boyson 1975); along with campaign networks (for example, *The Black Papers*, Cox and Dyson 1968, 1969). A number of important trends emerged in the production of knowledge, whereby the funding of independent high quality social science research was cut by the UK government, and education research in particular was criticised (for example, Tooley with Darby 1998), where researchers were required to conform to ideological agendas and the non-negotiable remits for commissioned evaluations or risk being denounced (see Gove 2013b). Notions of 'users' and 'impact' developed whereby evidence informed policy and practice was presented as a means of improving the quality of data and analysis, along with sending projects off shore (for example, Earl et al 2003) and funding preferred methodologies and methods (for example, Educational Endowment Foundation).

The intellectual work that packages and sustains the ERC both promotes and benefits from depoliticisation as an idea, process, and emerging outcome. Integral to the fabrication of rationales and espoused narratives is that the reforms to public education are democratising through notions of choice, accountability, and individualism in ways that distract from the strengthening of hierarchy and personal patronage. The shift from public politicised agendas and decisions towards privy practices is intensifying oligarchic club sovereignty through the dynamic formation and networking of private oligarchies in educational services:

Depoliticised privatism is evident in the relocation of decisions to quangos (for example, National College for School Leadership, Gunter 2012) and trusts (for example, MATS, Hughes 2019), where the academisation of a school excludes local democratic oversight. The provision of school places is therefore located with private individuals and within private organisations such as faith and business. There are now between 70 and 90 different types of schools in England (Courtney 2015), where MATs as networks of schools are private oligarchies who receive public money for strategically directing and co-ordinating the provision of education in schools. A Chief Executive of a MAT as a 'courtier' (Courtney 2017) epitomises policy enactment through oligarchic club sovereignty, where the CEO may decide not to allow a school to join that MAT because the type of pupils who attend could damage the brand (see Hughes 2019, 2020). Hierarchical control is strengthened through oligarchic association such as the Confederation of School Trusts (CST), where the private is recognised as a marketing problem and so the focus is on changing the narrative in two main ways: first, deflection away from the role of business in schools and MATs (Whittaker 2019); and second, redirecting attention away from 'excessive salaries' and how 'schools have been turned into personal fiefdoms', towards presenting MATs as 'education charities running schools' (Whittaker 2020: NP). Importantly, the CST is becoming government-like through positioning MATs as 'new civic structures' (Cruddas 2019: NP), issuing 'white papers' (CST 2019), and instigating a 'consultation' (CST 2021). The relocation of decisions away from the public means that dissent only matters when private and usually advantaged interests bring it to the attention of the public (with possible threats of litigation), through cases of children being 'off-rolled' (see Savage 2017), and moved to a different school in the MAT without consulting parents (Mansell 2021b).

Depoliticised corporatisation is evident in the intensification of shared product identities for children, parents, communities, and workforce between (for example, vision and values statements) and within (for example, school uniforms; use of streaming and banding) schools. While this has been a feature of the history of provision of and access to school places in England (for example, religious schools), the processes of corporatisation (for example, private owners, recruitment processes) have exaggerated the requirement for organisational unity and specified outcomes, and strengthened distinction and difference in relation to competitors (Gunter et al 2018). Oligarchic colonisation of the provision of taxpayer funded school places has marginalised and even removed educational professionals as club members, and intensified oligarchic occupation by faith, business, and philanthropy (Woods et al 2007). Obtaining and keeping a place as a member of staff in a school is based on a requirement to privately confess about individual performance (Ball 1990b), and compete publicly through data driven notions of superiority where equivalence is based on comparisons to non-public sector organisations and individuals. For the workforce, there are winners and losers: for example, contract termination for those who do not deliver according to requirements (Courtney and Gunter 2015), and the adoption of business qualifications (for example, MBA) combined with the purchasing of best practice business solutions to protect and enhance the school/MAT label (Gunter and Mills 2017).

Depoliticised populism is evident in the seeking and giving of consent for reforms to education that are presented as being in your interests (for example, parental consumer choice, higher quality education, responsive professionals, work-focused curriculum) but may not be in your interests (for example, entry to and keeping a place in a school based on competition; curriculum is limited due to the private views of those who 'own' and 'govern' the school or MAT). To be in receipt of and a beneficiary of philanthropic largesse generates emotional connections to having been recognised by someone more important than you as deserving of this investment (Gunter 2021). As noted in Chapter 2, private oligarchies can in effect become little monarchies, where hierarchical structures and cultures in MATs (CEOs) and schools (principals) are buttressed by leader-centric norms that someone more important and worthy should be in charge. Oligarchy therefore embeds the fiction of the veracity of a segregated system, and where political debate as citizens is eschewed in favour of accepting the natural order of things and applauding the efficiencies generated by 'deliverology' (Barber 2007a).

Within the education research community, a range of positions have emerged regarding doing important intellectual work for the ERC, as vital for adopting positions as assumed and co-opted oligarchic interests: first, professors in higher education develop knowledge production projects that are presented as politically neutral but that actually enable non-educational contentions to be translated, normalised, and to reach the profession through the promotion of the corporatised school as organisational management and leadership (Gunter 1997); second, professors have joined a growing consultancy industry that include major companies and named field leaders who develop and promote ideas globally (Gunter and Mills 2017); and third, a range of high profile education professionals collaborate with and have taken control of the changes and made them work tactically in classrooms and staffrooms and have enabled hierarchies to work in the interests of oligarchic club sovereignty (Hughes et al 2020). Over a period of 50 years, such work has served various networked groups and funders around government policy such as the New Right (see Angus 1993), and New Labour (see Gunter 2012) governments, whereby commissioned research and private lobbying has enabled education policy to remain consistently focused on pro-oligarchic agendas – not least the replacement of public education policy with private markets.

A political sociology of governing by knowledge production

Governing by knowledge production by successive UK governments for education policy in England demonstrates a strategy of *authorised violence*, where constitutional legitimacy has been used in order to create, sustain, and extend segregated services. The UK parliamentary system has been the site of a major insurgency against public services, where electoral legitimacy has been used to confirm eugenicist populism for national unity combined with demands for individualised freedom. Rebelliousness is presented as reasonable, and the identified delivery difficulties as troubling but resolvable.

Authorised violence is evident in a range of positioning and repositioning problem-solving projects: first, *preservation*, through maintaining segregation as normal and in the public interest (for example, retaining charitable status for private schools), not least by cultivating simulations of the included by the excluded in order to develop associative identity focused on the same interests (for example, espousing notions of parental consumer choice that are in reality faux choices); second, *renewal*, through developing new ways to improve and make segregation more effective and appealing (for example, performance leadership of the workforce, and establishing headteachers as equivalent to corporate executives); third, *restoration*, through re-introducing segregation to universal access services (for example, the revival of grammar school expansion enabling new stimulation for the private tutor market); and fourth, *expansion*, through identifying opportunities for introducing segregation to unsegregated sites (for example, academies at primary and secondary levels opened up as sites for capital accumulation). Such projects are in the interests of social, economic, cultural, and political elites where the conceit is that all can benefit, and while elites are heterogeneous, they share an instinct for sustaining advantage through the oligarchic occupation of the state. Indeed, as Wacquant (1996) has explained, state violence actually '*bears upon us all*', and this happens:

> in a myriad minute and invisible ways, every time we perceive and construct the social world through categories instilled in us via our education. The state is not only 'out there,' in the form of bureaucracies, authorities, and ceremonies. It is also 'in here,' ineffaceably engraved within us, lodged in the intimacy of our being in the shared manners in which we feel, think, and judge. Not the army, the asylum, the hospital, and the jail, but the school is the state's most potent conduit and servant. (xviii, original emphasis)

The school is the site where we learn how and why our bodies are/are not the problem, and how the rejection of certain bodies by the school rescues us from that problem. Hence from the 1970s onwards the inclusion–exclusion game in education policy became a site of oligarchic investment through the *illusio* of problem solving as the only game in town worth playing (Bourdieu 2000). This game is played through individualised and corporatised fabrications in the ERC where certain knowledge, ways of knowing, types of knowers, and displays of knowledgeability are used and produced to dismantle and ration high quality local public schools in order to protect elite educational provision that shelters and strengthens oligarchic interests.

The ERC promotes the ontology and epistemology of functional problem-solving where the identified issue is always a problem rather than problematic, and the answer is provided as the only solution. For example, integral to the ERC is that educational standards are not good enough, and so – like retailing – the educational product (pedagogy, the curriculum, and outcomes) must be standardised through performance measurement and then delivered through segregated provision (see Chapter 2). This is what Cox identifies as a '*problem-solving theory*' which he characterises as:

> It takes the world as it finds it, with the prevailing social and power relationships and the institutions into which they are organised, as the given framework for action. The general aim of problem-solving is to make these relationships and institutions work smoothly by dealing effectively with particular sources of trouble. (Cox 1981: 129, original emphasis)

Making the segregated system work better requires an isolated parent to focus on enabling an isolated child as 'my child' to do well by recognising that 'other people's children' are the problem – in Arendtian terms the fact of natality and plurality can be adapted and exploited through the actuality of needs-based separation. As Cox (1981) goes on to argue: 'the strength of the problem-solving approach lies in its ability to fix limits for parameters to a problem area and to reduce the statement of a particular problem to a limited number of variables which are amenable to relatively close and precise examination' (129). And so, statements about measurement, testing, and metrics can be judged according to constructed success–failure binaries, where teachers, children, and families experience 'hierarchical answerability' technologies (Ranson 2003: 461). Consequently, natality is actually regulated as only those who 'pass' the required test at the required level can actually think about and do something new, and plurality becomes rhetorical as only those who 'pass' matter (Gunter 2018). Metrics *per se* are not the issue, rather it is 'excessive measurement and inappropriate measurement' or 'metric fixation' that requires our attention (Muller 2018: 4). The authorisation of such forms of violence is what happened in the exam results fiasco in the summer of 2020 that opened this chapter – there is a conjuring of science and neutral algorithms but in reality, ideology determines beliefs about 'those' teachers and children. Consequently, problem solving often uses 'clever gimmicks which are only successful enough to make the problems temporarily disappear' and so it is only a matter of time before the consequences 'come home to roost' (Arendt 2003: 273).

The content and contentions of the ERC are a denial of the political process that Arendt characterises through a metaphor of sitting at a table: 'to live together in the world means essentially that a world of things is between those who have it in common, as a table is located between those who sit around it; the world, like every in-between, relates and separates men at the same time' (Arendt 1958: 52). Hence political power is about 'the human ability not just to act but to act in concert' (Arendt 1970: 44) on the basis of problem-posing through relational exchanges. This is what Cox (1981) identifies as '*critical theory*', whereby sitting at an Arendtian table enables ideas, facts, and opinions to be shared, listened to, and understood: 'it is critical in the sense that it stands apart from the prevailing order of the world and asks how that order came about' (129, original emphasis). In doing so, critical theory is practical because 'it approaches practice from a perspective which transcends that of the existing order' (130), where the approach is to focus on 'the social and political complex as a whole rather than to the separate parts' (129). This requires – in Arendtian terms – the recognition of spontaneity interplayed with the capacity to take responsibility and to exercise judgement while sat at the table, where teachers, children, and families (and wider civil society) engage in 'communicative reason' as a form of 'reflexive accountability' (Ranson 2003: 461). Listening, questioning, and talking things through is integral to such practice, where primary research exists outside of the ERC in ways that expose the fabrications and generate productive ways of knowing differently (for example, Wrigley et al 2012).

Following Arendt's (1958) table metaphor, who I/we want to sit down with, who I/we are allowed/required to sit down with, and where I/we sit relationally, has been authorised within the ERC. The notion of the public may be invoked by the ERC, but in reality segregated parenting and communities are vital to prevent political exchanges and understandings 'in-between people' (Arendt 2005). As Bourdieu (1994) identifies 'there is a struggle for monopoly over legitimacy' (37) in the field of education, and so where I/we sit and who I/we sit with is both structured in our embodied experiences and structuring in our current practices, where the inclusion–exclusion game plays to the advantage of the dominant over the dominated. Depoliticisation is vital to how the game plays out by either 'crushing' people together and/or 'insulating' people from each other at the 'table', and by creating the fear of removing the 'table' as an option for the majority, and making it a reality for only a few. Integral to oligarchic club sovereignty is the building of consent to the denial of agency and action through the use of authorised violence as a substitute for power (Arendt 1970: 87). This destruction of power means that the ERC as violence cannot persist within democratic forms of government because it is premised on the friend–enemy distinction that is being blurred where all become potential or actual enemies. Hence what emerges are forms of terror – examination results in the summer of 2020 – that Arendt (2009) recognised as being central to the conditions for totalitarianism (Gunter 2014, 2018).

Authorisation of violence within knowledge production requires a political sociology of sovereignty, particularly since 'the people' are meant to be sovereign (voting, public opinion, accountability to constituents) but such sovereignty is yielded to and controlled by oligarchic club sovereignty. Both Arendt and Bourdieu are concerned about the occupation of state institutions and how this location enables the nation to be imagined and enacted in ways that does violence to those within the state (Bourdieu 1990) and to the stateless (Arendt 2009). And in addition, they both raise questions about what it means to undertake thinking in ways that Bourdieu (1994) characterises as a form of '*hyperbolic doubt*' because 'when it comes to the state, one never doubts enough' (1, original emphasis). Hence they are both concerned not to normalise the categories and conceptualisations regarding what are and are not problems that the state generates, because such normalisations are integral to the authorisation process (Arendt 1958; Bourdieu 1994). Importantly, state institutions are a site of power (real and symbolic) and can be a site where power is evacuated, and violence replaces it. A person experiences a form of silencing either by being represented (for example, by a Member of Parliament) and/or a state contractor (for example, by a consultant). Arendt engages with this through a direct examination of sovereignty where she shares with Bourdieu the recognition of how domination operates to deny action and even provoke withdrawal from the public realm:

> The famous sovereignty of political bodies has always been an illusion, which, moreover, can be maintained only by the instruments of violence, that is, with essentially nonpolitical means. Under human conditions, which are determined by the fact that not man but men live on the earth, freedom and sovereignty are so little identical that they cannot even exist simultaneously. Where men wish to be sovereign, as individuals or as organized groups, they must submit to the oppression of the will, be this the individual will with which I force myself, or the 'general will' of an organized group. If men wish to be free, it is precisely sovereignty they must renounce. (Arendt 1977: 163)

Forswearing oligarchic club sovereignty means that whatever is thought, said, and done regarding education policy stops being an ERC as violent governing, and becomes a site of understanding and decision-making that recognises plurality, natality, and action within knowledge production. This therefore requires a political sociology of the polity, where I now turn to the idea of intelligent violence through the oligarchic occupation of the state.

4

Policy mortality

Introduction

Peacehaven Heights and Telscombe Cliffs Primary Schools were in the news in spring 2021 because parents and staff are campaigning to stop the schools being academised and run by a MAT. The parents want the LA to keep running the schools but the LA want to hand over the schools to a MAT. The first take-over attempt by a MAT was in 2019, and following the rejection of academisation by the schools, both school governing bodies were removed and replaced by Interim Executive Boards (with no parent or community membership), and this was approved by the Regional Schools Commissioner (DfE 2020). In response to the second attempt to hand the schools over to a MAT, a parent stated: 'East Sussex County Council have sacked our governors, they have shut our swimming pool, they have stood in the way of consistent leadership at the schools and put the interests of academy chains above those of our children' (Stringer 2021: NP). At the same time as this campaign was underway, Gavin Williamson, the UK Secretary of State for Education in England, gave a speech where he demanded that more schools should become academies: 'I want to see us break away from our current "pick and mix" structure of a school system and move towards a single model, one that is built on a foundation of strong multi-academy trusts, and I'm actively looking at how we can make that happen' (Adams 2021: NP).

Oligarchic occupation of the state determines the reality of what parental consumer choice actually means – parents may not want academisation and may distrust the consultation process as rigged, but depoliticised club alliances between oligarchic sovereignty in government with private oligarchies enable national policy to both marginalise local democracy and to outflank demands for citizen forms of participation. The irony in Williamson's speech is that the 'single model' of the LA system from the 1970s was attacked by the ERC, where the argument was made for the diversity of school place provision as being integral to the choice process and experience. Now that parents are rejecting academies, studio schools, and free schools in favour of retaining LA control they are being denied this choice (for example, Gunter 2011, 2018). The violence of the inclusion–exclusion segregation game has been legitimised and authorised through the ERC, and while education policy texts speak about 'improvement', 'effectiveness', and 'success', in reality, eugenicist populism means that public provision is premised on a segregation imperative in order to manage the ever-present danger of failure. Children will fail because they are deemed uneducable and so schools will fail, and society will fail because to try to educate 'those' children might arouse fear of the masses (Chitty 2007).

This chapter presents analysis from the EPKP projects that describes, understands and explains such policy violence as a form of *policy mortality*, whereby failure is a policy strategy rather than a consequence of risky innovation or poor tactical implementation. I deploy Arendtian and Bourdieusian thinking in order to examine the interplay between the state, public policy, and knowledge regarding failure as smart policy, as a form of *intelligent violence*.

Knowledgeable state

Oligarchic club sovereignty uses laws, policies, guidance, and taxpayer investment to make and prevent policy decisions, and this constitutes what Pearton (1982) characterises as the 'knowledgeable state', whereby policy regarding aims, content, and enactment is in relationship with knowledge production both within and external to the state. The state needs to be seen as knowledgeable in order to maintain legitimacy and authority, and so notions of listening, consulting, and responding are part of the policy repertoire. Pearton (1982) focused on warfare where the state is the 'overall policy-maker' and, through public revenue, 'finances the whole process' which secures planned outcomes. As such the state is a 'researcher' and so acts as a knowledge 'producer' and 'user' (254) with industry and universities regarding new technologies, where more recent analysis demonstrates how the state acts as a significant investor and underwriter in technological and medical research (for example, Massucato 2013).

The state has a monopoly over security, where rival centres of power and services are illegal, and potentially treasonous. It is recognised even by anti-state neoliberal knowledge producers that the state has to matter: 'the state has to guarantee, for example, the quality and integrity of money. It must also set up those military, defence, police, and legal structures and functions required to secure private property rights and to guarantee, by force if necessary, the proper functioning of markets' (Harvey 2007: 2).

Importantly, oligarchic occupation of the state has used the processes of depoliticisation to fortify the centralised knowledgeable state. Indeed, 'if markets do not exist (in areas such as land, water, education, health care, social security, or environmental pollution) then they must be created, by state action if necessary' (Harvey 2007: 2). Consequently, the state is not actually 'reluctant' (Ball 2012), but rather the necessity of the state for oligarchic survival has been deployed variously as 'manager' (Clarke and Newman 1997), 'evaluator' (Neave 1988), 'regulator' (Moran 2003), and 'contractor' (van den Berg et al 2020). Pro-oligarchic security and austerity policies interplay, where the state continues to matter even at a time when the state is seemingly divesting itself of costly accumulated responsibilities and assisting capital accumulation by new service providers.

The strengthening of the centralised knowledgeable state in education policy is evident in a range of ways, where governments govern through legislation and legal sanctions for non-compliance, with an acceleration in the use of legislation. Tomlinson (2005) notes that between 1944 and 1979 there were three Education Acts, but from 1980 to 2005, 'some 34 Education Acts were passed, with hundreds of accompanying circulars, regulations and statutory instruments' (8). The current UK Department for Education website is full of guidance documents and information, with over 7,000 hits for academies that include detailed non-statutory (for example, DfE 2021b) and statutory (for example, DfE 2020) guidance. The Secretary of State operates as the 'high command' for the determination of preferred knowledge production through policy texts regarding priorities, schedules, and contracts. Research shows the relationship between the ERC and the personal knowing of those favoured by governments, whether elected (for example, Ribbins and Sherratt 1997) or contracted (for example, Gunter and Mills 2017).

For example, from the 1970s onwards oligarchic occupiers have extended and invested in autonomy as a justification for the existence and continuation of segregated school services. The policy problem was and remains the success of in-common schools at primary and secondary levels, where high levels of achievement and the development of children as persons challenged oligarchic dominance (Gunter 2018). The ERC continues to promote oligarchic notions of liberty as an intelligent solution to the contrived crisis of the common school, and this can be illustrated by Kenneth Baker, who as Secretary of State for Education and Science (1986–1989), led on school autonomy through the 1988 ERA. In an interview with Ribbins he explains how his own ideological positioning impacted:

> I certainly wanted greater choice. ... There was a huge continent of which was state education, catering for over 93 per cent of all children. Then there was private education, a relatively small island with 7 per cent. And there were no links between them all; no other types of islands or semi-continents. What we have done is to create a lot of semi-continents in the CTCs and in the grant-maintained schools. I was also very interested in the administration of the whole system. I had

been a business manager and was therefore interested in the mechanics of management. (Ribbins 1997a: 105)

Baker's experiences as a student, a business leader, an MP, and a school governor all impacted on this thinking about the need for vital interventions into professional knowledge and skills regarding curriculum, testing, and teaching training. He explains how policy was developed:

> A lot of the policies we developed were produced through a process of discussion, debate and examination around the table. I am a great believer in that way of doing things. But certainly the idea of grant-maintained schools owed more to me than I think to anybody else. I remember seeing Margaret (Thatcher) in the division lobby just before the Christmas of 1986 – we were discussing education in a general way – and I said, 'I want to try out an idea on you which would mean giving parents a bigger say on closures of schools, and on the possibility of schools operating outside of the local education authority as a result of a choice by parents.' And she said, 'What a very interesting idea. Please pursue it. I am broadly in sympathy with it.' … And so we developed the idea of the grant-maintained school. (Ribbins 1997a: 109)

For Baker, change had to be speedy and had to work. He claimed to understand the barriers:

> I wanted to release the energy in the system. An energy which was being constrained by all sorts of historic devices, of traditional ways of doing things. I genuinely wanted to energize people; to allow them to do the things they had always wanted to but could not within the existing system. I wanted to energize governors who wanted to get more involved in the management of the school. I wanted to enable business people who wished to do so to get involved. We were not going to achieve this by going through the local education authorities. I was quite clear about that. When you come to reform, something you have to decide is whether you basically try to do it from within or whether you do it from without. If you do it from within you've got to make quite sure that you're not seduced, as Keith (Joseph) was, by the system. The powers of seduction are enormous. The powers of inertia are enormous. (Ribbins 1997a: 109)

The interview transcript is a smart celebration of segregation to be achieved by dismantling local democracy, advantaging private oligarchies in business, and viewing the public as stratified consumers rather than as citizens. Importantly, disapproved-of change by previous Labour governments and LAs were negatively conceptualised, where the comprehensive school is presented as destructive of good schools (usually grammar schools) undertaken as 'a deliberate political vendetta' (92) and based on a false 'social nature' aim of all children attending their local in-common school (92). What is intelligent about what Baker says is not just the content and tone in regard to parents who had themselves attended a grammar school, but how what he said was listened to because he spoke about 'the realities that people experience' (Apple 2006: 27). Eugencist populism remains deeply entrenched in English culture and practice, and so the recognition that comprehensive schools meant that children were doing well even though they were not supposed to disrupted normalised hierarchies and the scramble for superiority.

The impact of such policy actors in senior roles in government on the development of the ERC can be understood through the conceptualisation of 'institutionalized governance', whereby oligarchic occupation enables contractual agreements with trusted individuals and associated interconnections (Gunter and Forrester 2009). Hence oligarchic occupiers such as Baker provide a glimpse into how the legitimising and authorising of violence within, by, and through the state takes place, where it is clear that those in formal roles require confirmation and validation internally within government (for example, Prime Minister; Treasury), the party (for example, groups such as No Turning Back in the Conservative Party), and external oligarchic interests (for example, the wider 'selectorate' through to specific elite interests such as faith and business, and even Baker himself who from 2011 has been setting up University Technical Colleges as providers of vocational education, Wilby 2011).

Institutionalised governance works through depoliticised privatism, corporatism, and populism by inviting oligarchic interests in civil society into policy making that is distant from direct political scrutiny and accountability. Such forms of depoliticisation are evident: first, consultants are contracted to conceptualise and present the reform agenda, for example, Local Management of Schools was designed by Coopers and Lybrand (1988); second, private sector providers enter the market as reforms require in order to provide educational services, for example, the CTCs set up from 1988 (Dale 1989b); third, philanthropic donors invest in products that they believe in and want to support, and provide governments with brand association, for example, the City Academies from 2000 were sponsored by individuals and companies (Gunter 2011); and fourth, education professionals who support the reform agenda are used as role models, with evidence of headteachers working to not only make policy delivery work but also to extend and develop it (see Kulz 2017; Hughes 2019, 2020). In addition, intellectual work is undertaken in ways that sustain the issues and create the cultural practices in which school autonomy is nested and protected. Hence think tanks provide ideas and sustain the rhetoric through pamphlets, conferences, and enabling supporters within Whitehall to be ready and able to speak up and about an issue (for example, Croft et al 2013); and international organisations such as the OECD interplay national and global agendas that promote particular ideas such as school autonomy (for example, OECD 2011). In addition, the grand ideas of a Secretary of State are translated into credible and viable new organisational and professional practices, where for example, Caldwell and Spinks (1988) provided the template to enable school autonomy to work, and companies such as Pearson have provided educational products to ensure that schools operate in a capitalist economy (Hogan et al 2016).

Institutionalised governance depends on the primacy of the state, where millions of pounds are invested to support and retain entry into government matters: from appointment to offices of state (for example, Baker and others as Secretary of State) to formal employment in Whitehall (for example, Michael Barber as Head of the Standard and Effectiveness Unit, SEU) through to invitations to join policy enactment consultations (for example, Hopkins 2001). Relationships are established and facilitated by people moving occupations between a range of organisations such as schools, universities, and private consultancy firms. Ways of knowing remain located in oligarchic beliefs and experiences, and have been veiled and enabled by technical evaluations, and the translation of commercial models of good practice into the school context (for example, DfES/PwC 2007). Esteem and acclaim along with rewards (financial, cultural through state honours) are given to knowledge actors in practice, business, faith, and higher education who collaborate with, promote and develop the preferred knowledgeable and ways of knowing. Attributions given to individuals and organisations as being 'in the know' and hence assuming, accessing, owning, mobilising, deploying, and exhibiting of intelligent knowledgeabilities are displayed in what is said and done in the right place at the right time.

Policy mortality and education policy

The individual and corporate fabrications regarding housing, poverty, assessment, and academies presented in the introductory sections of Chapters 1–4 have been produced for and by the knowledgeable state, and illuminate how the sorting and management of bodies is identified as the core concern for education policy. The puzzle for smart policymakers is not only to maintain and extend segregation but to create and nurture deceptions about change that is not change, and most certainly to prevent disquiet and potential opposition, not least through court cases and news reports that expose realities. Integral to this is the strategic use of *policy mortality* whereby the rhetoric is one of inclusive success (we are in this together), but in reality the strategy and tactics are premised on the divisiveness of failure: certain groups are characterised as failing (for example, the right wing press present public servants, whether teachers or judges, as 'the enemy', Phipps 2016); the fear of failure is integral to the production of quality processes and goods because it is causally linked to working harder (for example, right wing politicians present narratives of hardworking families as strivers who get up early to go to work, in contrast with feckless parents who remain in bed 'sleeping off a life on benefits', Jowit 2013); and, some children and teachers will fail as a necessary part of the process (for example, if 'we' collectively see or hear about failure then 'we' will learn from this and it will enable those who succeed to be vindicated by their superiority).

For example, the policy of failing schools cuts across both left and right ideological positions of parties who have held office in successive UK governments from the 1970s, and it has become so pervasive and normalised that it is described as a national and globalised 'movement' (Tomlinson 1997; Meyers and Murphy 2007). One daily newspaper reported: 'England's worst schools REVEALED – is YOUR child's school on the list?' (Miller and Evans 2019); with accounts of what this means: 'Failing schools face closure' (BBC 1998b), and 'Failing headteachers will be sacked if they can't turn schools around, says Education secretary Nicky Morgan' (Harding 2015). The ERC is so damning because such failure is not an example of the types of heroic failure to be celebrated as a legacy of empire (for example, Scott of the Antarctic), because the hitherto acceptance of failing heads, teachers, parents, and children illustrates the 'cultural malaise' that is responsible for the UK's decline (Barczewski 2016). Zero tolerance of failure is the message from these media headlines, but in play at the same time is the deliberate creation of the reality and possibility of a failing school as integral to the rescue of schools. This is *policy mortality* because it uses strategies and tactics that result in predicted and actual systemic, organisational and professional 'death'. The diagnosis tends to be partly organic in regard to how the DfE (2016) talks about schools being diseased as 'chronic failure' (105) and partly instrumental through images of malfunctioning with breakdowns of structures and systems by teachers who sabotage children's education. There can be restorative interventions from school improvement/effectiveness solutions (for example, DfES 2004), or a decision can be made to 'euthanise' the teacher, and/or student, and/or the whole school, and/or the LEA (Courtney and Gunter 2015). This can be illustrated through how one director of a major public education agency stated: "most of the bad schools are located in maybe thirty, forty LEAs that are not up to the job, and the only way you're going to raise the standards is to give the schools independence and appoint outstanding headteachers" (Project 15). In practice this means:

> 'what we do is to partner failing schools with high performing schools, because often these failing schools, about four hundred schools in the

country that we define as low attaining … many of these schools have not performed well in years, not made any progress. Probably half of them will become academies, be closed and become academies. Some might become part of a trust with a high performing school, but if the headteacher's no good, you've got to move them on. And typically with the academy programme, we just pay them a hundred thousand pounds and just have them go.' (Project 15)

Certification of life or death, functioning or broken, lies with a range of agencies and roles, but significantly the Ofsted inspection categories matter: 'Outstanding', 'Good', 'Requires Improvement', and 'Inadequate', the latter sub-divided into 'Serious Weaknesses' or 'Requiring Special Measures'. For schools that are deemed 'Inadequate' then, the interventions may not achieve functionality, and so the postmortem and inquest can generate a what went wrong analysis and/or can be fast tracked in order to close the school. The Ofsted framework is procedural and can be altered in ways that trip up schools that thought they were secure and playing the game in approved-of ways (Lightfoot 2020). Schools that used to be 'successful' and are now downgraded may appeal against an Ofsted category, and this has generated a consultancy industry in pre- and post-inspection 'in the know' preparation and follow up (Gunter and Mills 2017). While Howlett (2012) argues that the exercise of judgement about failure tends to demonstrate partiality and incompleteness, it is the case that in education the production and legitimacy of a judgement has become a scientific truth. Hence policy mortality is different from the 'disasters', 'fiascos', 'blunders' (McConnell 2015: 224), and 'mistakes' (Lupton and Hayes 2021) caused by design and implementation failures to deliver goals on time and on budget, rather it is a proactive structural and cultural practice designed to shape agentic thinking, attitudes and conduct about the spectacle of blame, shame, and acclaim.

Policy mortality raises questions about the interplay between knowledge production as policy intention and the realities of enactment. The law requires implementation fidelity but there are policies based on guidance rather than prescription (for example, Teacher Appraisal, see Gunter 2002), and so there are opportunities for professional expertise and localised policymaking (Bowe et al 1992). Dale (1994) brings important perspectives to the dimensions of what is legally required and what actually happens in classrooms through his characterisation of 'the politics of education' and 'education politics' (35). Importantly, 'the politics of education' is focused on '*the agenda for* education and the processes and structures through which it is created' (Dale 1994: 35, my emphasis). School autonomy has been *the agenda* used by successive UK governments *for* education in England from the 1970s onwards, and so knowledge production *for the agenda* of failing schools requires the study of the interplay of the state (government institutions, rules, and personnel) and potential allies (and enemies) within civil society (for example, parents, professionals, trade unionists, faith groups, researchers, consultants, business people). Integral to this is how and why 'education politics' engages with *the* agenda as *this* agenda through how the policy is read and engaged with in homes, streets, offices, and classrooms: 'practitioners do not confront policy texts as naïve readers, they come with histories, with experience with values and purposes of their own, they have vested interests in the meaning of policy' (Bowe et al 1992: 22). However, the date of this assessment of localised policymaking is 1992, and this coincides with the setting up of Ofsted, where the framework was designed to codify standards and processes, where compliance rather than professional judgement is officially required. Consequently, what matters are 'the processes whereby *this agenda* is translated into problems and issues for schools, and schools' responses to those problems and issues' (Dale 1994: 35, my emphasis). Much continues to be debated regarding agenda setting and delivery (see Chapter 9), but *the agenda* of the ERC becomes *this agenda* for schools through three main processes: the possibility and reality of a failing school is *weaponised* in order to reverse the gains made through investment in public education; is *calculated* where what constitutes a higher standard is both fixed and subject to change, and this is decided outside of classrooms and schools; and is *enacted* as a normalised practice through improvement and effectiveness technologies that depend on the reworking of professional codes of practice.

Policy mortality is evident in four strategic research themes within EPKP projects (Appendix):

Theme 1: System Design (and ongoing re-design) has been studied in a number of EPKP investigations (for example, Projects 1, 11, 16, 20), where doctoral projects show there is strong evidence of local strategic decision-making regarding academisation (Project 26, for example, Rayner and Gunter 2020), but at the same time there is also not only professional collaboration but also significant personal gains and losses made through leading the changes (Project 26, for example, Courtney 2015; Hughes 2020). Importantly, the EPKP projects show strong evidence of policy mortality through first, how knowledge production is weaponised within and against the profession, and can be illustrated by a chair of governors at an academy who proclaimed that "… I've really brought my experience of business into the academy" (Project 20). The ruthlessness of deal-making can be illustrated by an academy headteacher who in talking about the legal process for reviewing the staff and deciding whether they would have a job at the new academy, stated: "I absolutely 100% knew that I was not taking all them shit people out of the predecessor schools … I wasn't prepared to have them because I know that if you give me two rusty sheds at the bottom of the garden and excellent people, I'll give you a school" (Project 20). Second, is calculated whereby a headteacher of a successful comprehensive school reasoned that the plan for conversion into an academy following the 2010 legislation was based on the notion of "getting on the train before it left the station" where one senior leader stated: "I think the SLT viewpoint is that all schools will become academies eventually and you're better off being on board early on rather than later – I think it's a pragmatic approach. I think [the head] saw a possibility of gaining a higher profile for the school" (Project 26, see McGinity and Gunter 2017). Third, is enacted whereby academy conversion was undertaken without the assent of the students who were meant to be beneficiaries of the change, where my fieldwork notes at an assembly at the newly opened Metropolitan City Academy show that the children are the audience to professionals lauding the changes and telling them how lucky they were, and how this was different to what the children had told us in interviews, not least how school dinners were now more expensive and how they were forced to attend after school clubs (Project 16).

Theme 2: The Workforce has been studied in a number of EPKP projects that have been funded by research councils and charities (for example, Projects 2, 9, 15, 20, 23) and commissioned by local government (for example, Project 5); by agencies (for example, Projects 3, 6, 10, 12, 13); by unions (for example, Projects 17, 18, 19) and by central government (for example, 7, 8), where doctoral projects show professional commitment to students and high quality educational experiences and outcomes, where significant challenges to professional practices are charted and explained regarding educational services in England and internationally (Project 26, for example, Bradbury and Gunter 2006; Cain and Gunter 2012). This research shows that there is strong evidence of policy mortality through: first, how professionalism is weaponised through how system redesign is premised on school autonomy as causally related to innovative practice, but in reality those who are given this opportunity find themselves having to implement technological requirements (Gunter 2011). Second, it is calculated through how the workforce are required to engage in 'luxury leadership' either as the recognised special person who embodies exceptionality, or as the follower who inscribes the leader as superior and who may dare to emotionally and practically commit their career as a future CEO (Gunter et al 2018). Third, it is enacted through how headteachers as leaders, both leading and exercising leadership are required to dispose of educational professionals who do not deliver the right type of data. For example, following Collins (2001), one headteacher stated how they communicated compliance:

> 'You're either on the bus or you're off the bus. And if you're on the bus, then we'll do everything we can to help and support

you. But if you're not, then you're off the bus. And that's either through redundancy, through a restructure, through a change in roles … (or) … "do you know, what? This isn't the job for me, I'm applying elsewhere".'

Another headteacher says:

'It's all about the type of people, the right people and chucking out what wasn't needed and getting in what was. … And it's like football … if you buy the best players, you get some success. And if you don't get some success, the manager gets sacked. And I think a lot of what happens in schools is a bit like that.'

Staff, pupils, and parents have to buy into the vision and mission, as another headteacher stated: 'Staff who have fought it [the vision] are being given the message that they're not welcome here' (Courtney and Gunter 2015: 17).

Theme 3: Policy Actors have been studied in a number of EPKP projects that have been funded by research councils and charities (for example, Projects 9, 15, 20, 21, 23), through being written up as part of accreditation and/or through university funding (for example, Projects 1, 4, 22, 24, 25), and where commissioned projects (for example, Projects 7, 11) and doctoral projects (Project 26 for example, Rayner et al 2017; Hughes 2020) have provided first-hand experience of policy actors at work. This research shows that there is strong evidence of policy mortality through: first, how knowledge production is weaponised by policy actors to promote performance control as integral to breaking professional values in order to install business cultures and systems. For example, a headteacher explains how "it's a cold data-led profession, and I don't like that", and the reason given is that the relentless focus on numbers means that the realities of knowing and working with children and parents does not count (Project 15). In addition, another headteacher talks about how "a lot of the initiatives come fast and furious before the previous ones have even had time to embed themselves", and how this is the external installation of "industrial models" that lack the "human dimension" (Project 15). Second, is calculated whereby the fears of headteachers are visceral: "I think Ofsted obviously, you do feel threatened by that … and fortunately I've got a very good school and we are doing very well … but it must be difficult when you are in a school where the pressure is even bigger" (Project 15). Private consultants are actively involved in the calculation whereby those who have professional credentials are active in supporting the profession through the change: "I use the skills that I have and the experience I have to make things work for people that commission me" (Project 21). Third, is enacted whereby speedy changes, and what even supportive heads regard as ill-thought-through reforms, have to be delivered in schools. There are issues of workload whereby one headteacher talks about the Self-Evaluation Framework (SEF), and the idea is supported but "the amount of work that is involved in trying to do that properly is huge" (Project 15). What the EPKP data show is how the profession recognises important interventions that help them to do their work better: "I think Excellence in Cities is the best initiative I've ever come across'" whereas Teaching and Learning Responsibility posts "have been a very poor development" (Project 15). What the data also show is how the simplifications of policy requirements confront the realities of what it means to be an experienced professional, whereby headteachers know their schools and seemingly have little to actually learn from Ofsted inspection reports. Importantly, headteachers recognise how the enactment of policy actually destroys good schools, whereby one headteacher talks about the plans for an academy to replace a "failing school" in the locality, and so "I understand that the academy would have a lot of money poured into it, would have a lot of advantages, and yet I know all the other schools in the borough presumably wouldn't have that sort of advantage" (Project 15).

Theme 4: Knowledge Production has been fundamental to Themes 1–3, and has been directly studied in a number of EPKP projects (for example, Projects 4, 14, 15, 20, 21, 22, 24, 25), where my own doctoral projects (Gunter 1999, 2020a) and those I have supervised have given special attention to how knowledge is produced and used to categorise in ways that include/exclude (for example, Project 26 for example, Courtney 2015). This programme of research shows strong evidence of policy mortality through first, how knowledge production is weaponised whereby the model for the school leader doing leading and exercising leadership is recognised as being unacceptable, but that does not seem to matter regarding what policymakers in government think and want. One headteacher talked about transformational charismatic models that have failed (for example, Fresh Start Schools), and how the UK government prefer this model even though it is inappropriate:

> 'there are a limited number of charismatic people and we haven't got enough for every school in the country. I think secondly, it's not a model that works in terms of succession. If you go to a school where there has been a charismatic leader and they've left, it's a very hard act to follow.' (Project 15)

According to one headteacher the problem lies in the knowledge production process: "lots of good ideas, very hard-working people … but you think sometimes, well if you just sat down for a little while and thought about this, you could strip a lot of this out and get down to the real nitty gritty, but again it's the same problem, too many vested interests" (Project 15). The EPKP project data show that the fabrications nested in business models present a rationality that is exposed in the reality of doing the job, and this is calculated as a second feature through how the profession is positioned in knowledge production. As a senior member of the NCSL said: "the one thing we know that practitioners don't do is read research reports" (Project 15), and this characterises professional knowledge as what a 'practitioner' does, where that practice is actually and necessarily disconnected from the 'nitty gritty' of the impact of family and community poverty on learning as noted above, and the intellectual resources that have been developed within and by the field through researcher-professional projects. The NCSL had seminars with and for practitioners whereby listening to their 'wants', 'needs' and 'likes' enabled particular types of improvement and effectiveness research to be communicated and embedded in ways that may have considered the 'nitty gritty' but did not actually address it. Third, such knowledge is enacted through the focus on improvement, as one consultant stated: "with so much experience and data collection – there is a clearer view about what works ... so you can affect these improvements more quickly now depending on your circumstances" (Project 21). The focus on standards means that the 'nitty gritty' is what the data is saying rather than what the context is in which that data is produced, and so inconvenient evidence is discounted.

A political sociology of policy mortality

The four strategic research themes and the underpinning fieldwork evidence from the EPKP projects demonstrate the cruelty unleashed by the knowledgeable state through policy mortality as a form of *intelligent violence*. Those constructing and practising violence use and produce knowledge to play the normalised inclusion and exclusion game to win, and present ideas, practices, and imaginations in the ERC as an acclaimed intelligent response to the 'fact' of eugenicist populism. The data from the EPKP projects show how and why knowledge production has been and continues to be violent and produces violence through how policy is weaponised by using corporate and individual fabrications in order to destroy the notion of a *public* service; is calculated in order to introduce high stakes depoliticised risk and responsibility; and is enacted through performance delivery. Division within unity is promoted whereby sites of popular consumer activity are constructed through new 'types' of schools (Courtney 2015), where consumer demand and oversubscription of applications for a place in an academy is what is used to validate the violence being experienced by those who are playing the inclusion–exclusion game and those who are spectators (BBC 2007). What is particularly smart about this intelligent violence is through the acceptance of policy failure as the only agenda, not least how arguments against commercialised school autonomy are deemed to be ludicrous.

In Bourdieu's (1994) terms, capital investment matters, and in particular 'statist capital' investment in knowledge matters the most because '*the state is the culmination of a process of concentration of different species of capital*' regarding security, economy, information, and symbolism. It is not just that the state claims to be knowledgeable through the ERC, but how that knowledge is used 'to exercise power over the different fields and over the different particular species of capital, and especially over the rates of conversion between them (and thereby over the relations of force between their respective holders' (4, original emphasis). The ERC demonstrates how capital is invested to create, develop, and sustain the game in play in ways that that not only codify the *doxa* and communicate the *illusio* of the game worth playing, but also that shape the field terrain and borders regarding objective relations and struggles. Other ways of knowing to the ERC are variously ignored through to being denounced, where capitals can be devalued through this process, particularly evidence from independent primary research.

This inclusion–exclusion game is not only about the specifics and imaginings of the provision of and access to school places, but is about extending the private and limiting the public, and in doing so the actual playing of the game prevents the development of the agora as a productive site for political action in the public realm. Following Nixon's (2001) analysis of Bauman (1999), the agora is intermediate between the privacy of the home and the legislative politics of a public assembly, and as such it is a site where in Arendtian terms citizens can engage in plural-relational action in order to 'free themselves from limited interests and see the world in its many perspectives' (Bowring 2011: 29). This is seen as vital because it enables citizens to give recognition to plurality and natality regarding how differences and their resolution are made public and undertaken in public. However, in Nixon's (2001) terms, the agora is 'beleaguered' due to the ideological and practical insistence by oligarchic occupiers that private interests should withdraw from concerns other than those possessed as an individual (Macpherson 2011). Intelligent violence not only does damage to the lives of those in education services but to those within the wider *polis* who could and should be taking action to debate and resolve issues, along with exercising judgement and making promises.

The consequence of intelligent violence is that in Arendtian terms we begin 'to suffer under desert conditions' where 'the danger lies in becoming true inhabitants of the desert and feeling at home in it' (Arendt 2005: 201), and where human agency is subjected to the 'sandstorms' of 'totalitarian movements' (202). In other words, plurality and natality have been besieged and so 'what has kept those subordinate in line has been their lack of any means of resistance, and, above all, their belief in their own impotence' (Beetham 2016: 121). Educational services are being turned into a desert, where data from EPKP projects show how policy creates the possibility for children, parents, and the profession to escape to little 'improvement' and 'effectiveness' oases that are created to distract and soothe. Arendt (2005) argues that oases have to be more than a spa, because if they are not understood differently then: 'the oases, which are not places of "relaxation" but life-giving sources that let us live in the desert without becoming reconciled to it, will dry up' (203). The EPKP projects show that those living and working within communities and their schools do experience such arid conditions, but there is also evidence of taking action to expose and counter the ERC, with alternatives generated in order to live and work differently. Research shows the possibilities of creating and sustaining 'little agoras' in communities (for example, Topper 2011; Kennelly 2018) and civic-educational projects (for example, Gandin and Apple 2012), where there is 'a new way of being *together* (in difference) … a reorientation to that "political space" where the public and private meet' (Nixon 2001: 230, original emphasis).

I intend taking these ideas forward in Part II where I use fieldwork data and analysis from the EPKP projects to explain how and why the ERC is a form of policy violence (authorised, legitimate, and intelligent) and the possibility for alternatives generated by researchers in little agoras. The unfolding of the TPSF begins in Chapter 5 where I provide evidence from *Theme 1: System Design* in order to examine how and why policy actors (for example, ministers, officials, consultants, professionals, philanthropists, researchers, business owners, trade unionists) operate from different organisational/institutional *vantage points* that have different types of recognition and status. I then move onto Chapter 6 where through examining *Theme 2: The Workforce*, I examine how and why policy actors locate (and relocate) in knowledge production through deploying *viewpoints*. In Chapter 7 I investigate *Theme 3: Policy Actors* regarding how vantage points and viewpoints interplay to generate *regimes of practice*, and I develop this further in Chapter 8 by exploring how regimes operate through *exchange relationships* regarding what is or could be a public policy issue and how it might be addressed. In Chapter 9 I examine knowledge production within and against policy violence, and I further engage with the field of Critical Education Policy Studies (CEPS) to conclude the book (Chapter 10) by considering the possibilities of little agoras.

PART II

A political sociology of education policy in action

5

Vantage points

Introduction

MATs have been reluctant to take on schools where certain pupils and communities could damage the brand, and so there are schools that have become 'orphans' because no Trust will take them on (Mansell 2017). In addition, local authority schools have not all leapt at the lauded opportunities of voluntary conversion (Rayner and Gunter 2020) and there are cases of local resistance (see Chapter 4). The policy response has been to tempt schools by using a 'Try before you buy' scheme that enables MATs to take on identified failing schools (Dickens 2016: NP). Economic incentives that are 'time limited' are used to encourage schools to experience the membership of a MAT, where for the price of 'a service charge', a MAT will open its 'networks and services' with a school to demonstrate the benefits (Dickens 2021: NP). The use of targeted funding to lever system change is not new (McGinity and Gunter 2017) and currently it is premised on a form of benign coercion underpinned by the assurance that it is reversible, but in reality, schools and MATs become locked in, and so the actual conversion process with potential parental opposition is eased. The academisation of schools in England is incomplete (22 per cent primary and 68 per cent secondary), and so the remaining unconverted maintained local authority schools are a problem for UK governments that want to dismantle local democracy in favour of markets underpinned by eugenicist populist ideology. A huge contradiction exists whereby school, teacher, student, and democratic system failure are integral to education policy, and yet specific reform interventions cannot be seen to fail, and so those involved must navigate in choppy waters.

Investigating such matters through the EPKP projects requires explanation through the TPSF. This validates the importance of *vantage points* in education policy, or the organisational location of the person or group involved in public decision-making. Research within the EPKP projects demonstrates that the *core* is the prime vantage point, and I examine policy violence through *Theme 1: System Design*.

Education policy vantage points

Policy violence through the ERC is legitimised, authorised, and intelligent, and as such it is located within and dependent upon the recognition of vantage points by and for policy actors. Vantage points are organisational locations for decision-making that legitimise modernisation, authorise through governing by knowledge production (for example, departments of state through to consultancies through to homes), and are sites of intelligent knowledgeability that weaponise, calculate, and enact what needs to be known as worth knowing in order to frame and deliver vital reforms. Policy actors in certain vantage points identify what and whose knowledge counts, and hence intelligently limit the opportunities to understand and to think otherwise. Based on Fitzgerald and Gunter (2005) there are four main vantage point positions in education policymaking.

Core

This vantage point is located in the institutions of the UK state and is structured by public rules, cultures, and practices, and private interpretations of said rules, cultures, and practices. For example, primarily this is Whitehall, but historically this has included local authorities, schools, and universities. Such vantage points are: repositories of knowledges where some are codified, some operate by convention, and some are not recorded; knowings are facts, rules, systems, spreadsheets, beliefs, assumptions, and gossip; knowers such as ministers, researchers, and teachers; and knowledgeabilities or cultural practices, languages, modes of communication, architecture, offices, furniture, and titles. The core is stratified and dynamic, where within Whitehall there are different locations of and struggles for power (for example, No 10, Treasury), and there is dominance over other parts of the core (for example, universities and schools). The core protects dominance through the deployment of sovereign power not only over the core but other vantage points, where some policy actors who are privileged and safe have been institutionalised into the core, particularly through governing strategies that direct and deliver change through the judicious use of 'command and control', 'quasi-markets', and 'delegated responsibility' (Barber 2007b). Data from the EPKP projects show how negotiating positioning can be vicious, where one professor explains how s/he decided to be "absolutely independent" from political parties, and having declined an invitation to review a speech by Blair s/he was "cut out" from policy matters (Project 15). Alternative sites of potential control and autonomy can be tolerated but have tended to be closed down, and so Local Authorities and maintained schools have been marginalised, where acceptance of academisation and MAT control enables schools to submit to oligarchic representation and LAs to be rendered redundant. Universities as sites of commissioned evaluations by 'world leading' professors can be used to award status to evidence, but independent primary research and postgraduate study have been othered.

Privileged

This vantage point is located in the agency of individuals and groups within civil society as private and globalised oligarchies, who are enabled by reputation, achievements, and acclaim from those within the core. For example, privileged vantage points are used by professionals, philanthropists, consultancies, business, faith groups, think tanks, researchers, and charities, and they are: repositories of approved-of knowledge, ways of knowing, and knowledgeabilities that are held and demonstrated by favoured knowers. The privileged are dynamic where, for example, certain professionals may be selectively recognised by the core, while the profession as a whole can be marginalised and othered. Certain people and organisations can be institutionalised and so have opportunities to impact and deliver policy either in specific roles (for example, Cyril Taylor at the SSAT); EEIR researchers who lead on policy (for example, David Hopkins and the NSCL and the SEU); and professionals who are called in to 'turn around' failing schools (for example, Stubbs 2003). Groups and interests can be contracted to help frame and develop government policy such as consultancy firms (for example, PwC and academies and school leadership, Gunter and Mills 2017), individual entrepreneurs (for example, sponsoring academies, Gunter 2011), and faith groups (for example, city academies, Woods et al 2007). Data from the EPKP projects show that recognition by the core can strengthen the privileged vantage point where headteachers who led on GMS in the 1980s through to academisation from the 2000s can be attributed high status as effective leaders (Projects 20, 21). However, those involved do want to retain some independence, and so data from the EPKP projects show that 'famous' headteachers of successful schools did not always want to join the core regarding the work of the NCSL, and so while these heads benefited from policy they did not necessarily want to be publicly integrated into the core (Project 15).

Marginal

This vantage point is at a distance from and may be located outside of the formal state structures, and can include private and globalised oligarchies who may or may not be concerned with policy scoping and influence. Such vantage points are: repositories of knowledge, ways of knowing, and knowledgeabilities promoted by knowers that potentially could be relevant to the core. For example, resignation/sacking from a role in Whitehall moves someone from the centre to the periphery, and/or a change of governing party following a general election sees a change in oligarchic membership, and/or through events that make those on the margins either strategically or pragmatically relevant/irrelevant (see Beckett 2007; Gunter 2011). The margins are dynamic where there are the dispossessed who were core insiders and are now outside. For example, Reynolds (2007) having chaired the Department of Education and Skills Numeracy Task force in the 1990s, is highly critical of PM Brown's announcement of *Every Child Counts* initiative because it is not based on the evidence and strategy that had already been in operation before the committee stopped meeting in 2002. In addition, there are those who position in anticipation as ever-ready to accept contractual roles in core knowledge production as advisors, members of committees and/or as commissioned evaluators of government interventions (see Gunter and Mills 2017). The mantra of 'turning around a school' is a contractual opportunity for a range of policy actors, for example, the data from the EPKP projects show that headteachers can use the appointment to a failing school to reposition their professional brand. As one headteacher said in reviewing potential posts in a range of schools: "I was looking for a 'doer-upper'" as an opportunity to prove what s/he could do (Project 20), and so be worthy of privileged and core recognition. In addition, the construction of a failing school crisis generates mini-vantage points within a school where staff are required to position around the rescue narrative, where one teacher stated: "I've been very fortunate under his leadership" (Project 20).

Othered

This vantage point is located in the agency of individuals and groups within civil society who are private and globalised oligarchies, but who are positioned as unrecognised contributors to knowledge production, and if they are known by the core and the privileged, they may be ignored or even vilified. Such vantage points are: repositories of knowledge based on independent primary research with espoused ontologies and epistemologies where particular ways of knowing and knowledgeabilities are deemed oppositional to policy, and where knowers receive acclaim from their work (for example, professors in universities) but are positioned as irrelevant to policy or even enemies by the core (see Gunter 2012). For example, Tooley with Darby (1998) are dismissive of education researchers and their work as 'partisan' (28) and based on the 'adulation of great thinkers' (56). While the othered can be homogenised and so easily dismissed as irrelevant, in reality this vantage point is dynamic through knowledge production and reporting, and the othered may see their position developed through association with dissatisfied and excluded privileged and marginal policy actors. Importantly, trade unions have variously been in all four vantage points, where, for example, they have been institutionalised into the core regarding New Labour through the remodelling the school workforce policy and the Social Partnership; but also marginalised and sometimes othered by the UK Conservative Government during the COVID-19 pandemic.

While the four vantage points can be distinguished as identifiable sites of authoritative, legitimate, and intelligent decision-making, the dynamics of oligarchic club sovereignty means that borders can be simultaneously permeable and impermeable. There are a number of key features: first, *intersectional engagement*: a policy actor may remain in an organisational location but operate at the juncture of vantage points regarding informal discussions through to formal contractual relations between privileged and core vantage points, for example, a consultancy company that accepts a contract to deliver a policy intervention. Importantly, occupiers have shifted advisors and deliverers within the state from neutral career civil servants based on open-competition recruitment to corporate contracted consultants who provide privatised solutions to governing problems (Gunter 2020b). Second, *revolving doors*: people may shift vantage points, and this can operate in strategic policy whereby occupiers have invested in eugenicist ideas and the modernising genetic science promoted by advisors (for example, Cummings 2013) and policy enactors (for example, Young 2015) in order to maintain and extend segregationist normalities. Policy enactment demonstrates such shifts, where a headteacher such as Michael Wilshaw has been acclaimed for turning around a successful school (privileged) and is appointed to head up Ofsted (core) (see Kulz 2017), and Peter Hyman as Blair's speech writer (core) shifted from No 10 to working in a mainstream school (othered), and set out to privilege the school sector through academisation (Hyman 2005). Third, *exclusionary blocking*: policy actors can ensure that actual and potential rivals stay within marginal and othered vantage points, for example, the winning of commissioned evaluation projects (privileged), and how independent primary research is discounted (othered). Oligarchic occupiers are networked with the media (it is reported that Boris Johnson regards the *Daily Telegraph* as 'my real boss', Rawnsley 2021: NP), and lobby groups such as those located at 55 Tufton Street in London that are pro-market, anti-EU, and anti-climate change, utilise the privilege–core vantage point to promote and secure an anti-state agenda. The language of 'elite' and 'establishment' is used in pejorative ways in order to remove and replace research experts by those who are in effect members of the oligarchic elite and establishment. This is evident in how the major crises in oligarchic legitimacy, authority, and smartness-to-govern within and external to state institutions have been characterised and managed.

The dynamics of vantage point activity is evident in how children and parents are addressed as beneficiaries and partners, and can be rhetorically privileged through how the ERC speaks for the normative benefits of consumer choice and competition. However, children and parents are objectified by the core through the focus on aspirations as 'public interest' issues such as testing, where oligarchic occupiers insist rather than consult. In addition, eugenicist populism means that some parents and children matter more than others, and so the majority of children are marginalised, and some are othered. This is rarely admitted to as the ERC talks about standards for all and the closing of the attainment gap, where the media produce fabrications by treating all 'knowledge as an opinion' where expert data and analysis is 'balanced' with non-expert beliefs (Wren-Lewis 2018: 3). Ignorance is celebrated, facts and opinions equated, where Nichols' (2017) argument about the US resonates with the situation in England, where 'to reject the advice of experts is to assert autonomy, a way for Americans to insulate their increasingly fragile egos from ever being told they're wrong about anything' (x). Consequently, oligarchic occupiers present themselves as the problem identifiers and solvers, and deny legitimacy, authority, and intelligence from those who know otherwise. The capacity to be taught is shrivelling because mistrust as a public policy strategy is reworking the interconnection between the private and public realms that sustain and produce ERC fabrications. Hence, while research evidence demonstrates the causal relationship between poverty and underachievement (Raffo et al 2010), this is usually inaudible in the ERC, and where attempts to turn up the volume are dismissed as 'excuses' made by those who are positioned as 'the enemies of promise' (see Gove 2013b).

A case study of vantage points

The EPKP projects have produced research evidence and analysis that demonstrates the actuality and validity of vantage points (see Gunter 2011), and here I focus on *Theme 1: System Design.* This important theme connects back to my MSc dissertation project that examined the introduction of Local Management of Schools in 1988 (Gunter 1990), and has been the focus of ongoing studies into the provision and access to educational services in England (Gunter and McGinity 2014; Courtney 2015; Rayner et al 2017), and by examining the privatisation of education in England (Gunter 2012, 2018) and in Chile (Carrasco and Gunter 2019). What these projects demonstrate is that the ERC constructs and deploys system design as a state regulated but privately devised service through the promotion of consumer choice interplayed with marketised provision. The private sector commodifies educational products regarding brand, status, and outcomes, where the objective of the ERC is to discredit and dismantle public services education, to establish consumer choice options for aspirational parents who cannot afford fees but can mimic segregated private provision within the state system, and to residualise education services for the majority through cutting investment, deprofessionalising accredited teachers, and economising the curriculum and outcomes. I intend focusing on this policy violence through examining the relationship between the ERC and vantage points, and the setting up of Metropolitan City Academy (anonymised name) in the first decade of the 21st Century (Project 16).

Metropolitan City Academy (MCA) is one of the initial group of City Academies from 2000 that were designed by New Labour (1997–2010) to inject innovation through school autonomy and independence:

> For too long, too many children have been failed by poorly-performing schools which have served to reinforce inequality of opportunity and disadvantage. City Academies will create new opportunities for business, the voluntary sector and central and local government to work together to break this cycle and improve the life chances of inner city children. (Blunkett 2000a: NP)

The plan was for radical change in cities, where the prospectus called for sponsors who 'may be businesses, individuals, churches or voluntary bodies, or partnerships within or across these categories, and willing and able to establish a school for the purpose' (DfEE 2000b: 8). The separation of the provision of and access to school places from the local authority was regarded as vital for improving standards, whereby private sponsors illuminate the depoliticisation of decision-making:

> They appoint a majority of the governors; they control the school estate; they have unambiguous responsibility for management and appointments; they instill their ethos and expectations; they develop – within broad parameters – their own curriculum; and their budget comes as a single block grant from the government to allocate as they think appropriate, with no intermediaries taking a top slice on the way. By the standards of state-funded schools at home and abroad, this is a high degree of independence. (Adonis 2007: NP)

Initially, sponsorship was up to £2m (in funds and in kind, for example, expertise, abolished in 2006) where such investment was integral to the modernising shift from taxation to philanthropy, with role models to inspire hope in disadvantaged communities. The MCA replaced two comprehensive schools where falling rolls due to middle class flight combined with a lack of investment in education and the wider community had impacted negatively on student output data that is used to determine standards (for example, attendance and punctuality of children and teachers, and examination results). In addition, the political culture where the academy is located had hitherto resisted the financialisation of service provision and everyday life, and so were required to experience a major rupture in provision and access to education in order to break embedded attitudes to work, aspirations, and family life. The project was funded by the British Academy and set out to study the establishment of the MCA through interviews, observations, questionnaires, and primary sources that took place between 2007 and 2008.

The data from the MCA project demonstrate that the core vantage point is where the key decisions were made to close two schools, and to fund and invest in an academy with new staff and make an 'offer' to the community that was framed as modern and vital. In order for this to happen, private commercial sponsors were brought in by the core in order to promote intersectional engagement, where the ongoing shift from paying tax to public philanthropy was fostered. As one sponsor stated: "I've got a view that if you've managed to do well in life and someone has given you a leg up you owe it to give several other people a leg up" (Sponsor 1). Sponsors were involved not only through funding but to ensure the imposition of modernised practices from a privileged vantage point of knowing how to run education as a business, and how the community could demonstrate approved-of dispositions regarding how to raise capital and to market products: "a generation of students who are better educated and more enterprising and will regenerate the area" (Sponsor 3). Professionals who staffed the school had to reject the LA and adopt business performance practices, and as such were protected by the core and the privileged from those who had been othered and marginalised in the community and the predecessor schools. While the ERC was deployed to present the MCA as a modernising opportunity for all children and parents in the locality, in reality, it was a disciplinary process of assimilation into economic practices required to turn welfare dependent communities into reliable and biddable workers for those who stayed, and aspirational entrepreneurs for those who left. Notably, sponsorship was recognised as integral to capital accumulation, where one teacher stated: "we are going with books or software because they've got their finger in companies that have these books or software."

The data gathered about the setting up of the MCA is illustrative of policy violence through how vantage points demonstrate forms of legitimised, authorised, and intelligent violence.

Legitimised violence is evident in a range of ways in which the core characterised the context, scoped the problem, and provided the solution to that problem. The closure of the two predecessor schools sent the signal that comprehensive schools with open access by the community were failing because they were under local authority control, and that the preservation and intensification of segregation (under the New Labour banner of diversity) was the reform imperative. The MCA was established as non-selective but in order to operate in an urban region with falling rolls there was a need to compete for students at key transition points (at 11 and 16 years of age). Such competition not only meant the brand had to appeal to existing parents (and be part of the cultural change to prevent further decline) but also to parents who would not normally see the predecessor schools or the catchment area on their list as an option for a school place. The processes used to do this were located in the ERC, where problems are portrayed as behavioural, for example, attendance by pupils and teachers was identified as a problem that needed fixing fast. Notably, local children and parents were characterised as in deficit and in need of conversion to a better and more worthy life as that demonstrated by the core and the privileged vantage points: "a number of children were coming through, either from single parent, difficult homes or where English wasn't the first language spoken at home, and children arriving at secondary school without literacy and numeracy" (Sponsor 2). Investment from the core through Building Schools for the Future (BSF) (a new school building was planned) and corporate sponsorship meant that the social and economic capital of children and families could be revalued by changing "the perception of education in the community" (Sponsor 2).

Problem solving was through the discrediting of one hierarchy, and its replacement by a modernised hierarchy that is validated by corporate sponsorship and governance, and through new logos on letters home and webpages. Education professionals in the two predecessor schools, local networks of headteachers, and the LA where subjected to exclusionary blocking and so could no longer be allowed to determine the purposes and standards of education. Parents and children had to obey a contract through acceptance of a uniform that allowed no individuality (including branded bags and coats), and of an enrichment curriculum that was *de facto* a compulsory lengthening of the school day. The core therefore determined the supremacy of the privileged corporate vantage points regarding their wealth, networks, and biographies that often showed 'rags to riches' role models with inspirational stories, and rooted legitimacy not only in philanthropic 'I want to give something back' accounts but also recognition by traditional privileged interests such as higher education as sponsors. Hence the professionals at MCA where appointed on the basis of controlled revolving doors, and were put under the control and protection of corporatised sponsors through the academy governance system, where the job of the professionals was to deliver the right type of data in order to demonstrate a worthwhile investment of money and reputation, and depoliticised regulation through Ofsted and other core scrutiny visitors determined tactical delivery agendas, and how data would be presented and interpreted.

Integral to the new hierarchy was the 'leaderisation' of the organisation. The establishment of an entrepreneurial vision based on what staff and students identified as 'command and control' from the top, meant that all are identified as potential and actual leaders operating according to a procedural and delegated agenda. The focus was on identifying and training 'middle leaders' as integral to connecting classroom practices with the requirements from the core and privileged vantage points. Key to this tactic was to close down sites and opportunities for professional discretion and judgement by embracing innovation as different from anything that did or might have taken place in the two predecessor schools, and for those new to the profession, the focus was on their opportunities to conform in ways that would be career enhancing. The children were positioned as enterprising leaders in classrooms and in teams, and events within and external to school were used to create a sense of disassociation with their home community, combined with potential aspirations to accept corporate cloning.

Authorised violence is evident in private matters regarding what is known and is regarded as worth knowing. The ERC is personalised by the sponsors and espoused as truthful opinion, hence the leader-centric CEO role is transferred from the business world into turning a school around, where corporate knowledges allow sponsors to speak on professional matters: "I would like to see more formal testing of children actually earlier, soon after they enter secondary school to help the schools diagnose what the remedial problems are and for people to be able to have a much better understanding of the value-added" (Sponsor 1). The new House system was based on a sponsor who thought it worked well in the private school where his/her own child was being educated, and that the approach to pastoral care would help children deal with broken homes. In addition, fabrications abound in the data, for example, "teacher training is something that's been probably not done terribly well historically", and "there'd been very little change or experimentation in education in state schools since the comprehensive system was introduced" (Sponsor 1). The 'freedoms' awarded to academies regarding the curriculum does mean that more experimentation was taking place in school, where staff spoke of coming up with an idea and being given permission to run with it and to learn from it. Hence single sex classrooms for certain subjects were set up without engagement with the research evidence, almost as if such experimentation had validity because it was locally authorised. Within the MCA there is evidence of how such 'good ideas' were necessary to establish provision as different: "you take an idea from somewhere, it could be anybody's idea, and you have a go at it and it doesn't work, you just scrap it and start again" (Principal). The strategy for what is recognised and counted as a good idea created a buzz within the school, but in reality control lies externally with the core in association with the privileged sponsors, and so what is new and original in classrooms is about tactical delivery of elite agendas. What used to exist is wrong, with the aim to show families and the community a better way.

Students and staff spoke about the experience of these forms of violence: first, the students had mixed experiences, where teamwork and more choice were appreciated, with recognition of more investment in technology and new teachers, but there are dissenting voices regarding the cost of food in the canteen, behaviour management, over-testing, and how the children said: "they don't understand like we're still kids and not adults". The children provided insights into how they have experienced speedy change, where one student said: "the headteacher ... kinda thinks this is a private school ... (and has) got to know that this isn't an area where people may talk properly or people dress appropriately and stuff", and where another engages in resistance against compulsory 'after school' enrichment: "I'll be honest I just walk out the gate". Second, the staff also gave accounts of a range of experiences, where recognition and celebration of achievements was welcomed, where one teacher spoke about "leadership is very open". However, another teacher characterised the culture as "leadership by diktat"; there is no union, and one teacher said, "the atmosphere at (MCA) is one of fear" and "people are walking on egg shells" because staff are told what to do and if they don't deliver they are called out in public.

The MCA is a product of and a contributor to policy mortality, whereby the comprehensive system had to be declared a failure locally by visitors from the core (Ofsted judgements, Whitehall officials visiting to examine the case for the MCA) and by privileged vantage point investors in order to legitimise and authorise the academies programme. In addition, the city academies had to produce data that allowed them to be declared as successful in order for policy to be given a new mandate at a forthcoming election, and this required other successful schools to be challenged and threatened in the marketplace through segregated secession. Forms of intelligent violence are evident in the ongoing struggle to demonstrate to the core that the remit of city academies was being delivered, and how locally the 'new kid on the block' was making a difference to the production of corporate thinking and practices within the community. This was summed up in the use of the word academisation where children, parents, and staff at MCA as an independent state school were enculturated into the demands of the ERC, where data from external and internal inspection determined identity and potential, where children at MCA now actually meet targets: "this is academising them into wanting to achieve" (Vice-Principal). Such achievements were also based on operationalising the fear of failure through making local intelligent interpretations of how higher standards are demonstrated. For example, MCA (along with other schools) made good use of the equivalence of BTEC with GCSEs (Level 2 BTEC First Diploma is equivalent to 4 GSCEs), and so MCA could demonstrate speedy improvement in how many students at 16 had achieved the national benchmark of five A*–C grades at GCSE.

Such fabrications are not unique to the academies programme as the ERC generates savvy calculations about positioning in the inclusion–exclusion game in education policy, where it is clear in the data that the improvements at MCA could have taken place under the LA and certainly in the predecessor schools. What those predecessor schools required was at least the same level of investment in buildings and resources as the academies programme, and the same freedoms regarding the provisions of the national curriculum and staffing. In addition, those who are sponsors for the academies programme could have invested in the locality and opened up their networks to children and teachers without having oligarchic privileges as a result, and certainly might have paid higher tax to fund education rather than engage in philanthropy.

Furthermore, while the MCA is secular, it is located in an urban region where parents invest in faith schools as privileged sites for both social mobility and conservatism, and so there is recognition that the entry of the academy into the local market generated potential tensions. Staking a claim for entry by the MCA into provision by hitherto privileged local vantage points is based on securing othering and marginalisation for provision in the local area. The MCA was viewed as aggressive and the MCA characterised competitor schools and sections of the local community as similarly hostile. Policy mortality was weaponised, calculated, and enacted through how the MCA faced potential failure from schools that the MCA needed to actually fail in order to be successful. The language evident in the data from senior staff and sponsors is one of 'battles' and 'wars' in regard to setting up and stabilising the MCA, where the status as independent was defended from the core: "I don't want to play with that lot in London if you know what I mean" (Principal), and shielded against new innovations such as the emerging pressure to join what at the time was called a 'chain' in order to share services. This external hierarchy of academies in a chain developed into MATs, where the LA was replaced in terms of funding and support by a depoliticised private system encouraged by the core. The MCA is now in a MAT.

Summary

Investigating the relationship between the state, public policy, and knowledge production in the production and preservation of the ERC demonstrates the importance of a political sociology of vantage points. The case example from EPKP *Theme 1: System Design* used in this chapter shows that policy regarding the provision of and access to school places through the academies programme and the process of conversion known as academisation is related to knowledge production for and within the core interrelated with privileged vantage points. The origins of academies and MATs lie within the legitimate, authorised, and intelligent policy violence of those who occupied the core that set up the MCA, where scaling up for full conversion of all schools in a parliamentary system requires schemes such as the 'Try before you buy' initiative that opens this chapter. The MCA as educational provision outside of LA control was a product of a shared core-privileged vantage point that provided advantages for all involved, and this is in contrast with local schools still under LA control. In due course the MCA was taken over by the MAT as the new core-privileged vantage point, and so the MCA swapped submission within one hierarchy for another.

Policy violence presents academisation as vital for social mobility, and yet modernisation is based on segregated exclusion (Chapter 2); as vital for problem solving, and yet governing is based on segregationist technologies (Chapter 3); as vital for policy success, and yet the reality of policy mortality is based on segregated 'deserts' (Chapter 4).

While vantage points are the starting point for TPSF education policy analysis, research requires an investigation into the espoused views of those who seek recognition, and so I now turn to the importance of mapping and understanding the viewpoints of those who inhabit vantage points.

6

Viewpoints

Introduction

It is estimated that 'two in five children living below the poverty line are not entitled to free school meals' (Butler 2021: NP), where during the COVID-19 pandemic food insecurity intensified leading to the increased use of foodbanks in England. The Trussell Trust has reported:

> As more and more people across the country face destitution – meaning they are unable to afford the absolute essentials to eat, stay warm, dry and clean – the Trussell Trust warns need for emergency food is expected to rise further still, this winter and beyond. Food banks in the Trussell Trust network face giving out more than 7,000 food parcels every day in December. The charity says many families already at breaking point face the fallout of the £20 per week cut from Universal Credit payments that hit this autumn. This is on top of rising fuel costs during the coldest season, as well as soaring inflation. This is forcing many families deeper into poverty, the charity says, and is leaving people facing impossible decisions where their only option is to either skip meals to provide food for their children or heat their home. (The Trussell Trust 2021: NP)

The precarity of work combined with austerity cuts and inflation means that families are increasingly depending on food parcels at home and free school meals for children in school term time. After being rebuffed by the UK government, the footballer Marcus Rashford secured a policy U-turn by successfully campaigning for immediate support for: 'the provision of meals and activities to low-income families during school holidays and the expansion of the healthy start voucher scheme', and he continues to argue for longer term change through 'a full-scale review of the free schools meals system' leading to 'a meal a day' to all school pupils in England in financially struggling families' (Butler 2021: NP). This speaks to the reality of the working poor whereby families are not being paid a living wage, and so are toiling hard to put food on the table, where subsistence is additionally threatened by Brexit and COVID-19. A different elucidation of the Rashford campaign is located in the ERC as an enduring Thatcherite legacy project focused on naming and shaming 'benefit cheats' (Keay 1987). For example, Steve Baker, Conservative MP, argued on Twitter that allowing free school meals in school holidays 'passes responsibility for feeding kids away from parents, to the State. It increases dependency' (Weale 2020: NP). Blaming parents is a pattern in the reports about foodbanks, where Darren Henry, Conservative MP, made the statement about families at a constituency meeting: 'When they go down to the food bank, what they struggle with is maybe being able to manage their budget' (Gregory 2019: NP). The core vantage point of being from the governing party enables the promotion of arguments for the acceptance of the sovereign individual as a means of building support for anti-civic welfarism, and while Rashford is potentially privileged (status, income, fan base) he is actually marginalised because his philanthropy is rooted in his own narrative about his mother's experiences of raising her family in poverty.

Investigating such matters through the EPKP projects requires explanation through the TPSF. This validates the importance of *viewpoints* in education policy, or the knowledge production position of the person or group positioned in vantage points. Research within the EPKP projects demonstrates that *normative functionalism* is the prime viewpoint, and I examine policy violence through *Theme 2: The Workforce*.

Education policy viewpoints

The conceptualisation of education policy viewpoints is based on Arendtian (1958, 2005) scholarship regarding how a person presents the self within the public realm, and seeks to understand what others say. The formation, communication, and action in regard to viewpoints is premised on plurality, and as human beings each is unique but we share humanity and natality – we are all born into the world with the capacity to do something new through relational engagement (Gunter 2018). Policy violence requires an espoused viewpoint of ideas, beliefs, opinions, evidence, and arguments that deny such action, natality, and plurality. Policy actors who position within or are positioned into core and privileged vantage points all display viewpoints that variously legitimise the modern, provide authority and authorising for governing, and exhibit the required intelligence to imagine and secure change in ways that are weaponised, calculated, and enacted. Policy actors present and vouch for permitted viewpoints, and denounce and ridicule not only different viewpoints but also the capacity to form and voice such viewpoints. Indeed, policy actors who are marginal and othered have viewpoints where the sources and practices of and for legitimacy, authority, and intelligence are located differently, and hence the core not only challenges the actual espoused viewpoints but also the validation of those ideas and arguments.

Understanding viewpoints begins with knowledge production in the social sciences, and based on my engagement with Fay (1975; Gunter 2022), I argue that there are three ontological and epistemological positions: positivist, interpretive, and critical:

Positivist approaches assume that the world is objective and observable, and can be described and explained through facts that enable prediction to operate, hence in education policy, good practice is located in linear models of strategic development planning.

Interpretive approaches assume that the world is co-constructed through how people subjectively experience, read, and create relational exchanges through values, hence in education policy research there are non-linear models in collaborative team planning.

Critical approaches reveal suffering because the world is socially, economically, politically, and culturally unjust because it is rigged in favour of oligarchic private interests, hence in education policy research there is an activist agenda that not only identifies how and why positivist and interpretive positions fail to secure equitable change on their own, but also present alternative inclusive ways of enabling participation in decision-making.

These positions in knowledge production have generated four main viewpoints in the education policy field, and these are presented in Table 6.1.

Positivist knowledge production has generated a *functional science* viewpoint where what is thought, said, and done is based on outcome measures regarding what does and does not work, and the efficient and effective processes for delivering the correct data. For example, Ofsted commissioned a meta-analysis into the 'determinants of school effectiveness in secondary and primary schools', and produced 11 organisational factors that have been influential in policy scoping, design and enactment (Sammons et al

Table 6.1: Knowledge production and viewpoints

Functional science	Production of cause-and-effect measurement data that demonstrate the requirement, validity, and processes of the change.
Normative instrumentalism	Interplay between the efficacy and potential of normative ideological beliefs about what needs to be done and the technologies required to effect approved-of change.
Narrative description	Espoused and storied accounts (individual and group) of lived realities and experiences of change at a moment in time or over time.
Critical social justice	Identification and commitment to reveal and work against inequity and for social justice at a moment in time or over time.

Source: Based on Gunter 2012, 2016

1995: 5). However, while investment in such functionality has dominated education policy, this has been called 'pseudo-science' by some insiders (Barber 2007a: 79), where the endurance of ideology combined with a failure to provide definitive and reliable causal explanations has led to the deployment of *normative instrumentalism*. This means that the gaps in evidence are filled with inspirational packaged claims about what works as the right thing to do in order to functionally deliver as required, and this can be the site for the production and communication of simplification, mimicry, and fiction. The interplay between the rhetorical use of evidence as functional science and the declarations of normative instrumentalism has produced forms of *normative functionalism*. For example, a school can be 'empowered' (Hargreaves and Hopkins 1991) and 'intelligent' (MacGilchrist et al 1997), and while teachers have the most impact on student outcomes the leader-centric reform agenda retains its primacy in the messages delivered to the profession (Leithwood et al 2006).

Interpretive knowledge production has generated a *narrative description* viewpoint where what is thought, said, and done is based on recognising the validity of experiences and how change is experienced by those who deliver it and have to live with the consequences. Such narratives can raise concerns about the impact of reforms by headteachers (for example, Arrowsmith 2001) and can enable reform delivery (for example, Coles and Southworth 2005). Narratives can be colonised by normative functionalism in order to include approved-of role models and inspirational victory stories (for example, Clark 1998), and while the legitimacy of accounts by children, parents, and teachers are evident in primary research (for example, Czerniawski and Kidd 2011) this is either missing or is objectified in policy agendas (for example, Taylor 2009).

Critical knowledge production has generated a *critical social justice* viewpoint where what is thought, said, and done is based on exposing inequity through narrative descriptions that not only provide accounts of what is real for children and adults, but is activist through working on what needs to be done in order to challenge power structures that deny agency. Social justice viewpoints connect access to and experience of educational services to structural inequalities (for example, Chitty 2007; Raffo et al 2010), and present new agendas that demonstrate how working for a different approach to human beings is possible and desirable (for example, Smyth 1989; Fielding and Moss 2011).

Interpretive and critical forms of knowledge production have not only made visible the viewpoints of those in othered and marginal vantage points but also have been conceptualised as standpoints: 'despite their marginalized status, those who are systematically oppressed nonetheless possess some kind of epistemically privileged knowledge that both reflects their experience of oppression and places a special transformative role in resisting the very structures of oppression that generate that experience' (Wilson 2018: 213). Such knowledge production is evident through survivor accounts of the ERC (for example, see the accounts of Black Africans who attended Eton, Evaristo 2022), where giving recognition to viewpoints as *standpoints* not only validates experience, but also makes visible how and why a policy actor can take action in the public realm with others. Standpoints espoused by students, teachers, parents, and communities regarding class, race, disability, gender, and sexuality are dangerous for the ERC, and this tends to be handled mainly through policy violence from the core vantage point that promotes and invests in functional science but ultimately is dependent on normative functionalism.

Hence the ERC demands evidence about what works, but this is underpinned by ideological tropes about the human condition that may or may not be overt, and may use selected narrative descriptions to generate relatability to the argument being made. Indeed, standpoints can be appropriated and fabricated by the core in order to assert that the real oppressors are teachers and bureaucrats who are failing aspirational children and families, while the actual oppressors present themselves as liberators. For example, Gove (2013a) spoke to the Social Market Foundation in February 2013 where he attacked comprehensive education by using the case of the TV reality star, Jade Goody, who had died in 2009 and had left a legacy of investing in private education for her children. He used Gramsci's political analysis to attack the 'progressive education' that he claimed had let Goody down in her school days and she had rejected for her children. Importantly, he did not engage fully with the ideas regarding how Gramsci actually set out to politicise the working classes 'so that they would have the tools to challenge and overthrow the political elites of his time', and where 'Jade Goody's problem was not that schools failed her, but that she lived in a capitalist society that only needs a certain degree of training for its basic workers' (Thompson 2013: NP). Hence Gove's attempted standpoint engagement with Gramsci is partial and is based on a misrepresentation of Goody, where the actuality of Gramscian ideas and Goody's experiences are not in the interests of Gove or the Conservative Party either within or outside of government.

Othered vantage points tend to be excluded on the basis of unsafe or hostile viewpoints, where researchers who expose the standpoint knowledge production of children and teachers are scorned. For example, about a month after Gove's Social Market Foundation speech he responded to a letter signed by 100 educational researchers to *The Independent* about education reform (Garner 2013) by replying in an article in the *Mail Online* that attacked university departments of education by labelling alternative viewpoints to his own as 'Marxists', and 'the blob' (Gove 2013b: NP). Governments who have found independent primary research to be an unpleasant and unjustified interruption to policy have found support from those within the research community to demonstrate that education research is futile as no one reads it (Budge 1996), and/or have pursued policy through privileged networks rather than through evidence (see Gunter and Mills 2017). Furthermore, funding for independent primary research through the UK research councils has been cut, and so viewpoints from non-core vantage points based on thinking and speaking differently have been censored.

A case study of viewpoints

The EPKP projects have produced research evidence and analysis that demonstrates the actuality and explanatory validity of viewpoints, and here I focus on *Theme 2: The Workforce*. This important theme connects with my professional biography as a teacher in schools and higher education, through to independent primary research (for example, Gunter 2012) and commissioned research (for example, Thomas et al 2004), where I have studied professional identity and work over time in regard to policy interventions into the composition of the school workforce and professional practice (for example, Butt and Gunter 2007). As Moran (2003) argues the relationship between the teaching profession and the club has varied over time, but what the EPKP projects demonstrate is that the ERC continues to attack the status of teachers as professionals and reward school leaders as role models for disciplining the profession, not least by depriviligeing teacher knowledge and skills through a focus on codified experiential training and measurable delivery technologies. Accountability to parents and communities has shifted from democratic systems (through a director of education for the locality who is accountable to elected representatives) to market commodification (for example, through a school leader and/or MAT who is accountable to the market and to depoliticised appointees in head office in a distant location). I intend focusing on this policy violence through examining the relationship between the ERC and viewpoints, with a specific focus on the reforms to the school workforce at the turn of the century (Project 7).

The teaching profession had been at best marginalised and at certain times othered by successive governments (Gunter 2008), and so on taking office in 1997, New Labour inherited a demoralised profession that was identified as a potential barrier to their planned reforms to standards (DfEE 1997), particularly the 20 per cent of new teachers who left in their first two years (Ofsted 1999). The 1988 ERA had transformed schools into small businesses where usually 80 per cent of the budget was spent on staff salaries, and income streams were dependent on pupil enrolment, philanthropy, and bidding for projects. This required high stakes non-educational work where professionals had to be preoccupied with market branding and positioning combined with a performance imperative through Ofsted inspection categories, national league tables, and reports to funders. School autonomy required the relocation of work from the LA to the school (or to companies, for example, supply staff) where investment in new staff (for example, business managers) and skills (for example, data management) were related to corporate leadership. Ten years on from the 1988 ERA, New Labour inherited serious workload issues as evidenced in a range of reports (PwC 2001; STRB 2002; Smithers and Robinson 2003, 2004): 'Teachers and headteachers work more intensive weeks than other comparable managers and professionals … Headteachers' own workloads are higher than average – by some 300–400 hours a year' (PwC 2001: 1–2). Workload was not just about the volume of high priority tasks but also how the speed and intensity of reform initiatives had to be handled without support or sufficient resources. Exhausting workload meant that not enough people were entering the teaching profession, and where the age profile of in-service teachers demonstrated that there would be a predicted shortfall of 30,000 by 2006 (Ross and Hutchings 2003; Stewart 2003).

The New Labour government adopted the viewpoint that the problem was behavioural – teachers need to be incentivised to change; organisational – teachers had to work smarter and be accountable for standards; and ideological – teachers had to be modernised by breaking away from professional cultures and practices. A programme of interventions was launched, where as noted in Chapter 1 (Box 1.1) the ERC demanded as an appropriated standpoint that it is 'teachers', and seemingly no one else, who must meet 'the challenge of change' (DfEE 1998): first, the codification of professional practice as leader–follower, adopting corporate forms of transformational leadership (see: DfES/PwC 2007) in a redesigned diverse system of school place provision (see Chapter 5); second, the adoption of process and outcome data to demonstrate delivery efficiency and effectiveness of pedagogy and assessment at the right standard (see: DfES 2004); third, the introduction of performance related pay (see: DfEE 1998); fourth, the use of training and accreditation according to national standards (see: TTA 1998); and fifth, the introduction of National Strategies (for example, Literacy, Numeracy) to make interventions into teaching and learning with pedagogic resources and guidance on effective practice through personalisation (see: DfE 2011). Issues about workload were scoped and the requirements for change laid out in *Time for Standards. Reforming the School Workforce* (DfES 2002), where the development of the ERC under New Labour was based on commissioned evidence to inform policy and practice.

The plan was to demonstrate that change was vital and possible, and so in 2002 the DfES commissioned a consortium led by Pat Collarbone at the London Leadership Centre to conduct the *Transforming the School Workforce Pathfinder Project* (TSWPP), by developing and enacting a change management model through pilot projects in 32 schools in England led by an internal Change Management Team (CMT) in each school, supported by visits from external School Workforce Advisors (SWA). The focus was on the profession thinking radically about maximising time invested in teaching and learning, producing evidence about how human and physical resources could be managed more effectively and efficiently, and using additional resources to trial the creative use of Teaching Assistants, a school Bursar, and ICT hardware and software (for example, all teachers having a laptop) (see Collarbone 2005). The DfES also commissioned an evaluation of the TSWPP from a team at the School of Education, University of Birmingham (Project 7), who conducted a pre-pilot baseline survey (questionnaires and interviews) with all staff in the 32 schools during April and May 2002 (in addition, nine schools were identified as comparator schools). The DfES received a baseline report (Thomas et al 2002), and individual schools received a bespoke report to help them produce an action plan by the end of June 2002. Each school implemented their change plan from September 2002, and at the end of the pilot project in 2003 the questionnaire and interviews were repeated, with a final change measurement report including case studies for the DfES (Thomas et al 2004), and each school received a second customised report on the outcomes of their action plans. The data gathered about and for the TSWPP is illustrative of policy violence through how the viewpoints adopted demonstrate forms of legitimised, authorised, and intelligent violence.

Legitimised violence is evident in how the New Labour project scoped, defined, and set out to solve the problem as 'remodelling' that would 'transform' the school workforce. The conceptualisation and label of 're-modelling' suggests there is an actual 'model' that needs technical structural changes in order to improve functionality and aesthetics, or what has been called a 'makeover' (Gunter and Thomson 2009). Such ontological and epistemological positioning tends to be used regarding building repair and renovation, where design and resources are deployed to adapt, adjust, and transform space and decor. Consequently, *re*-modelling required the existing model of the teacher to be rendered deficit, where Circular 2/98 *Reducing the Bureaucratic Burden on Teachers* was published in June 1998 and listed the 25 Tasks 'that teachers should not routinely do', such as collecting money, classroom display, invigilating examinations, and ICT trouble shooting and minor repairs (DfES 2002: 36). These tasks could be handed over to others, where the label of 'school workforce' was adopted to include teaching assistants, clerical staff, and the use of professionally trained business, building/campus, ICT, and HR managers.

While the removal of the 25 Tasks was broadly accepted as important and achievable through the TSWPP, there are significant implications, not least through how not doing certain work without focusing on various viewpoints regarding the purposes of teachers and teaching meant that the very idea of the teacher as educator was called into question. For example, at the time of the TSWPP, a document entitled *Workforce Reform – Blue Skies* was reported to have come from the DfES and seen by the *Times Educational Supplement*, where it examined the idea that the school of the future would have only one qualified teacher who would be the headteacher – hence teaching and learning could be supported by adults who could be 'bought in from agencies and seconded but need not be qualified' (Stewart 2003: 6). Some TSWPP pilot schools did trial TAs undertaking whole class teaching and marking, and while experiences were varied the reality of appointing non-accredited teachers had a post-project legacy and was encouraged by successive Conservative led and majority governments from 2010 in Free schools and then widened to Academies with consequences for equity (George 2019). While formal training and accreditation currently remains in place for teacher supply, the establishment of Teach First (TF) from 2002 demonstrates the enactment of the viewpoint in favour of experiential training, and while TF applicants currently have to have a degree, the current chair of the House of Commons Select Committee on Education, Robert Halfon (Conservative MP for Harlow), has argued that graduate status for teachers is a barrier to advising children about their studies and careers (Cunliffe 2021). Interestingly, interviews with the children in the TSWPP schools provided evidence to counter this emerging ERC viewpoint, whereby while TAs were appreciated by children from 5 through to 18 years of age, and they do know the difference a graduate and accredited teacher makes. An A-level student noted the obvious, that studying physics required a physics graduate to teach the course. The main outcome of removing graduate status from the profession would be to remove access by children in the state system to such knowledge and expertise within school and ultimately to access higher education.

Legitimised violence is exercised by the core in contractual alliance with privileged individuals and consortia through framing and adopting an ERC viewpoint based on knowledge production that asserted the importance of both functional science to pilot and evaluate the relocation of the 25 tasks, but also normative functionalism illustrated by a mantra of 'capturing hearts and minds'.

The TSWPP invested in a change management model of 'Mobilise, Discover, Deepen, Develop, Deliver' (Collarbone 2005: 79–80) that was based on corporate charismatic and organisational systems thinking (each headteacher of the 32 pilot schools received a copy of Fullan 2001). The data demonstrate that the profession in the 32 schools (and the nine comparator schools) could reduce their working hours. In 2002 the average hours per week was 54, and by 2003 it was 52, with a reduction of '3.7 hours per week in the primary schools, 3.5 hours in the special schools and 1.2 hours in the secondary schools' (Thomas et al 2004: i), and gains were made through investment in TAs and ICT, and a range of innovative practices evidenced in the case studies (Thomas et al 2004; Gunter et al 2007).

While important gains were made, there are important issues to raise about the ontological and epistemological foundations of the TSWPP, not least that basing remodelling on a narrow problem solving viewpoint, meant that the project assumed that rational change management processes and outcome data would shift attitudes, alter behaviour, and so improve job satisfaction. However the data show that: 'there was no systematic relationship between job satisfaction and hours worked' (Thomas et al 2004: i), or in other words, the number of hours worked may not be the issue. The data show that it was the type of work that the profession was forced to do post-ERA in order to survive professionally that was the problem. Furthermore, the research field had evidence of narrative descriptions and social justice standpoints as sources of professional job satisfaction (for example, Webb and Vullaimy 2006), and the evaluation of the TSWPP generated data about the experiences of what it means to be a teacher at a time of neoliberal dismantling of public services education, and how teaching is and needs to be activist (Butt and Gunter 2007). Researchers had already identified the consequences of normative functionalism on teachers, whereby Ball (2003) talks about the consequences of the 'terrors of performativity'. Indeed, Smyth (2017) uses Sennett's (1999) analysis of the changes to work as 'corrosion of character', whereby just as bread makers no longer actually make bread but push a button to produce a loaf, teachers are required to metaphorically operate a learning machine by delivering learning packages, and producing outcome levels for specific key stages. The TSWPP project set out to do this through the installation of electronic whiteboards (EWBs) for whole class teaching, and while there is positive evidence about the impact of this technology, the evidence also shows that in primary education decisions were made about pedagogy whereby whole class teaching may not be appropriate and so the EWB was not switched on (Thomas et al 2004; Gunter et al 2007).

A second and connected problematic issue is that the TSWPP was designed to undertake remodelling as a form of change management as a 'pathfinder' project that would present the one way forward that could be scaled up from the pilot schools to all schools. The 32 schools were chosen by the DfES, and they were enthusiastic finders of new paths; however, the TSWPP presented a model of organisational change that depended on an investment in resources regarding new staffing, ICT hardware and software, and capital projects (for example, new offices for new staff). The security of the gains made in the 32 schools and the roll out across England would require additional investment in schools, and this is evident in the espoused standpoints of those who had made the TSWPP work in day-to-day practice:

'There are sustainability issues beyond the life of the Project. The teaching staff will soon get used to the level of support they have been given' (Senior Manager).

'You can't set up systems that people rely on and then let the money dry up. It will definitely need more money to keep these initiatives going' (Support staff). (Thomas et al 2004: 1iv)

The national roll out of remodelling across England (discussed later) had to take place without additional resources, and so while a path had been found it was the case that continuing to walk on it for the pilot schools was a challenge. Ironically, the data from the evaluation that demonstrated productive changes could not actually be used to support and defend the roll-out of policy because schools that had to be convinced to follow the path did not necessarily have the resources to start the journey.

Authorised violence is evident within the TSWPP through how the core viewpoint was depoliticised, where the ERC based on normative functionalism meant that knowledge production was conducted as if there was nothing to debate – all that mattered was to secure the enthusiastic delivery of changes that used and produced the right type of data. The TSWPP was tightly regulated by the Department, whereby action plans produced by each of the 32 pilot schools had to be approved, and hence while the CMTs were meant to think creatively it was subject to core vantage point say-so. Such depoliticised policy processes are particularly evident in how 'units' were set up to control, deliver, and regulate educational reforms, some within the Department such as the Innovation Unit and the SEU, and some that were external but under the control of the Department such as BECTA, NCSL, and the TTA (which became the TDA from 2005). Such units worked and reworked the ERC to be in line with New Labour strategy, and so helped to regulate the work of the change management teams and school workforce advisors in the TSWPP, and in the post project national rollout of remodelling across England.

However, these depoliticised units did not challenge the segregated school system, and hence enabled privatism, corporatism, and populism to develop oligarchic club sovereignty that restored education as a private good, where the workforce had to put school brand identity above professional knowledge. Teachers had to consent to reforms that were said to be about improving their workload but in effect did not examine purposes and practices of teaching in communities where major economic disinvestment had been taking place for decades. Workload is not just a technical and behavioural issue but is about critical engagement with services and families in real life contexts, and this type of work has little to do with the 25 tasks. Hence investment in laptops speeded up work but did not make work more meaningful: 'there had been a substantial increase in access in 2003 compared with 2002: 51 per cent of special school teachers and 64 per cent and 49 per cent respectively of primary and secondary school teachers' (Thomas et al 2004: xxviii), but the data also showed that 'there was no consistent relationship with increased access (to ICT) and total hours worked by teachers' (Thomas et al 2004: i). What seemed to happen was that workload was not so much reduced as relocated in the working lives of teachers:

> 'I now leave at 4 pm and collect my own children. I used to leave at 6 pm. I collect, feed and bath them and by 8 pm I can use my laptop. This has not reduced my workload but it has reorganised it, and it has remodelled my life' (Senior Manager). (Thomas et al 2004: 1xvi)

Change management actually meant tactical local delivery of changes decided elsewhere, and while the evaluation report demonstrates some significant developments, the project team also picked up examples of local intelligent experimentation that was disconnected from professional codes of conduct and research evidence (Thomas et al 2004). For example, in one school, cover for absent teachers was handled by putting teaching and learning packages online, where children would be sent to the newly designed library. Books were removed and computers installed, where one TA would support a potential group of over 100 children. Security guards patrolled in order to ensure that the children did not do damage to the hardware (removing a roller ball from the mouse). Children could find that they spent the whole day in this 'learning centre' due to how the coincidence of staff absences impacted on their timetable.

These forms of legitimised and authorised policy violence enable understandings about how and why the TSWPP demonstrated policy mortality, whereby teachers were identified as potentially failing and had to meet the challenge of these failings through being managed to change in prescribed ways. This intelligent violence was disconnected from the research into education policy and practice at the time, and while a range of approaches to change positions were available for policy actors, the focus was on sustaining current power structures and cultures through controlling participation through surveillance, performance audits, and team work (Gunter et al 2007). The underlying ontology and epistemology of the TSWPP meant that normative functionalism enabled change to be controlled and delivered, and hence weaponised – 'this has to happen or I will be failing children and I will be a breach in contract', calculated – 'I need to accept how I am in deficit and what I need to do to improve', and enacted – 'I need to produce data to prove that standards have improved through remodelling'. Linear process and outcome delivery change management models could score quick wins in the pilot schools, but a number of issues arose regarding deeper and longer-term change.

A National Agreement was signed by employers and unions in January 2003, with the subsequent publication of *Time for Standards: Consultation on Implementing the National Agreement* in April 2003. This allowed for contractual changes regarding covering lessons for absent colleagues and guaranteed planning and marking time, with training for support staff. This National Agreement was signed 6 months before the measurement data had been collected from the pilot schools, and so it was not an evidence-informed policy. The evaluation of the TSWPP was rendered a part of the background literatures (for example, Blatchford et al 2009; Hutchings et al 2009) or even written out of history (for example, Easton et al 2005; Ofsted 2005; Wilson et al 2005; Easton et al 2006). The National Agreement was boycotted by the NUT due to the planned transfer of the 25 tasks to support staff that could increase teachers work, lead to non-qualified people teaching rather than supporting the teacher, and/or may not happen due to the funding crisis in education (Curtis 2003; Revell 2003). Nevertheless, the National Remodelling Team (NRT) that was located at the NCSL under Pat Collarbone's leadership, was overseen by the Workforce Agreement Monitoring Group (WAMG) made up of the government, unions (not NUT), and employers. While there is evidence of productive changes in schools regarding organisational change (for example, Ofsted 2005; Easton et al 2006), the longer term impact has been affected by austerity budgets from 2010, with cuts to the very support staff that had been integral to the TSWPP and National Remodelling (Skipp and Hopwood 2019).

There are a number of inconvenient truths about the eventual failure of the TSWPP that need to be noted: first, that it was premised on a normative functional viewpoint of change delivery, but was unable to actually capture the 'hearts and minds' of teachers due to the lack of engagement with narrative description viewpoints as mediating change, or with critical social justice viewpoints as working for change. As one teacher stated about the TSWPP:

> 'The job is still hard because of what is expected of us, such as league tables. The project has not removed the demands, there is still the issue of accountability. I still feel frustrated about having to comply. The project has not removed the people related issues, and how we cause stress.' (Thomas et al 2004: 1xvii)

In other words, the regulation of work continued, where teachers who engaged in narrative descriptions wanted to be consulted, and demanded professional rather than technical accountability, but they found that the

TSWPP did not engage, and hence the gains made were unlikely to be embedded. Historically, research shows that teachers and headteachers espouse different viewpoints about reform initiatives (for example, Grace 1995; Gunter and Forrester 2010), and while the 32 pilot schools were on board with the project, they were, as noted, ultimately let down by the fact that the project had an end date. Interestingly, the project gave the staff in the pilot schools a new sense of confidence to tactically control their work because they had learned that challenging bureaucracy through the 25 tasks could actually be used by the profession through how they resisted other reform changes. Notions of critical social justice and professional activism were evident in the data, but working for a different type of change from that which the TSWPP model demanded actually required a re-politicisation of the workload issue as a public matter. Importantly, professionals from 2010 used their 'new freedoms' from projects such as the TSWPP and national remodelling to challenge austerity (Ferguson 2019) through the adoption of problem posing within the agora. Oligarchic club sovereignty would not countenance such developments, and the COVID-19 pandemic created the opportunity to refocus the profession back onto controlled delivery management.

Summary

Investigating the relationship between the state, public policy, and knowledge production in the production and preservation of the ERC demonstrates the importance of a political sociology of viewpoints. The case example from EPKP *Theme 2: The Workforce* used in this chapter shows that policy regarding the purposes and practices of educational professionals is related to knowledge production as the normative functionalist viewpoint that is preferred and acclaimed within, for, and by the core and privileged vantage points. The interventions made into teacher's work lie with the legitimate, authorised, and intelligent policy violence of those who use club sovereignty to appropriate selected standpoints, and so deny and prevent relational exchanges that problem pose, and hence rework identities into data determined delivery performance. The example of children living in poverty that opens this chapter is characterised as an excuse used by state-dependent parents and under-performing teachers.

Policy violence presents workforce reform as: vital for social mobility, and yet the workforce is itself segregated and invested in intensifying segregated services (Chapter 2); vital for problem solving, and yet governing by knowledge production for the workforce is based on the operationalising of segregationist technologies (Chapter 3); vital for policy success, and yet the workforce under the endemic threat of policy mortality labours to survive in segregated 'deserts' (Chapter 4).

While the viewpoints used by those who are positioned in different vantage points are vital for education policy analysis, research requires an investigation into networked interconnections, and so I now turn to the importance of mapping and understanding the regimes of practice of those who inhabit vantage points and espouse viewpoints.

7

Regimes of practice

Introduction

On 21 June 2021, the UK Department for Education that governs education in England published a tweet in which they pronounced 25 June as 'One Britain One Nation Day', 'when children can learn about our shared values of tolerance, kindness, pride and respect', with the support of the then Secretary of State, Gavin Williamson (Harding 2021: NP). The celebration included an 'anthem' for all children in school to sing on the appointed day, with the repeated chorus line: 'We are Britain and we have one dream, To Unite all people in one great team'. Verse two sings out: 'A nation survived through many storms and many wars, We've opened our doors, and widened our island's shores, We celebrate our differences with love in our hearts, United forever, never apart' (OBON 2022: NP). This proposed 'national event' raises questions about how and why the core vantage point of the Department for Education is inter-related with privileged vantage points such the former police inspector Kash Singh who is promoting the anthem in his capacity as the Chief executive and Founder of the campaign group 'One Britain One Nation' (OBON). The anthem shows how the core vantage point uses normative functionalism to fabricate conformity and approved-of identity through how histories and current experiences of living in the UK are included/excluded in the curriculum. Ironically the lyrics encourage disunity because Britain is not the UK, and so Northern Ireland is excluded, and it was reported that most schools in Scotland would be closed for the summer vacation on the day of celebration (Harding 2021). Geography and the UK constitution put to one side, the words and event conflate (and confuse) nationalism with patriotism, and as such the narrative description and critical viewpoints and standpoints of those who are marginalised and othered on the basis of eugenicist populism and nationalism are unrecognised. Surveys show that a third of children have 'heard someone be racist at school' (Gayle 2020: NP), and there are cases of people who moved to and raised families in the UK from 1948 who have experienced the actuality or threat of deportation that is known as the Windrush Scandal (BBC 2020b). Those who have taken the knee at sporting events in order to challenge racism have faced criticism from the Home Secretary for engaging in 'gesture politics', and where 'football fans have a right to boo the England team' (Stone 2021: NP).

Investigating such matters of preferred knowledge producers through the EPKP projects validates the importance of *regimes of practice* in education policy, or the objective relationship between those who occupy particular vantage points and espouse certain viewpoints in ways that demonstrate a shared agenda. Research within the EPKP projects demonstrates the primacy of *state regimes*, and I examine policy violence through *Theme 3: Policy Actors*.

Education policy regimes of practice

Policy violence requires policy actors who scope, design, enact, and sustain the ERC, where regimes of practice control what is thought, said, and done, in ways that reach into everyday activity in classrooms and the lives of families. Policy actors who are located in certain vantage points and who espouse particular viewpoints form distinctive 'regimes' by engaging in associative practices, and this is 'constructed through informal bargaining and the "tacit understandings" of its members' (Harding 2000: 55). It is therefore vital to describe and explain the practices of policy actors who inhabit vantage points and promote viewpoints, where Bourdieu's (1990, 1992, 1998, 2000) logic of practice and thinking tools are helpful in identifying the policy inclusion–exclusion game in play. Importantly, regimes draw boundaries and actively include and exclude regarding what is known, how it is known and why it matters. While policy actors may be occupationally located in distinctive organisations (for example, public institutions, private businesses, charities, universities) it is the case that shared dispositions and agendas are necessary for regime formation, where forms of authority, legitimacy, and intelligence are interplayed with recognition/denial of credible expertise and trustworthiness. Table 7.1 presents three main types of regimes of practice:

Table 7.1: Knowledge production and regimes of practice

Regimes of practice	Knowledge production for the ERC
State	Policy actors in the core vantage point who frame policy based on a functional science interplayed with normative instrumentalist viewpoint, and who form, shape, and use a regime of practice for governing.
Satellite	Policy actors in the privileged vantage point who accept and support the framing of the state regime viewpoint, and who are formally and informally invited into the state regime of practice to champion governing.
Star	Policy actors in the marginal and othered vantage points who challenge the state regime viewpoint, and who form alternative regimes of practice through critical and activist viewpoints.

Source: Based on Gunter 2012

All regimes of practice exist and operate in relation to the state – they are either *the* state regime, or operate as satellites *for* state regimes, or are stars that 'shine a light' *on* state and satellite regimes, and so illuminate regimes that are officially rendered dark *by* the state and satellite regimes. State regimes dominate as they represent, protect and enable oligarchic club sovereignty in ways that are promoted as governing in the interests of all. Those who are located in the state regime as the core vantage point and those who are invited into the public institutions of the state from favoured privileged vantage points in civil society, all espouse viewpoints that deem them to be recognised within the dominant regime of practice.

State regimes of practice

Policy actors in the knowledgeable state form a governing regime of practice as the means of protecting and advancing oligarchic club control, and may invite participation from privileged knowledge actors in civil society. Here I scope two state regimes.

Conservative Privatisation Regime (CPR)

The Thatcher and Major governments (1979–1997), the Conservative-led Coalition (2010–2015), and the Conservative-Brexit governments (2015–2017, 2017–2019, 2019 onwards), have produced and sustained an ERC that is about replacing public education policy with markets. Depoliticisation through the privatisation of, supply of, and demand for school places is directly related to ministerial strategy (see: Ribbins and Sherratt 1997); privileged thinkers and narrators (for example, Lawlor 1988) and professionals (for example, Boyson 1975). While civil servants were integral to the core vantage point in the 1980s, the deprivileging process is evident in the contracting of consultancy firms (for example, Coopers and Lybrand 1988), and the enhanced privileging of those who accepted invitations to join the policy process (see Gunter 2020b).

New Labour Performance Regime (NLPR)

The Blair and Brown governments (1997–2010) produced an ERC that is about modernising markets through re-politicisation of education as a site for investment, but also intensified depoliticisation through diversity. The interplay between re- and de-politicisation is directly related to ministers, where Blunkett (New Labour's first Secretary of State for Education, 1997–2001) had read Bobbitt's (2002) arguments for the market state, and 'was reported to have found Bobbitt's thesis on the remaining role of governments very appealing' (Tomlinson 2005: 6). In addition, advisors (for example,

Barber 2007) along with privileged thinkers and narrators (for example, Giddens 2000), researchers (for example, Hopkins 2001), and professionals (for example, Munby 2019) were crucial to the regime. As a minister said, "we were good at recruiting good heads to be civil servants, you'll know that from looking in the Standards and Effectiveness Unit, they were ex-heads" (Project 15). The depriviledging of career civil servants intensified (see Gunter and Mills 2017), while invitations were issued to the privileged with approved of viewpoints to enter the core (for example, NCSL, see Gunter 2012), and to undertake commissioned projects (for example, Earl et al 2003) that provided 'discursive and legitimatory work' (Whitty et al 2016: 46).

While members of these two state regimes enter and exit the core vantage point in regard to elections and the mandate of a manifesto, the viewpoints used to shape and amplify the ERC endure beyond the ballot box with a shared focus on depoliticisation and the financialisation of knowledge production in regard to consultancy firms (for example, PwC 2009), employees in delivery agencies (for example, Taylor 2009), and researchers, whereby school effectiveness serviced both Conservative New Right (Angus 1993) and New Labour (Gunter 2012) governments.

Satellite regimes of practice

Previous and potential policy actors outside state regimes tend to position themselves at the margins ready to be invited in, and/or seek to distinguish their practices by forming alternative relational oligarchic regimes. This can be illustrated by the School Leadership Satellite Regime (SLSR) which includes partnerships between those who work in schools, local authorities, higher education, and businesses, regarding professional practices and engagement with change. The SLSR focuses on the impact of reforms on professional practice, and developed training through an initial focus on administration, then shifted to management, and then leadership (Gunter 1999, 2004). The SLSR declined from the 1980s, where members were left behind due to their focus on postgraduate programmes for educational professionals and partnerships with LAs. The CPR (from 1979, and then from 2010) and the NLPR (1997–2010) privileged those who focused on organisational leadership, improvement, and effectiveness, and key people joined the state regime through various advisory, employment, and commissioned research contracts. For example, Pat Collarbone had been a headteacher, set up the London Leadership Centre, and led the national roll-out of workforce reform, and she then set up Creating Tomorrow consultants (2008–2018) (see Chapter 6; Gunter and Mills 2017). A second example is from Hughes et al (2020) who examined the career of KT Lawrence as a CEO of a MAT, and how his entrepreneurial disposition took time to be recognised as a teacher, but his time came when he shifted in Arendtian (1974) terms from being a pariah in a public system to being a parvenu in a privatising system of schools. These two examples show that operating in border territory is fruitful, but it can also be very risky. For example, Beckett (2007) tells the story of how headteacher Des Smith was paid £500 a day as a consultant by the SSAT, and how as a recognised 'superhead' he had 'been taken up by Sir Cyril (Taylor) as a suitable headteacher to introduce potential sponsors, and had worked with the company Capita' (30). However, he was reported in the national media promising national honours in return for donations regarding academies. He was arrested by the police and questioned, and members of the government 'disowned him' (30).

Star regimes of practice

Those who position or are positioned in othered vantage points tend to hold narrative description and social justice viewpoints. Here I give attention to the *Policy Research Regime* (PRR) of policy actors from universities, schools, local authorities, and unions who frame their position as policy sociology (Ozga 1987; Ball 1990a). This regime is located in the 'policy turn' from the 1980s (Deem et al 1995), where policy sociology grew in relation to Thatcherism and neoliberal ideas (Halpin and Troyna 1994), and developed in relation to post-Thatcher legacies (Whitty et al 2016). Notably recognition and acclaim were through research centres, special interest groups in national and international research societies (for example, BERA; EERA), editorial boards, and funding by the BA, ESRC, EU, and Leverhulme. This enabled the policy processes and impact of Thatcherism to be subject to scrutiny in a range of projects (for example, Grek 2013), with groundbreaking texts (for example, Ball et al 2012), where the contribution was to problem pose regarding pupil voice (for example, Fielding 2006); the profession (for example, Helsby 1999); organisational leadership (for example, Hatcher 2005); and system reform (for example, Whitty et al 1998). Such research not only examined and theorised the realities of the impact of reforms on schools and the profession (for example, Ball 1990a) but also revealed and developed alternative ways to enhance public services education (for example, Wrigley et al 2012). An example from the EPKP data shows how a minister in the NLPR explained how the government used their own research rather than engage with the wider research community: "we found it difficult to work with that bit of the research community and the irony was they were often a politically left research community" and the minister goes on to blame these researchers because "it almost pushed us onto the right-of-centre research community" (Project 15). Importantly what is characterised (incorrectly) as partisan or politically left research was critiqued by this minister for failing to warn the government of the consequences of their education policies: "I hold them a bit responsible for not actually saying, 'look, this is where you shouldn't be going ... and in the light of that, this is the research you need to look at'" (Project 15). Such an account does not fit with events, not least the persistent attack on the PRR (for example, Tooley with Darby 1998, see Ribbins et al 2003), where the vantage point of social science research in elite universities and the social justice viewpoint that connected classrooms with wider social and economic structures was regularly othered, not least because it revealed evidence of elite control of and by the state regimes and their satellites.

A case study of regimes of practice

The EPKP projects have produced research evidence and analysis that demonstrates the actuality and validity of regimes of practice (see Gunter 2012), and here I focus on *Theme 3: Policy Actors*. This important theme connects to my career-long study of the field of educational leadership (for example, Gunter 1999, 2012, 2020e) in regard to the professional biographies of those who have been actively involved in the relationship between the state, public policy, and knowledge. This includes studies of knowledge production (for example, Gunter 1997, 2016); along with policy actors in different vantage points and espousing different viewpoints (for example, Gunter 2013). I first developed regimes of practice for the *Knowledge Production in Educational Leadership* project (KPEL) to examine the inclusion–exclusion game in play (Project 15, Gunter 2012). The argument remains that for the privatisation and depoliticisation messages of the ERC to be enacted, then policy actors who were credible with the profession had to be involved. Such policy actors were a product of and located in a segregated system, where school improvement and effectiveness could be justified through benign presentations of social mobility and meritocracy in ways that deflected attention from the reality of eugenicist populism. Consequently, regimes of practice are different from network analysis, while the latter is focused on mapping connections between policy actors, I argue that regimes are focused on the knowledge production practices for and within actual policy interventions (that do or do not secure change).

For example, the NLPR intensified the *doxa* of headteachers as corporate leaders, doing leading and leadership. The *illusio* or 'fundamental belief in the interest of the game and the value of the stakes which is inherent in that membership' (Bourdieu 2000: 11) was articulated by a minister: "we always knew we couldn't do what we wanted in education unless we turned around leadership" (Project 15, Gunter 2012: 19). The ERC had a functional role in order to ensure that the suite of reforms would be delivered in schools (for example, DfEE 1997, 1998), but at the same time the approach to leadership had to be made attractive to the profession. Consequently, the promotion of corporate and performance transformational leadership was coherent with models developed to deliver business autonomy for schools from 1988, and on taking office in 1997 this model fitted with the commitment to school improvement and effectiveness (Barber 1996). Indeed, in 1998, PM Tony Blair told a conference of newly appointed headteachers of the plan to establish the National College for School Leadership (NCSL) by 2000: 'our best heads are superb, but we need more of them', and he went on to say: 'top business invests heavily in training their high-flyers and senior managers. So do the army, the police and other parts of the public sector … but when it comes to headteachers, whose jobs are at least as demanding, we do far less' (BBC 1998a). As a senior civil servant said: "our feeling was that we had a lot of headteachers who were effective but almost effective by chance" (Project 15). The NLPR set out to make significant interventions into the purposes and identities of educational professionals, where the Department considered models from outside of education such as The Royal Military Academy Sandhurst, and Ashridge Strategic Management Centre, and from within education contact was made with the London Leadership Centre, where a key issue was how to scale up training provision to cover England.

A prospectus for the NCSL was published in 1998, where expressions of interest were invited, leading to a competitive tendering process (DFEE 1998), and by 2000 the NCSL for England was launched with the official opening of the conference centre on the Jubilee Campus of the University of Nottingham (with nine regional centres) in 2002 (NCSL undated: 3). The NCSL declared its aim to 'provide a single national focus for school leadership development, research and innovation', and to 'be a driving force for world-class leadership in our schools and wider community' (NCSL undated: 3). Such aims were to be achieved through, first, research: 'seeking out, sharing and building best practice through research and learning networks'; second, virtual college: 'providing online support through our website and online communities'; and third, programmes: 'developing and delivering programmes that meet the needs of school leaders at every stage in their careers' (NCSL undated: 3). A range of activities were developed (see Gunter 2012), and in summary they include a take-over of the administration of the NPQH (aspiring heads), HEADLAMP (newly appointed heads), and LPSH (experienced heads) training programmes (see Ofsted 2002), and the development of new programmes (for example, Leading from the Middle). These programmes were located in a codification of a professional career in a *Leadership Development Framework* with five stages: 'emergent leaders', 'established leaders', 'entry into headship', 'advanced leaders', and 'consultant leaders' (NCSL undated: 11). Projects were commissioned in order to ensure that research fitted with education reform requirements from the Department. The College set out to base its activity on evidence with a functional science viewpoint

(Hopkins 2001), but the failure to produce such evidence meant that the normative functionalist viewpoint dominated: 'effective school leadership is driven by beliefs' (NCSL 2006: 3) that are consistent with the ERC and government policy.

The data gathered about and for the KPEL project is illustrative of this policy violence through how state and satellite regimes of practice participated in knowledge production that evidence forms of legitimised, authorised, and intelligent violence.

Legitimised violence is evident in the associative practices within the NLPR in the core vantage point in Whitehall. Knowledge production was based on the personal beliefs of those who held public office, from Blair as PM through to the Secretary of State, Ministers, Civil Servants, and Advisors – they knew that the leadership of the headteacher mattered, as a senior civil servant stated: "we know really good heads make a big difference" (Project 15). In addition, the government needed headteachers to be transformed and to accept their role in the transformation of the profession in order for reforms to be delivered. Again, the senior civil servant stated about governing education: "you don't do that just by having diktats in Whitehall about what has to happen, you need school leaders on the ground who are going to make it happen" (Project 15). These personal beliefs (Blunkett and Morris had worked in educational services, and of course everyone involved had a view because they had been to school) were developed and justified through the control of knowledge production, whereby the Department commissioned projects as 'state of the art' reviews of school leadership practice (for example, Earley et al 2002; Stevens et al 2005; DfES/PwC 2007; Day et al 2009), and seemingly ignored or othered research that claimed that there was a belief but no evidence of a direct causal link between the headteacher and learning (Hall and Southworth 1997), and had shown that teachers are the most significant cause of student outcomes (Hallinger and Heck 1998).

The NLPR within the Department and in alliance with No 10, the Cabinet Office and the Treasury determined that there would be a College (DfEE 1998), and I used primary sources in the public domain combined with a Freedom of Information request to obtain the documentation regarding the setting up of the NCSL (Project 15). A named civil servant (CS1) acted as 'Project Manager' for the NCSL, and the documents show memos and emails with ministers, civil servants within and external to the Department, and with outside legal advisors. There are a number of features about the setting up of the NCSL that demonstrate the practices that constitute forms of legitimised violence. The first one is how the modernisation agenda required a complete break with previous practices in different vantage points, and so the ERC wrote history in a particular way, with statements such as: 'up to now leadership development has lacked coherence, direction and status' (DfEE 1999: 2). Importantly, the NCSL was set up without due regard for all the work that had taken place (for example, School Management Task Force, 1990) or was taking place at the time in regard to research and professional development (for example, Bush et al 1999). The way that the modernisation agenda operated is also evident in the associative practices within the Department whereby a senior civil servant (CS2) wrote to the Private Secretary to Her Majesty the Queen: 'I wonder if we might consider the possibility of Royal College status for the National College for School Leadership', with the argument that 'Royal status would put teacher development on a par with many comparable professions' (CS2, Letter 22 November 1999). On being informed of this, CS1 replied by noting that Royal status had already been rejected: 'we are looking to set up the College as a modern, forward-looking organisation rather than tying it to a more established image. Certainly when (name of civil servant) touched on the possibility of Royal status in much earlier discussions with Ministers and No 10 there was little enthusiasm' (CS1, Letter 23 November 1999).

A second example of legitimised violence is how the NCSL was legally established in ways that enabled centralised control of purposes and activity. The NCSL was set up as an executive NDPB and this meant that Ministers would not only appoint the first Director but all future Directors, the Governing Council, and provide the remit and funding while using terminology such as 'arms-length' as the means of empowering appointees to be responsible and accountable for day-to-day activity (CS1 Memos 20 April and 29 April 1999). The Department issued 'remit' letters from the Secretary of State to the Chair of the Governing Council of the NCSL which included ERC statements produced by the NLPR that permeated across policy and justified public funding:

> Leadership and vision are crucial to raising standards and aspirations across all our schools. (Blunkett 2000b: 1)

> Inspirational leadership in schools is crucial for delivering the government's educational agenda. (Kelly 2004: 1)

Expectations for and requirements of the College are clearly laid out:

> I look to the College to develop proposals for my consideration for training and development events and programmes for school leaders designed to address the major challenges facing schools today. (Blunkett 2000b: 2)

> I expect the College to develop its role as a powerhouse for high quality research on leadership issues directly related to actual practice in schools. (Blunkett 2000b: 3)

> I would like the College to give particular attention to how heads in particular can be helped to tackle practical management issues that can give rise to unnecessary bureaucracy and workload within schools. (Blunkett 2001: 5)

> The key priorities for the College's work 2007–08 should be: succession planning, redesign of NPQH, and the development of new models of leadership. (Johnson 2007: 2)

The evaluation of the NCSL in the 'End to End Review' report noted that while progress is recognised, the Secretary of State raised concerns about activity that is threatening central control. The case is made for how 'activity must be both evidence-based and proportionate to College capacity' (Kelly 2004: 2), and so the College needed to be reined in, and hence there is a need for a 'close alignment between the College and the Department' (2). An important development is noted with the setting up of 'a sponsor unit in the DfES' in a 'gatekeeper role' to monitor and check what the College is doing (Kelly 2004: 2), and a year later it is clearly stated that 'the College should seek the prior agreement of the NDPB Sponsor Unit in the Department Workforce Group before taking on any significant new work during the year' (Kelly 2005: 3).

The NCSL was the creation of and controlled by the NLPR, whereby in 2008 Children's Services was added and it became the National College for Leadership of Schools and Children's Services (NCLSCS, for brevity known as the National College). When New Labour left office in 2010 the CPR began to dismantle and disinvest through austerity budgets and the deregulation of professional accreditation (for example, the NPQH had been made compulsory for new heads in 2009, and this was removed in 2012). The National College became an Executive Agency within the Department in 2012, and so day-to-day control was undertaken by the Department (The Governing Council was abolished). In 2013 it was merged with TDA and became National College for Teaching and Leadership (NCTL, for brevity known as the National College), and in 2017 the NCTL was closed and the functions were taken over by the Department (Whittaker 2017).

Authorised violence is evident in the associative practices between the NLPR in the core vantage point of government and those policy actors who were invited into variously design, develop, and enact policy at national through to classroom levels. Such invitations are evident in open calls or expressions of interest, such as the NCSL (see DfEE 1999), through to particular people and organisations, where capitals were staked by professionals (for example, Clark 1998); unions (for example, Miliband 2003); consultancies (for example, DfES/PwC 2007); researchers (for example, Hopkins 2001), supra-national organisations (for example, Huber et al 2007), and universities (for example, universities of London, Manchester, Newcastle hosted regional centres for the NCSL). Practices revealed dispositions or *habitus* to use vantage and viewpoints to play the game of oligarchic positioning with energy and optimism. Opportunities existed to secure influence, jobs, and win bids for commissioned projects and training delivery, whereby the NLPR controlled objective relationships within what was a complex field of research and practice.

As already noted, Departmental control of the NCSL was seen as vital, and the primary sources show how professionals were positioned by the NLPR. A key issue was funding whereby the plan was to set up a charitable body to fund the National College building and activities, and to sign up a named internationally renowned businessperson and philanthropist: 'as a potential sponsor and securer of sponsorship' (CS1, Memo, 29 April 1999). The various memos and emails report that one potential sponsor had 'raised a question of whether we were considering mutuality as a model for the College' and following an investigation into what this would mean it was rejected as a way forward. Importantly, it was identified that 'mutuality' meant that 'an organization is owned by its customers – like building societies and the co-op', and this would mean that the NCSL would be owned by the profession. This was eliminated as an option:

> We certainly want to establish a vigorous alumni organization for the College – this would be part of the important benefits of networking and sharing good and effective leadership practice and experience. In the longer term, it is an attractive model for the College to be owned and run by its alumni. However it is clear that we are not in that world yet and would not be for some time, perhaps as long as 10 years. (CS1, Memo, 29 April 1999)

About a week later, the situation was confirmed: 'we would need to be satisfied that it was *safe and sensible* to hand the College over to its alumni and that they would run it properly for the benefit of parents and pupils, who as the Secretary of State says are the principal stakeholders' (CS1, Email, 7 May 1999, my emphasis). Consequently, authorisation is centralised through the electoral mandate and the sovereignty located in the NLPR control of Whitehall, and this disconnects the profession's direct relationship as a source of expert and accredited sovereignty from parents, children, and communities. The primary sources do not include the detail of events, but by February 2000 it was confirmed that the named businessperson would not have a formal role. While the School Leadership Charity was registered on 24 August 2000, it was deregistered as a charity on 12 February 2002 (it remained a dormant company, and was then struck off on 21 February 2002).

Whoever was to be invited into the NLPR had to accept the terms and conditions for associated practices that rendered the profession as the objects for reform intervention. Consequently, the NLPR developed the ERC through the NCSL as a site for privileged vantage points to be invited to support and enable the core. This included a range of people who would engage in ways that were regarded as 'safe and sensible' members of the NLPR: from industry such as Richard Greenhalgh (Chief Executive of Unilever, UK) as Chairman of the Governing Council; from local government such as Tim Brighouse (Chief Education Officer, Birmingham City Council) as member of the Governing Council, and Heather du Quesnay (former Director of Education for Hertfordshire County Council and the London Borough of Lambeth) as Director; from schools such as David Jackson (former Headteacher of Sharnbrook Upper School and Community College, see Jackson 2000) as Director of Research, and Toby Salt (Headteacher, St Anthony's School) as member of the Governing Council; from consultancy Tony Mackay (Director, Centre for Strategic Thinking, Melbourne, Australia) as member of the Governing Council; and from higher education, David Hopkins (Dean of Education, University of Nottingham) as member of the Governing Council.

A significant example of how the ERC was shaped by 'safe and sensible' NLPR membership and practices was through the establishment of a Think Tank chaired by David Hopkins with the brief to design a new framework for developing school leadership (Hopkins 2001; NCSL 2001). The Think Tank had a membership that is firmly located in the NLPR, and included – in addition to key NCSL staff such as Heather Du Quesney and David Jackson – key New Labour personnel such as Michael Barber, and project leaders such as Pat Collarbone who led on remodelling (see Chapter 6), with people from consultancy such as Tony Mackay, and from business such as Nigel Portwood from Pearson Education and Hugh Mitchell from Shell International Petrol Co Ltd. The SLSR is represented by Professor Geoff Southworth as visiting professor (and who later took over from David Jackson as Director of Research), with headteachers from a range of schools including Michael Gibbons, from Trinity School in Carlisle (and later he became the first Chief Executive of The Innovation Unit in the Department). The meetings included seminars with invited speakers, where 'Ten Propositions' as imperatives for the 'Leadership for Transforming Learning' were developed:

Proposition One: School leadership must be purposeful, inclusive, and values driven

Proposition Two: School leadership must embrace the distinctive and inclusive context of the school

Proposition Three: School leadership must promote an active view of learning

Proposition Four: School leadership must be instructionally focused

Proposition Five: School leadership is a function that needs to be distributed throughout the school community

Proposition Six: School leadership must build capacity by developing the school as a learning community

Proposition Seven: School leadership must be futures oriented and strategically driven

Proposition Eight: School leadership must be developed through experiential and innovative methodologies

Proposition Nine: School leadership must be served by a support and policy context that is coherent, systemic, and implementation driven

Proposition Ten: School leadership must be supported by a National College that leads the discourse around leadership for learning.
(Hopkins 2001: 8–15)

These propositions are nested in business models of corporate transformational leadership and its translation into a school improvement model vital for behaviour and organisational change (see Gunter 2016). The espoused viewpoint is leader centric, and so accepts leading as an elite function that is both held and delegated, and leadership as a power-over process in order to deliver reforms to meet the standards agenda – it is consistent with *teachers: meeting the challenge of change* (DfEE 1998, see Box 1.1).

Importantly Proposition Ten demands that the NCSL 'leads the discourse', and this required the control of knowledge production regarding what is known and what is worth knowing, and how functional and normative research and scholarship were funded in order to support the delivery of policy within schools (see Gunter 2012). This operated in a number of ways: first, the direct exclusion of vantage points and viewpoints that would open up issues for debate and seek to locate children, families, and professionals as democratic citizens rather than as stakeholders (Fielding 2006), where the plurality of knowledge traditions and purposes in regard to change do not feature, and where researchers who were working on values (for example, Richard Bates), power (for example, Bill Foster), and on activism in regard to communities (for example, John Smyth) and inequality (for example, Jill Blackmore) (see Smyth 1989), are missing from the final report. A second approach is to create activity such as conferences, online seminars, webpages, and the funding of projects (see Gunter 2012) and the publication of books (for example, Coles and Southworth 2005) in ways that enabled the NLPR to both set the ERC agenda and to control how it is read and understood. For example, the list of ten propositions mentioned previously are full of 'must' this and that, but they are open to interpretation and so are potentially defendable when challenged. However, challenges are unlikely from within the NLPR, and so while Proposition Two can be read in different ways, there is no recognition of the modernisation of school leadership in an unmodern segregated system. The establishment and operation of the NCSL is an example of depoliticisation whereby important issues such as the inclusion and exclusion of children through discriminatory school admissions are removed from public sites of debate and primary research, and are identified and resolved in ways that only require tactical enactment within the school. This is the technology that enables the profession to be trained and accredited as 'safe and sensible', and this connects with system redesign (Chapter 5) and workforce reform (Chapter 6) that emphasises what is characterised as 'best practice'. Furthermore, while the NCSL was subject to ongoing government monitoring and evaluation as evidenced in the formal remit letters, its research programme was not subject to independent peer review (see Gunter 2012).

These forms of legitimised and authorised policy violence enable understandings about how and why regimes of practice demonstrate intelligent forms of violence. Public money was invested and accounted for on the basis of a defendable approach to knowledge production – the NCSL and its activities were based on evidence and arguments from internationally renowned knowledge workers in universities and supra-national organisations, and productively engaged with by policy actors in schools, homes, communities, businesses, unions, local government and think tanks. However, in the 17 years that the National College operated, it is clear that its existence and functions were integral to how policy mortality operates: the NCSL weaponised school leadership in ways that made everything an issue for leaders who had to lead and exercise leadership in a particular way; it was calculated in the presentation of leadership propositions, training, and accreditation that was consistent with and could further develop the ideologically determined ERC; and it was enacted in language, systems, titles, and pay grades through how everyone from children through to ministers were identified and organised as potential and actual leaders of anything and everything. As one school administrator stated: "We are all leaders. We're leading the children, we're leading each other and we're all growing together" (Project 20). Professional titles such as headteacher, teacher, head of year began to disappear and were replaced by principal, senior leader, emergent leader, and middle leader (Gunter and Forrester 2008). Everything that was said and written spoke to everyone as leaders, and so everyone was responsible even if it was not their responsibility.

The NCSL was required to create school leadership premised on the reality and potential of failure, and so the job of headteacher was established as high stakes where accountability and responsibility were key to professional dispositions, and this had impact where professionals variously accepted and actively developed the ERC through their engagement. For example, one headteacher explains "I was invited four years ago to a meeting in London by the DfES ... and there were about 200 of us there nationally, and we had been identified as being transformational leaders" (Project 15). In addition to being consulted by the Department, the professional went on to explain how the headteachers had collaborated to make policy work. For example:

> 'And so we are now a Foundation School. We took a lead role in becoming an Extended School long before it was the trendy thing to do. ... A couple of years ago we also came out of contract for County grounds and cleaning, so we also directly employ staff. And we are about to come out of County catering, so to have the autonomy. I want a school that is different to everyone else's.' (Project 15)

Alignment with policy is evident in a range of projects (for example, Hughes et al 2020), but this work also shows that while the NCSL was premised on the complete colonisation of field intellectual and practical work, it actually failed to do that. An NCSL insider stated:

> 'It is probably worth saying that government is always looking for quick solutions to immediate problems, and I do think that there was some sort of hope that overnight the College would transform the world of school leadership and therefore the policy of schooling ... and we were constantly struggling with an expectation that there would be a quick answer.' (Project 15)

However, there is clear evidence of values and practice-based resistance to what was being required by policy and the NCSL as the delivery arm of that policy. For example, one headteacher talked about the impact of policy mortality and how "the biggie was having to implement government policy when you didn't agree with it. I found that very, very difficult" (Project 15). Another headteacher related it to values:

> 'it's still that thing about you know, one, making sure that every child actually can thrive in terms of our social democracy, and two, making sure that you create a sense in which you open up what it counts to be successful in terms of a learner rather than just five A–Cs, and, three, that you have an absolute remit to work in a sense of social justice and community and to build up fairness and a model community so

that you model something in a sense which you yourself can approve, appreciate and enjoy.' (Project 15)

Such a refusal to abandon professional values had been characterised by the Department as evidence of how the profession was not yet sufficiently 'safe and sensible' to own their own college and training, and while educational services were depoliticised in order to close down or relocate educational debates, it is the case that alternative sites of knowledge production remained.

Summary

Investigating the relationship between the state, public policy, and knowledge production in the production and preservation of the ERC demonstrates the importance of a political sociology of regimes of practice. The case example from EPKP *Theme 3: Policy Actors* used in this chapter shows that policy regarding the professionals as leaders and followers (along with parents, children, and communities) is related to knowledge production for and within state regimes located in core vantage points and espousing normative functionalist viewpoints. The interventions made into identities of educators in order to produce transformational leaders and followers lie within the legitimate, authorised, and intelligent policy violence of regime activities, where the example of fabricated history that opens this chapter is the outcome of how the core-privileged vantage point and normative-functionalist viewpoints operate to control policy agendas through regimes that practice to preserve oligarchic club sovereignty.

Policy violence presents 'leaderisation' as: vital for social mobility, and yet the elite leader role is actually integral for the normalisation of hierarchical segregated services (Chapter 2); vital for problem solving, and yet governing by knowledge production for leaders, leading, and leadership uses approved segregationist technologies (Chapter 3); vital for policy success, and yet leaders are required to make policy mortality work efficiently and effectively, and so are invested in segregated 'deserts' (Chapter 4).

While regimes of practice are vital for education policy analysis, research requires an investigation into the interchanges and deals, and so I now turn to the importance of understanding the impact of exchange relationships within and between regimes by those who inhabit vantage points and espouse viewpoints.

8

Exchange relationships

Introduction

In June 2021 it was announced that Eton College had signed an agreement with the Star Academies MAT to open three selective sixth forms in the Midlands and North of England, with the aim from 2024 to 'fast-track young people, often from deprived communities, to the UK's most academic universities' (Dennett 2021: NP). The plan is that:

> the new colleges will admit 240 students each per year and will offer many of the educational and extra-curricular opportunities available to pupils at Eton College itself, including knowledge-rich teaching from some of the country's most respected subject-specialists, access to talks from high-profile speakers, academic essay prizes and debate clubs, Oxbridge-style tutorial sessions and the chance to learn Latin. Some of these students' teaching will be delivered virtually by Eton staff and students from the new colleges will have a chance to attend Eton College annually for a Summer School. (Star Academies 2021: NP)

There is nothing in this list of activities that Sixth Forms in schools and colleges in the public sector do not do and cannot do, but what is different is that both organisations in this scheme are beneficiaries of privatised independence from democratic accountability, but at the same time are dependent on public funding from the taxpayer. For example, Eton charges annual fees of £44,000 generating an income of £51 million, plus £8.1 million in donations in 2020, and has charitable status which means it receives 80 per cent discount on its rates bill (cutting from £831,600 to £166,320 in 2020, Rushton 2020: NP). In addition, while reports show that private schools give bursaries, they 'are spending millions more on giving affluent middle-class families fee discounts than on children from disadvantaged backgrounds' (Henry 2018: NP). A change in the law in 2006 required charitable status for private schools to be linked to sharing facilities with local state schools through to formal partnerships facilitated by the System Partnership Unit (Fairburn 2019), and so the price of hefty tax exemptions and other privileges means that private schools undertake civic philanthropy in the public interest as missionary work with those less fortunate. Oligarchic club sovereignty not only protects and enhances its own interests through adjustments to concessions, but also intensifies the authorisation and legitimation of segregation in the state system through smart schemes.

Investigating such matters through the EPKP projects requires explanation through the TPSF. This validates the importance of *exchange relationships* within and between regimes of practice regarding the security and dynamics of the ERC. Research within the EPKP projects demonstrates the primacy of *personal-cultural contractualism* in the exchange relationships by the state regime with satellite regimes based on rhetorical functional science and shared normative instrumentalism, and I examine policy violence through further developing my analysis of *Theme 3: Policy Actors*.

Education policy exchange relationships

Policy violence requires actual or at least the appearance of consensual enactment, and as such it depends on agreeable exchange relationships within and between regimes of practice. In education policy there are a range of tangibles that are exchanged, for example, people, money, ideas, language, narratives, activity, evidence, experiences, and skills, along with recognised intangibles such as status, reputation, image, and networks. Potential risks of under-performance (for example, partial or non-delivery of policy and the consequences that come from this, such as losing an election) are insured against by deploying mutual trust through to various forms of subjugation. Exchanges are premised on a form of modernising utility whereby a job can be designed and done by those who accept and develop the ERC as individual and corporatised fabrications, where non-educational innovations designed to improve education can be presented and engaged with (Gunter 2020e). Regimes form around shared problem identification, solution dispositions, and espoused truths, and engage in associated practices regarding investments in careers, reputations, and resources, and manage potential and actual interstitial encounters in the knowledge production involved. Regimes are structured and operate according to formal and informal contractual relationships between policy actors whereby vantage point authority and legitimacy interplays with viewpoint framing and articulation.

The EPKP projects are premised on regimes undertaking governing through contractualism based on the legality of formal remits, and the informality of entrusting risk and responsibility to recognised vantage points and approved-of viewpoints. Policy actors who engage in exchange relationships invest public resources into occupational roles and ideological positions that enable knowledge production to be structured and used to scope and promote ERC agendas. Thus exchange relationships move theorising beyond the social networks of who knows who towards the actuality of what Goodwin (2009) identifies as 'the power of agents to realise

Table 8.1: Knowledge production and contractual exchange relationships

Forms	Purposes are to…
Personal	Secure obligations and opportunities
Employment	Do a job of work
Project	Deliver outcomes
Socio-political	Secure stability
Cultural	Empowered contractualism

Source: Based on Gunter and Mills 2017

their intentions' and the importance of 'the effects of the structured terrain on which networks operate which shapes, constrains, and enables the strategies of actors' (682). Table 8.1 presents contractual exchange relationships in evidence in education policy.

All five forms of contractual exchange relationships in Table 8.1 are evident in education policy making by the UK government for schools in England.

Personal

State regimes form and develop (sustaining, fracturing, repositioning within and outside) regarding how the club works by knowing people *personally*, and hence through contact people can generate experiences, create memories, and vouch for each other as being located in approved vantage points with preferred viewpoints that are on message. In a high-stakes risky context, it is the case that trust and reliability are important, where personal friendships, likes, and dislikes also feature. One minister explained how the government knew that policy would happen:

> 'And so you do it by putting Michael Barber who as an ex-Labour politician, as well as an academic, but had worked for the Tories as well, you put him in charge of the Standards and Effectiveness Unit. Now we did that so that we knew then that there was somebody going to be giving us decent stuff on school effectiveness, and what we also knew because we asked for it to happen, and we made sure it was happening, that the people that were recruited to the SEU were frontline deliverers.' (Project 15)

The club works by forms of relationality that is about knowing people (or getting to know people), but is more than this as it is about a sense of shared interests within and for various projects. Even though policy actors may not have met before or may never actually meet each other in person, they actually *know* someone is or is not one of us. This is vital for securing tangible gains from the trading of ideas as products, through to status and the acclaim generated by certain people being associated and involved, and keeping other 'types' out. Hence consent is personal where enactment is dependent on how clubness operates.

Employment

State regimes offer *employment* contracts to work within Whitehall and/or its sites of depoliticised policy delivery either in the department (for example, SEU) or managed by it at arms-length (for example, NCSL, TTA). Those in public office alongside officials and invited participants engaged in policy debate, as one senior civil servant stated about the NLPR:

> 'I think one of the things about the Department was that it was a great time for discussion and policy development was taking place kind of all over the place, so we would regularly have strategy away days for example, where Special Advisors would be present with senior civil servants, with Ministers, Secretary of State, and it was a really exciting exchange of ideas and thinking.' (Project 15)

Employment can be a form of co-option to a club approved role (either temporary or longer term), and this can be through contracts issued to enable particular people to enter government, for example, Barber, and then Hopkins as Head of the SEU; and into the government system for example, Jackson, and then Southworth as Directors of Research at the NCSL. Munby (2019) describes how he was appointed to the Director role at the NCSL and then CEO at CfBT 'in spite of my lack of school leadership or commercial experience' (265), and he shows that in regard to the NCSL role the PM's office tried to block his appointment as he had not been a head teacher. Nevertheless, they reconsidered as he was vouched for, and so consent can be personal, and it is also official through signing on the dotted line with a commitment to deliver.

Project

State regimes offer contracts for commissioned evaluation and/or training design/delivery *projects*. This enables private companies (for example, PwC 2008) and teams from universities (for example, Day et al 2009) to undertake projects that scope a problem and/or provide evidence and recommendations. As one Secretary of State from the NLPR said to us about universities and research: "we saw them almost as a service industry to government", and while subsequent reflection had generated the view that "they never should be that and they never will be that", it is the case that the production of a particular type of evidence for policy was the key priority (Project 15). Policy actors in a state regime may be clear about what they want but may not be clear about the details of how this might be achieved, and so policy actors from satellite regimes are enabled to network into various competitive consortia in order to communicate how policy can be delivered. Importantly, while each contract may be a stand-alone 'one-off' it is the case that particular people and groups tend to be identified as preferred providers with a track record for helping ministers and civil servants to understand what is possible, and so they will fund options that are conducive to policy delivery. Consent is personal and legal but also active in regard to agendas and the requirements for enactment.

Socio-political

State, satellite, and star regimes engage with *socio-political* contracts that are integral for democracy and the rule of law to operate. While the law and regulation structure relationality, it is the case that forms of imagined agreement are about bringing stability to human conduct (and is distinct from the Hobbesian notion of the 'state of nature'), whereby I or we 'agree to not only engage in certain activities, but also to take on the obligation to regulate one's own behaviour in an appropriate fashion' (Hindess 1997: 14–15). There is evidence of regime activity premised on this social contract, whereby the logic of practice within state, satellite, and star regimes operates on the basis of broader rules of the game. While frustrations can and do exist within and between regimes, not least those who are located in marginal vantage points (and so may have lost personal, project, and employment contracts), there is general adherence to a wider socio-political contract regarding legality. Nevertheless, there is recent evidence of corruption in the wider public sphere in regard to state regimes and education policy (for example, Thomson 2020). Hence consent and enactment are dependent on how the legality of employment and projects are engaged with by the personal, but as already noted (see Chapter 1) the reliance of personal integrity of playing by the rules as 'chaps' is under threat (Blick and Hennessy 2019).

Cultural

State regimes have invested heavily in *cultural* contracting that is known as contractualism. From organising and governing a state through to a single public institution within the state, researchers have identified the use of contracts in order to govern the individual (see Rawolle et al 2017). Bodies, identities, and practices are regulated at an individual or private level that is made public through the use of a contractual agreement: 'the requirement for the individual user of a service both to choose what it is they require of that service, *and* to make that choice explicit in such a manner that it can be determined whether the service has responded effectively to that choice or not' (Yeatman 1994: 2, original emphasis). Not only does this manage risk but it also elides contradictions generated through structural injustices, and it does this through enabling the individual to be responsible and accountable. Data show this in a range of ways, with one example of a middle leader in a school demonstrating corporate certainty by explaining their understanding of leadership:

> 'in my opinion leadership is to try and inspire people to do well in their work and to want to do well in their work and to see the positive aspects of their job and to try and provide them with the tools to be able to do their job to the best of their ability.' (Project 20)

In other project schools we found a high degree of cohesion, for example, "I feel valued at work" and "I am really happy at work", where one middle leader at Birch Tree stated: "If you are not seen as being supportive on school policies and you are not supporting the school ethos, it doesn't look very good" (Project 20). Such statements illuminate a number of issues, not least how the person in the organisational middle role assumes emotional and practical obligations for how their colleagues feel about their work and hence do their work, and the need to communicate endless positivity. In this sense the distribution of leadership as a popular model in the 2000s and 2010s is interpreted by the headteacher as "we've got more responsibility devolved further deeper down into the structures" (Project 20), and so the focus is to put the onus for change and outcome data onto everyone's shoulders – whether staff or students. This is quite visceral, where at Birch Tree school, a senior leader stated: "the remit I have been given from [headteacher name] is that at the next Ofsted we have outstanding at teaching and learning, so basically my job is to get us there" (Project 20). Contractualism is based on consent as a form of individualised self-calculation within exchange relationships, whereby there is a need to be seen to fulfil a remit for contract delivery but also to (a) offer to take on the provision of services that previously were the responsibility of the state, not least local government; and (b) insure the self against the loss of a contract (and services) that previously the state provided, not least public terms and conditions of service (see Shamir 2008; Peters 2017). While contracts are presented as a rational form of regulatory control, what is emerging is a form of contractualism that is replete with individualised struggling for positioning and acclaim for the self and hence relational advantage.

State regimes enable oligarchic club sovereignty to be preserved and enhanced within public policy, where personal and cultural forms of contractual exchange relationships have come to dominate. In order for the core and privileged vantage points to remain secure, and functional-normative instrumental viewpoints to be legible and credible, then state regimes need contractual relationships with satellite regimes that buttress oligarchic occupation through being onside, and with star regimes that are permanently othered as irrelevant or even dangerous. Cultures of permanent vulnerability and coercive disposability as a disciplinary process for everyone underpin exchange relationships, and while private club oligarchies can walk away, it is the case that parents and children who depend on public education, and educational professionals who are committed to public education, are required to navigate and to learn very quickly how to survive and cope with policy mortality.

A case study of exchange relationships

The EPKP projects have produced research evidence and analysis that demonstrates the actuality and validity of exchange relationships (see Gunter and Mills 2017), and here I focus again on *Theme 3: Policy Actors*. This important theme connects all of the data collection and analysis I have been involved in (Appendix), whereby a range of exchange relationships are in evidence between professionals and children (for example, Thomson and Gunter 2006), between professionals within schools (for example, Hall et al 2012), between professionals and others (for example, Gunter and Mills 2017), and between policymakers in government and policy actors in other vantage points (for example, Gunter 2012). Data demonstrate that the construction and development of the ERC is actively dynamic through how what is thought, said, and done is located in a range of exchange relationships by people in the same and different vantage points, with espoused (as well as silent) viewpoints, and interconnected within regimes of practice. I intend focusing on this policy violence through examining the relationship between the ERC and exchange relationships through drawing on the data from a range of projects, but in particular, the *Kingswood High School (KHS) Innovation Project* (Project 11).

The energetic complexities involved in contractual exchange relationships can be captured through a mapping of waves of policy interventions into educational services, and the way particular policy actors have been characterised and involved. An overview map is presented in Table 8.2.

Table 8.2 outlines trends in the positioning and repositioning of policy actors: first, the stance of the UK government from overseer to dominant regulator, local government from democratic partner to marginalised, underfunded, and othered 'who?', and supra-national organisations from observers to actively being involved in framing and speaking about and for globalised standards; second, the purposes of educational professionals

Table 8.2: Change and UK education policy for schools in England

	Recovery: Investment from mid-1940s to 1960s	Austerity: Oil crisis from Mid-1970s to 1980s	Investment: Banking boom from 1990 to 2000s	Austerity: Banking collapse from 2010s onwards
Children	Educated	Workers	Aspirational	Workers
Parents	'Who?'	'Natural experts'	'Consumers'	Gamblers
Community	Investors	Dis-investors	Investors	Dis-investors
Profession	Educators	'Problems'	Remodelled	Deliverers
Business	'Indifferent'	'Concerned'	'Consultants'	Providers
Local government	'Active partners'	'Squeezed'	Ineffectual	Who?
UK government	'Oversees'	Assertive	Dominant	Dominant
Supra-national organisations	Marginal	Emerging	Compelling	Instrumental

Source: Based on Dale 1989a: 115

from public experts to corporate deliverers of outcome data to enable marketised choice; and third, the privatised status and contribution of parents from citizen partners to consumers living in communities whereby public disinvestment determines attitudes to taxation, and businesses have shifted from indifferent users to philanthropic and corporate providers of educational services.

What is being exchanged is a combination of support (for example, votes) and acceptance (for example, there is no alternative), where policy violence is sanitised and sanctioned through promises for improvement, access to world leading services, and fulfilling the aspirations of 'your child'. Importantly, the security of oligarchic preservation and restoration projects are evident in how exchange relationships enabled the ERC to be worked and reworked by included and excluded policy actors based on eugenicist populism as advantageous privatised libertarianism. The ERC stressed national rebuilding in the post-war period, and for a short time the dominance of the civic project meant there was a possibility of democratisation based on the educability of all children underpinned by the welfare state and NHS. However, the UK continues to struggle with post-imperial identity, and consequently knowing your place in the economy and learning to market the self and to take risks in markets was re-cultured and strengthened as the core purpose of attending a segregated school that is framed as 'meeting your needs'. A combination of moral imperatives (what is right and decent) and consumer rights (privatised choice) trumped citizenship rights, where the immediacy of anti-civic gains was made popular through the marginalisation and othering of alternative knowledges. For example, Margaret Thatcher's Conservative Party won the 1979 election on a manifesto that stated: 'we must restore to every child, regardless of background, the chance to progress as far as his or her abilities allow', where a good school place is equated with segregation: 'We will halt the Labour government's policies which have led to the destruction of good schools; keep those of proven worth; and repeal those sections of the 1976 Education Act which compel local authorities to reorganise along comprehensive lines and restrict their freedom to take up places at independent schools' (Conservative Party 1979: NP). Elections for the UK House of Commons are processes that allow the oligarchic occupiers to restore and retain dominance, where state regimes traded with satellite regimes in ways that control knowledge production. Table 8.2 illuminates an anti-politics trend, and to paraphrase Appadurai (2017) it seems that parents, children, communities, and business were not only increasingly fed up with democracy but were also enabled through elections to become fatigued about democratic values, process, and outcomes. Importantly, schools continued to choose children, and so while parental consumer choice is based on fabricated lies, it did not seem to matter as people voted and practiced against their own interests (Gunter 2018).

Personal-cultural contractual exchange relationships have come to dominate. All educational issues have become personal and private marketised choices – to decide as a consumer what your preferences are, and as a provider to decide whether to invest in educational products. This of course is a fabrication because eugenicist populism means that everyone is known before they are born due to family inheritance, and so all children, parents, and communities are known for what they are and what they can achieve and contribute. Nevertheless, the impersonation of superiors has become a personal-cultural practice, whereby all parents and children are required to act in a club like way, and to demonstrate that they know and are known and so they are worthy or unworthy potential/actual members of the club. The personal segues into cultural contractualism whereby exchanges are based on individual choices, responsibilities, and insurances that are about and for the individual, and where risk is mediated through the 'offer' that is framed and guaranteed in the formal 'contract'. When this does not work, then parents and children can be ridiculed as 'freeloaders' who are over dependent on the state and/or fulfilling the eugenicist typing assigned to them, regarding 'what do you expect of them?' However, the situation may not be that simple, where non-compliance by a school place provider means that personal networks can be broken, and campaigns including actual and threatened litigation can be undertaken by parents in order to force contractual conformity in ways that focus on reputation and market status (for example, parental challenges to the offer and removal of a school place, Gunter 2018).

Such policy violence within and for contractual exchange relationships is evident in the data from the *Kingswood High School (KHS) Innovation Project* (Project 11). KHS was a successful comprehensive school under the control of the LA, and this was recognised by Ofsted as well as by parents and children, where one parent stated in an interview: "our children love school, and they get up in the morning and go. There is a buzz about the school, a sense of life. They are always trying something, and they attract new teachers. Those who have done their GCSEs want to come back here to do A-levels" (Gunter and Thomson 2004: 5). This 'buzz' was due to a dynamic approach to change whereby the planned focus was on establishing a culture of first, achievement and improvement through examining different approaches to teaching and learning; second, expectation and innovation through examining the curriculum; and third, personalised and responsible learning through extending student choice of and within learning.

The school operated within the law but established local policymaking through a number of projects, and a formal evaluation was commissioned by the Innovation Unit in order to identify the school improvement strategy underway, and hence learn the lessons for scaling up across the system. This evaluation included a range of questionnaire and other data collection from students, staff, parents, and governors, observation of lessons and meetings, and a study of documentation. The outcome was formally reported to the Innovation Unit (Gunter and Thomson 2004), and the school then supported the Students as Researchers Project (SRP, Thomson and Gunter 2006, Project 11), a NCSL funded project on middle management (Fitzgerald et al 2006, Project 12), and doctoral student in residence through an ESRC CASE studentship (McGinity 2013, Project 26).

Research undertaken by and within KHS contributed to the idea and reality of local policymaking as a researching school, where an approach that speaks to the idea of contractual exchange relationships was developed. There are four main approaches to the researching school regarding who sets the agenda (school or outsider such as the government) and the purposes of that agenda (to bring about externally demanded improvements or to fundamentally challenge and change power processes): agenda *setting, evaluation, following*, and *delivery* (McGinity and Gunter 2012). The research at KHS shows strong investment into their school-based local policymaking, where the school set its own agenda and evaluated progress and outcomes. Agenda setting and evaluation are evident in how the school determined its own priorities for pedagogy and the student experience, and invested resources into independent primary research as a learning opportunity for staff and students with a commitment to embrace the findings and analysis in order to review progress and determine next steps (see Fitzgerald et al 2006). For example, the Students as Researchers project (Project 11) is illustrative of how the school actively wanted children to understand and develop their role in enquiry, where through action research they could design a project, collect, and analyse data, communicate it to staff through in-service sessions, and actively lead change. Staff and students were concerned about the over dependency on content at the expense of creative thinking and analysis, where it was recognised that children have a valid contribution to make to the aims and practices of improvement. Importantly, the school was able to identify how external contractual exchange relationships could be framed and enacted in ways that would support the school's own innovation agenda. For example, the headteacher was antipathetic to the LA as a potential limitation on the school's development, and while he had similar concerns about the Department in London, he recognised that the ERC had to be engaged with. The head successfully negotiated with the Department that the school would not take on one specialism (for example, a language school, or a sports college), but as a comprehensive school the curriculum would have multiple specialisations *within* the school (McGinity and Gunter 2017).

While the headteacher handled potential policy violence through presenting such local innovations to the Department, it remains the case that government interventions required agenda following and delivery. Consequently, change is directly linked to externally determined improvement that provides data that demonstrates the efficacy of those interventions. The ERC promotes what is known and is worth knowing, where the core vantage point controls viewpoints, and who is invited from privileged vantage points into the state regime. The core requires this to be replicated at local level, where vantage points, viewpoints, regimes, and exchange relationships are focused on headteacher and senior staff as the organisational core, who control policy enactment through the privileging of the workforce, students, and parents, and the endemic potential for marginalisation and othering for unwelcome viewpoints, regimes, and exchanges. Hence forms of localised policymaking tend to be based on tactical interpretations of what was required within context – often described as 'wiggle room' – and so delivery may require some technical adjustments. There is strong evidence of such agenda following and delivery at KHS where the focus on achievement was governed by external requirements to target children who were not producing data to demonstrate the right standards; and in lesson observations we identified the endemic framing of learning in regard to the demands of various data production requirements, where the children may not present themselves as independent learners because they have learned to hand over responsibility to teachers as being in control of what they need to do in order to pass an exam.

The tensions between school and government initiated and enabled projects is a vital site for understanding policy actors, contractual exchange relationships and regime membership. Legitimised violence is evident in how KHS set out to lead its own change agenda but in reality, the school was located in a marginal vantage point, and as a comprehensive school under LA control it was potentially othered. Marketisation impacted on the school, where it is located in an affluent area whereby wealthy locals used private education without due regard to the high quality of education at the local school, and considered it to be the school for those children from the estate on the other side of town. This contextual situation is important, where the data show that the school set out to use its own agenda setting in order to establish itself in a higher and more privileged vantage point. The 2010 legislation that allowed successful schools to convert to academy status was an opportunity for the school to legally break away from the LA as a perceived brake on development (not least through how the school as an academy would receive more funding), but also to mimic the notion of independence that was a key feature of the provision of educational services in the town. The ERC presented the comprehensive school as 'a cancer at the heart of English society' (Adonis 2012: xii), and configured academisation as a liberation narrative for successful schools to break free of the national curriculum and national workforce terms and conditions.

The beneficial realities of academy conversion were preached to those who were prepared to be converts, and because KHS had helped to shape specialist schools policy, they explained how they would continue to do that: "We're at the cutting edge of where schools are nationally. … It's an exciting time to be here. It feels like the beginning of something that could be growing arms and legs and could become a model for other schools around the country" (Headteacher, McGinity and Gunter 2017: 103). Importantly, the local MP was a member of the Cameron cabinet, and this personal connection was used to access resources and to demonstrate that the school was on-board with policy following and delivery:

> I suppose what [name of local MP] has enabled us to do ultimately is get in front of [name of the parliamentary undersecretary for education] as we did this week and get him to say ok, what you are doing is absolutely what we want, we will find a way of fitting you into a funding stream. If I am being perfectly honest, probably that would have been quite difficult to get that without [name of MP] opening the doors in the first instance. But we always know, it's not necessarily what you know it's who you know, sometimes … but I don't think he would have done us any favours unless he was personally convinced that this was actually going to deliver real positive outcomes. (Chair of Governors, Gunter et al 2018: 124)

This is tactically astute, and is supported by recognition of the need to join the academies programme because: "currently the Department won't engage with schools that aren't academies. … So the DfE wouldn't have dealt with us if we weren't converting" (Headteacher, McGinity and Gunter 2017: 104). This is an example of authorised violence whereby the privatised decisions within school did the work of national policy, and where the accumulation of capitals by the headteacher with the Department over time (funding by the Innovation Unit; redesign of specialist school status) meant that the violence towards the comprehensive school as a successful idea and reality was misrecognised (McGinity and Gunter 2017).

Agenda setting and evaluation through primary research in partnership with universities by KHS could be seen as establishing rival centres of knowledge production, and this could damage the newly acquired privileged status with the Department and influential national policy actors. Hierarchy matters, where taking on academy and studio school status, with choice being used to differentiate between an academic and vocational curriculum, enabled the comprehensive school to be formally segregated on the same campus. There was no independent research evidence to support the academies programme from 2000 or its extension to successful schools from 2010, and there were examples at the time where schools in similar situations in other parts of England networked in order to retain local and public education (Gunter 2011). However, it seems that personal-cultural contractualism was evident in how national school based policy decision-making operated at KHS, where there was acceptance that the following and delivery policy agenda would be advantageous.

The research partnership with KHS itself was not only based on forms of personal and cultural contractualism, but also political and social exchanges. The only state secondary school in a town was an important civic-public service, where professionals and locals assumed that a school and the education service as a whole was too important and too big to be allowed to fail. The agenda setting and evaluation was synchronised with agenda following and delivery as an intelligent form of knowledge production in order to protect the pupils, families, and staff. However, such exchanges were based on civic security and dependency, but as already noted, from the 1970s onwards the intensification of policy mortality means that local policymaking has been a site for the erosion of the reality of a high-quality local school for all children (see Table 8.2). The school was located in the reality and fear of failure – the comprehensive school in general had been too successful and so had to be demonised in ways that spoke to an aspirational community that bought school places from the private sector but always had an un-informed but influential opinion about KHS. The school itself had been on track to fail, and had been turned around by the headteacher who had not only adopted the informal 'wiggle room' approach to local policy making of national policy interventions, but had also shown some independence from the ERC regarding local strategy. However, the school had to be reminded of pervasive failure in the system, with the requirement that the school match the predisposition to develop local policy with the requirement to follow and deliver. Local modifications may be tolerated but local strategy was not. While in 2001 the school was evaluated by OfSTED as 'a good school', at the next inspection in 2006 it had slipped to 'satisfactory', where the inspectors noted that the school's self-evaluation was wrong because it had judged itself to be 'good'. In other words, the school had given attention to local policymaking through agenda setting and evaluation, where the inspectors reported that in certain named subject areas the school had let its grip on standards slip. By 2011 the school had restored the Ofsted judgement as a 'good' school, and was then closed in order to establish an academy.

Summary

Investigating the relationship between the state, public policy, and knowledge production in the production and preservation of the ERC demonstrates the importance of a political sociology of exchange relationships. The case example from EPKP *Theme 3: Policy Actors* used in this chapter shows that local policymaking and knowledge production is primarily located in personal-cultural contractual exchange relationships. While policy actors at KHS set out to operate productively through their own improvement agenda based on and informed by research, they recognised that they had a marginal vantage point and that the school as a maintained comprehensive was increasingly othered by those within and aspiring for core and privileged vantage points. Indeed, the case of the partnership between Eton College and Star Academies MAT that opened this chapter shows how the core works with the privileged to extend the fabrication of privilege to maintain their interests. Exchange relationships with the core and associated privileged vantage points are based on the acceptance of academisation as inevitable, and so validated the fabrications of oligarchic club sovereignty.

Policy violence presents local policymaking as vital for social mobility, and yet it is national policy-making that dominates in the exchange relationships within and for segregated services (Chapter 2); as vital for problem solving, and yet governing by knowledge production for local policymaking enables a successful comprehensive school to be dismantled through accepted segregationist technologies (Chapter 3); as vital for policy success, and yet local policymaking is focused on preventing policy mortality and so intensive examination data collection is about improving segregated 'deserts' (Chapter 4).

While exchange relationships in relation to vantage points, viewpoints and regimes of practice are vital for education policy analysis, research requires an investigation into the knowledge production processes within Critical Education Policy Studies (CEPS). Importantly there is a need to examine the intellectual histories within CEPS in order to understand the relationship between research and practice, and what this means for vantage points, viewpoints, regimes, and exchange relationships.

9

Critical education policy studies

Introduction

In the wake of the abduction and subsequent murder of Sarah Everard by a serving police officer in London in March 2021, the issue of physical and reputational violence against women has become a focus of intense and sustained public debate. People came forward to give testimony, and included within this are accounts about how and why educational organisations can be unsafe. This is not new, where name calling and double standards are regarded as: 'ordinary, expected and public' (Bell 2008: 3). However, McBain (2021) reports that the failure to engage seriously means that the Everard and other cases has now produced 'the reckoning' illustrated by the public response to 'Everyone's Invited', an Instagram account set up in June 2020 by Soma Sara, a 22-year-old UCL graduate, to gather anonymous accounts of sexism and sexual abuse at UK schools, and she goes on to say:

> By early April it had collected thousands of testimonies (by late September it had 54,000) which implicated some of the country's most prestigious schools in perpetuating what Sara describes as 'rape culture'. By this, she means the normalization of sexist jokes, sexual harassment and online abuse, which creates the conditions for more extreme violence. In March students at Latymer and Highgate, two private schools in London, staged walkouts to protest rape culture. In June, Everyone's Invited released a list of almost 3,000 English schools that had been named in testimonies: around one in ten schools, state and private. (Soma Sara)

The segregation of the provision of and access to educational services means that the habitual rank ordering of the self and others is based on individual and corporate fabrications that demean and damage everyone. This physical and mental violence is evident in schools, and policy violence creates, sustains, and routinises it. Successive UK governments have a stake in segregated provision: in the name of modernisation the unmodern that sexualises female bodies is perpetuated as legitimate; governing by knowledge production authorises the acceptance of sexual savagery; and intelligent knowledgeabilities are deployed under the banner of aspiration but are used to keep bodies in their predetermined and correct place. McBain's (2021) investigation has unearthed how oligarchic club sovereignty creates and co-constructs segregated advantage and disadvantage within and through the ERC. While these issues are addressed through independent primary research in CEPS (for example, Chitty 2007; Ball 2013; Gunter 2018), it is the case that the field is replete with research ideas and practices for and about education policy that do not engage with policy violence.

Investigating such matters through the EPKP projects requires explanation through the TPSF. This validates the importance of *intellectual histories* in education policy, or the knowledge resources, the available ways of knowing, the recognition of those who are knowers, and the knowledgeabilities that demonstrate that someone is in the know. Intellectual histories of and for CEPS demonstrate different conceptualisations of criticality in knowledge production, where research within the EPKP projects demonstrates the primacy of *entrepreneurialism*, and I examine policy violence through *Theme 4: Knowledge Production*.

Research positioning in CEPS

Taking an intellectual history approach to knowledge production is a career long theme in my work, and it shows that CEPS is plural in regard to the traditions and the purposes of knowledge, and how change is engaged with and theorised (Gunter 2016, 2018). However, the TPSF analysis in Chapters 5–8 shows how the core vantage point determines which intellectual history matters, espouses and requires a normative functionalist viewpoint, and forms state regimes that use personal and cultural exchange relationships with privileged satellite regimes. Consequently, those who occupy the core vantage point engage in knowledge production for the ERC that is awash with actual and grandiose fabrications, where a study of policy texts shows that UK governments do have problems with evidence and analysis.

For example, the 'Mythbuster' (DfE 2010) document was produced by the Conservative-led Coalition government (2010–2015) to justify the extension of the academies programme from failing schools towards the removal all schools from local democratic control (Gunter 2011) (see Chapters 5 and 8) . The key task for the ERC was to demonstrate that the academies programme was working to rescue what is euphemistically called schools in challenging circumstances, but could also liberate successful schools from the local authorities that may have created the conditions for success but ultimately had to be condemned as a brake on privatised autonomy. The 'Mythbuster' document is a model for how the ERC takes on such duties, where it stated that student outcomes in academies showed the 'rate of improvement' on the 'number of students achieving 5 A★–C grades including English and maths'

Table 9.1: Criticality in education policy research

Policy positions	Meaning of policy positions	Position criticality questions the...
Description	Narrative of structures, events, and people	accuracy of narratives, and presents alternative accounts.
Science	Empirical measurement regarding reform delivery	evidence base for professional practice, and promotes data production for reform delivery.
Entrepreneurialism	Normative products for trade and profit	denial of markets in public systems, and promotes markets.
Scholarship	Empirical and conceptual research	ideological underpinnings and impact of reforms, and presents the evidence for social justice.

Source: Based on Gunter 2016, 2018, 2020d

was 'five times faster than the national average' (DfE 2010: 1). However, the actual evaluation report by PwC (2009) makes it clear that there is no 'simple uniform "Academy effect"' because 'there has been a more complex and varied process of change' (8), and in addition, primary research shows that academies were teaching different children to the predecessor schools (see Gunter 2011). In other words, a 5-year commissioned evaluation by PwC for the previous New Labour governments (1997–2010) was selectively used in order to justify an ideological policy shift from the academisation of failing schools to successful schools that was not actually evidence-informed, but seemingly needed rhetorical decoration.

Oligarchic club occupiers use and abuse data in order to create, refresh, and sustain the ERC. This has implications for researchers in CEPS, where positioning in relation to oligarchic club sovereignty as revealed by the TPSF is related to how criticality is conceptualised and engaged with. Table 9.1 presents four main positions of criticality. I now intend examining these four positions.

Policy description

Policy description is based on positions that give accounts of what the situation is, what has happened and what it means for people. Oligarchic occupiers selectively use descriptive forms of criticality in order to present a version of events that is legitimate, authorised, and intelligent, and this can be made public in speeches and manifestos where versions of history, sense making about events, and the policy imperative is made obvious, and can be *ex post facto* through the publication of memoirs and diaries. Criticality is about declaring a truthful experience, but the ERC depends on descriptive fabrications. For example, Astle and Ryan (2008) published an edited collection co-written by those who had a stake as policy actors in the academies programme. In the Foreword, Adonis (2008) makes it clear that the authors are 'convinced' that 'these new independent state schools represent a decisive break with past failure and a chance to shape a fundamentally better educational future for our country' (v). The ERC requires such certainty in order to be persuasive.

The EPKP projects are full of data that demonstrate how policy actors engage in this kind of experiential theorising about their advocacy position, particularly through espousing who is friend or foe. There are concerns about the way UK education policy for schools in England is experienced; one headteacher explains: "I think it was 91 initiatives last year, and things change very quickly at very short notice" (Project 15), and another states: "I feel it just gets worse and worse, that no matter what you do and no matter what progress you make, it's always not good enough" (Project 15). Such professional accounts of the challenges of a permanent revolution of reform have also been reported through biographical interviews (for example, Ribbins 1997b). What such accounts show is huge investment in making the reforms work, but also how policy actors who determine the reforms do not engage with the actual experiences, and so claim to be responding to headteacher 'wants' but in reality, they shape the meaning of those 'wants'.

This is illustrated by one leader of a major government education policy agency who promotes headteachers as business leaders based on the legitimacy, authority and intelligence of business models:

> 'You learn on the job. Well, the other book I think is essential reading on this whole subject is *Good to Great* by Jim Collins. He defines the quality of good leadership as the ability to get the wrong people off the bus and the right people on the bus in the right seats. And I think, personally I think that sums up exactly what a real leader is about.' (Project 15)

And while business writers may not have been in a school since they went to school themselves it does not stop this speaker using the relevance of practice to accept and discount particular kinds of knowledge producer:

> 'I think university education departments tend to be too theoretical, and that's why [name of university] has very close relations with the [name of organisation], and they are tailoring their support work to what headteachers say they want, rather than some professor of education saying this is what people should know, and he or she hasn't been in a classroom for, you know, never seen a school in a long time.' (Project 15)

Such a declarative position about who is right and who is wrong can be illustrated by data from the SPSO project whereby the headteacher at Birch Tree espouses the pro-academy narrative by disparaging the predecessor schools and the staff: "the two schools the academy replaced were dreadful" with one labelled as "truly shit", and this was because "I knew that local authorities were about levelling down and I really relish the independence of the academy" (Project 20). The narrative is a version of history that promotes business autonomy as vital for innovation, whereby the public system of laws and regulations as the duties and responsibilities of LAs and headteachers in partnership is ridiculed as a means of enabling headteachers to do *what they want to do*.

Policy description therefore enables and supports an account of practice that is essentially about what a headteacher *wants* or *does not want*, and this has been constructed as risky but solvable, and made urgent with tangible activities to do right now. For example, within CEPS there is an epistemic tradition that is known internationally as *Educational Administration (EA)* and in England it is *EMAL (Educational Management, Administration and Leadership)*, where a core feature is the creation and analysis of a binary between theory and practice (Gunter 1999, 2004, 2016). Professors talk about how policy creates new challenges, where EMAL's descriptive criticality is premised on supporting the professional as leaders and managers, with support for the NCSL's remit to enable government policy to be enacted in schools. One professor explains involvement with the NCSL:

> 'their research function has made a major contribution to the field and we know now that NCSL funds about fifty per cent of all the research in our field in this country and obviously, had they not been there, we would have had fifty per cent less research done, less research opportunities … I've had three evaluation contracts and one research contract with the NCSL … so I've had really quite an extensive involvement with NCSL since the beginning, so I'm broadly supportive of it.' (Project 15)

However, another field member raised concerns:

> 'A lot of people … in the early 2000s got into getting money out of the NCSL to do research projects in different ways and there was a lot of money there. It was great, but the nature of the research they wanted done was quite narrow. It fitted their purpose, and why shouldn't it, they were funders … so any other research that was as important but didn't instantly focus on school outcomes wasn't particularly encouraged.' (Project 15)

In addition, the EMAL community increasingly recognised that descriptive criticality was being occupied by international consultancy firms, where one professor identifies how taxpayer money was being spent on reforming performance management and teacher effectiveness in schools through a major contract with a consultancy company: "not only did they earn a huge amount for this" but,

> 'it's not the only thing they've earned lots of money from, through some of the leadership programmes they've developed for the National College, they've also milked the system, and governments have rather naively ... are prepared to pay lots of money to get what they think is going to meet the requirements, their policy agenda.' (Project 15)

Importantly, this consultancy firm also developed software as a result and was selling this to schools, and so government funded research created a commercial product that was being sold for profit.

In summary, policy description is an important part of criticality in the EMAL field whereby the official versions of reality (history, problems, challenges) are accepted and made to work, with opportunities for career advancement that require members to adopt commercialised identities and practices to meet the 'wants' of headteachers. However, policy description has been and continues to be a site for colonisation, particularly by policy science and policy entrepreneurial forms of criticality. It is to this that I now turn.

Policy science

Policy science is based on research positions that ontologically and epistemologically make demands on policy actors to move from descriptive criticality to energetically acceding to the findings and recommendations from improvement (see Stoll and Fink 1996) and effectiveness research (see Sammons 1999). Oligarchic occupiers selectively use scientific data to challenge the narrated faulty behaviours in the profession so that the change imperative is legitimate, authorised, and intelligent. Data from the EPKP projects demonstrate how policy actors present causal statements and evidence (for example, visions of a better world) to demand a shift from description to adopting prescriptions for new behavioural and organisational change. One headteacher talked about members of the school improvement research community: "I think they have made themselves available and they have not hidden in ivory towers, and I think that is very laudable" (Project 15). Importantly, what is integral to getting the job done differently is 'the concentration within school effectiveness upon "problems as taken"' and this is vitally different from 'problematizing problems' in policy scholarship (discussed later) in order to avert 'the kind of values debate that disabled

British sociology in education in the 1970s in which the nature of problems and of knowledge was revitalised with catastrophic results' (Reynolds and Teddlie 2001: 100).

Policy science presents evidence and strategies for identifying headteacher and professional *needs*, and making changes to how people think, what they say, and what they do. Within CEPs there are interconnected epistemic traditions known internationally as *Educational Effectiveness and Improvement Research (EEIR)*. Data from professors who work on change and organisational improvement, and the production of data about school effects illustrate distinctive but also shared purposes:

> 'I think I'm an old-fashioned school improvement person ... interested in strategies that improve, yes that do improve outcomes, measurable outcomes, but mainly things that improve the quality of experience.' (Project 15)

> 'coming from an effectiveness point of view I'm looking at things that make a difference. So if you look at those factors, something that keeps coming up is leadership ... I mean there is talk about all the other things, like climate, yes that's important but where does that come from, largely from leadership.' (Project 15)

Descriptive criticality can only get a professional so far, and so professionals need to engage with the EEIR knowledge base. Such knowledge production is varied but purposes are consistent: "I have deliberately tried to locate myself at that intersection between policy, research, and practice, and it's not been a very comfortable place to be, actually, you don't make a lot of friends there and you make a lot of enemies there" (Project 15). The activity in these junctural spaces is evident in UK government funding for knowledge production projects (for example, Sammons et al 1995; Day et al 2009), and EEIR members not only took up roles in the UK government (for example, Barber 2007a; Hopkins 2007) but also made the adoption of improvement and effectiveness for education policy an explicit commitment (for example, Barber 1996; Reynolds et al 1996). The EEIR community supported and enabled education policy, where one professor talks about the focus on: "trying to get the results of research into effective national policies" (Project 15). Another explained how prior to the setting up of the NCSL the ground work was being done through engaging with Michael Fullan's approach to the leadership of change:

> 'I would be given papers by Fullan to edit, which were then taken to ministers in different forms, and Fullan was brought in and directly

placed in front of ministers and asked to put forward points of view about school leadership and the role of school leadership in school improvement.' (Project 15)

Overall, the data show that EEIR experience as core policy actors was differentiated: some reached national government in the Department or even No 10, while others worked directly with the NCSL.

Field members talk about proactively working to focus on effective classroom teaching, curriculum initiatives such as numeracy and literacy, and the effects of leadership. For example, an EEIR professor states:

> 'The resources going into education have also increased since 1997 … all of that's drawn attention to leadership and of course that was officially recognized with the creation of the National College for School Leadership, and not just leadership of a headteacher but leadership development for senior management teams, for middle managers, there's *Leading from the Middle, Working Together for Success* of the senior management teams … new roles like Consultant Leaders, the idea of Federations and so on. I mean, there's a whole lot of change going on. So I think it's a whole range of things that have led to that realization but I think the school effectiveness-improvement research has been part of that because it's consistently drawn attention to the role of heads.' (Project 15)

While this intensive activity was important and generated income and prestige (chairs, journal editors, awards) the interplay between descriptive and scientific criticality is important. Some EEIR field members expressed their concerns at the adoption of target driven performance headship by UK government policymakers for schools in England, where "diktats don't work in schools and if leaders want teachers to develop they have to trust and give other people roles in leadership, they have to be prepared to tolerate mistakes" (Project 15). The tensions between securing the methodological rigour of effectiveness studies interplayed with people and values issues of improvement studies is crucial here, whereby epistemological conflicts are in evidence. Making a difference in practical terms for effectiveness scholars is about using the knowledge base about school effects, whereas improvement gives recognition to common sense: "I'm very theoretical and conceptual, but I'm also very pragmatic … I'm driven by how we can improve the performance of schools and institutions in a very practical way" (Project 15). In summary, policy science sets out to be useful and relevant to the structuring and shaping of organisational behaviours and conditions through investment by the core, but with some recognition that causation may not be able to be evidenced, and that local contexts require intelligent interpretations.

Policy entrepreneurialism

Policy entrepreneurialism is based on 'know-what' and 'know-how' positions that package and repackage forms of criticality located in description (heads 'want' answers to how to deliver policy) and science (heads 'need' to follow the school effects data and so adopt the behaviours required for improvement). As one consultant stated: "we're not hugely academic, we're very much about pragmatic leadership" (Project 15). Oligarchic occupiers selectively use entrepreneurial forms of criticality in order to be recognised as being responsive to the profession and providing evidence-informed solutions from world leading experts, but also to ideologically generate notions of choice that privilege personal and contractual exchange relationships, and so marginalise and other those involved in independent primary research in universities and schools. Traded criticality is what I have termed 'Jurassic Management' (Gunter 1997), with a focus on espousing a vision of the provision and access to school places that is a private matter (for the school as a business, for a family as the site of consumer choice), and are presented in ways that is in the interests of the public and profession to buy into emotionally, and practically.

Data from the EPKP projects demonstrate how policy actors design and create market pressures for such products. As one education company representative stated:

> 'we wouldn't be where we are in this country in terms of leading the world on leadership and education if it hadn't been for people like [name] and me pushing, campaigning, lobbying, persuading, influencing for the last ten years … you know, we were consulted in terms of whether there should be a National College to start with.' (Project 15)

The products (with brand images and reputations) can include the person as someone who has innovative ideas, who can do a particular job (for example, facilitate an event, conduct an evaluation, provide the knowledge base for a policy intervention, set reform agendas such as succession planning for school leaders) through to professional development materials that may respect the idea of experiential theorising but set out to politely convince that another way is desirable and possible. As one business consultant stated, his/her role was to enable "the increasing transferability of important ideas from one culture to another without creating resistance when you're doing it" (Project 15), and another stressed how their organisational models regarding workforce motivation and leadership are credible because "I think that ours are tested, I think ours are practical" (Project 15). Credibility comes from being in the private sector, where paying for knowledge production is equated with quality and worth the public investment. The data show that professors have declared forms of prestige based on having 'escaped' from a public researcher into a private consultancy company, but at the same time they rely on a combination of the professorial title and biographical experience of having worked in schools in order make the case for applicability within practice:

> 'so in many ways it's applying, interpreting, making accessible, making relevant that I see my work as focusing on, and I still do, and what I try to do, I think, is to pick up on key issues and then say here's what they might look like in school terms.' (Project 15)

The EPKP projects have also shown that professionals are endemically disappointed by the ERC because what they are promised as advantageous actually does damage through the creation of enactment contradictions and dilemmas. Indeed, while policy interventions may fail (for example, different types of autonomous schools are introduced and withdrawn, see Courtney 2015), the underlying ideas (for example, marketised segmentation and segregation) are resilient and underpin new products to ease professional concerns and generate energetic delivery. Policy entrepreneurs confront such matters. One education company representative talked about how they enabled secondments and mentoring for senior leaders and heads in business, and so,

> 'they go back in energised, can do, taking back in some very interesting models, realising that performance management systems in schools are pretty bad, but the performance management system they were part of in a company has actually got quite exciting things to offer them, and then they come up with their own model for school.' (Project 15)

Products are vended in ways that headteachers will like because they are essential to meeting policy demands by resolving problems that the profession has been told they must deal with. This is enabled through the co-option of headteachers as state consultants who integrate experiential theorising with the behaviours needed for improvement and effectiveness in order to deliver policy: "one of the things I did for the National College was to traipse around the country introducing workforce reform, and that was really good because I could talk about all the ways I'd actually released the staff in [school name] from doing cover" (Project 15). Those in the private sector also sell tactical solutions based on "credibility and having that in-school experience" (Project 23), and this is liked by schools as customers because "I am there to provide solutions that match the outcomes they're seeking" (Project 23).

Within CEPs there is a complexity of *Policy Entrepreneurs and Popularisers* (PEP), some are located in epistemic positions in EMAL and EEIR but who have left formal employment in a university or school or local authority (resigned, retired, made redundant, see Gunter 2017) to set themselves up in business, and some have different career trajectories and operate outside of these networks as sole traders through to global consultancy and product businesses (see Gunter and Mills 2017). For example, one professor says:

> 'I've been a pragmatist in that if an opportunity's come my way to research I've done it, even if it's not necessarily been at that time a particular interest, it's come about like that. I mean academies was not something that I was attracted to, but the opportunity was there and it seemed a good opportunity and I took it.' (Project 15)

Another says: 'We have been good at identifying an emerging trend, and getting stuff out on it, and then that stuff dies fairly fast ... (in fact) ... my books have a short shelf life' (Project 15).

An education company consultant says:

> 'the processes you need to be a successful organisation are generic, you know, HR, the way you manage people, the way you set your strategy, the way you have your aspirations, the way you articulate that, the way you market yourself, the way you manage your finances, you know, this is leadership and management and whether you've got peas in a pod or widgets in a machine or people in a hospital or people in a prison or people in a school. It's the way you apply the management processes that will provide the context, but the skills are generic.' (Project 15)

These are illustrative of how scholarship is eschewed in order to obtain and retain a privileged vantage point with opportunities to join the core; recognised and approved-of viewpoints are espoused with the possibility of connecting to a state regime, particularly through engaging in exchange relationships that sustain and intensify personal and cultural contractualism.

PEP are varied in identity, purposes, and practices, but there are some shared articulations: one established private consultant who was vital to bringing business management to education stated about his/her role as "having a finger in a whole lot of pies, and acting as a sort of bee fertilizing from one to the other" (Project 15). This person acted as a role model for those currently working in educational services who are attracted by consultancy work: "my feeling is that there are a group of us who you know think about as being, I don't know, connectors, networkers, facilitators, consultant advisors, you know, whatever" acting as "brokers" rather than having appointed organisational roles (Project 15). What this actually means in practice is that formal contracts can be negotiated, but there can also be calls for immediate support from a school through to the Department to advise, sort, and deal with a situation. What matters is that the person controls their availability as a virtue: "I feel I have the total freedom as a freelance consultant, I can choose which projects I want to do, I can choose who I want to work with" (Project 15). While there is plenty of evidence of work in classrooms with individual teachers through to work with national policy makers, a pattern in the data is how entrepreneurial forms of criticality are determined and shaped by personal thoughts and ideas, and what the person likes and dislikes, and how this is distinctive from critical researchers who are deemed to engage with "criticism for criticism's sake, and doesn't actually offer anything in its place" (Project 15). Indeed, private consultants talk about how they reject the research quality issues required to work in a university, particularly the accountability involved in national audit systems (for example, REF in the UK). One professor stated that going private meant that the income from the contract would not be top-sliced by the university, and so "clients get value for money" (Project 15). At the same time a consultant in an international company stated that they could do speedier work than those working in universities (not least because they do not have to do teaching, supervision, research, and publications, and be subject to intensive high risk internal and external performance management), but took a different position on value for money as s/he talked about how the world had changed whereby schools were now prepared to pay premium rates for private sector models. However, these large companies are recognised as an emerging problem for those who work as individual consultants or in small companies:

> 'I worry about the role of some of the people like [name of consultancy company] and other business organisations, and the ease and the joy with which the government buys them in and thinks they've got the answers, well, no they haven't, they've got interesting ideas, but [they have to] be used carefully.' (Project 15)

In summary, policy entrepreneurialism may illustrate shared dispositions regarding criticality about and for the profession and schools as organisations, but there are distinctive positions within the privileged vantage point regarding the scale and size of operation, and how commodified knowledge production for the ERC is dependent on personal and contractual exchange relationships that link vantage with viewpoint and regime membership. Policy entrepreneurialism has come to dominate the meaning of criticality by colonising policy description and science as a means of opening up public services to capital accumulation, and by eradicating the thought from professional practice that there could be alternatives to deal-making.

Policy scholarship

Policy scholarship is based on challenging the ERC regarding evidence and policy prescriptions (for example, Gorard 2018), along with studies about the technologies of knowledge production and the attacks on public services education (for example, Ball 2007). Importantly, 'what counts as critical depends on what counts as dominant' (Parker and Thomas 2011: 422), and so research is 'independent' in terms of the freedom from ideological control (funding, remit, and design), and is 'primary' in regard to dealing with first hand educational issues through empirical and conceptual investigations. Oligarchic occupiers have variously ignored, discounted, and ridiculed policy scholarship (for example, Gove 2013b), and have done this through demanding a different form of research (for example, DfEE 2000a), and by subjecting research councils to austerity cuts. Indeed, the ERC depends on ideological as well as pragmatic fabrications to both dismiss and discount research, and to promote policy based on a cocktail of professional wants, needs, and likes. Censorship can come from a range of directions where one professor talked about an invitation to speak at a conference, where s/he was told that "one of the two English people on the organizing panel were desperate to block me. So this is quite an insight into how the field protects itself" (Project 15). Another professor has written about her experiences, whereby Reay (2020) describes what happened when research with Lucey that demonstrated how savvy parents invested in market advantage for their children was reported in the national press (Russell 2002):

> a seconded education academic at the then DfE phoned both of us on behalf of the New Labour government to ask us to retract our findings. Over a series of phone calls, she berated us for our 'unscientific' qualitative research (we had a sample of 454 students), and harangued us for publishing work that challenged New Labour's school improvement policy. (Reay 2020: 820)

This type of interference has been evidenced through empirical research (Gunter and Thomson 2006), but where data from the EPKP projects demonstrate that policy scholarship remains vibrant and resilient in spite of these attacks, with evidence of challenging how the ERC positions criticality and independent primary research (for example, Rudduck and McIntyre 1999).

Policy scholarship is concerned with examining, giving meaning to, and explaining professional practice and the reforms to the provision of public services through major projects funded by the ESRC (for example, Ball et al 2012), charities (for example, Gunter and Mills 2016), and Europe (for example, Ozga et al 2011). The interplay between policy texts, interviews, and theorisations of data located in the social sciences enables policy scholars to operate within professional practice in schools and universities through to undertaking research, and supervising doctoral projects. For example, headteachers conceptualise leadership as different from the NCSL, as one headteacher stated: "I like the intellectual rigour of being a head. It's very challenging and you have to deal with some very thorny issues" (Project 15). What is valued is knowing and trusting valued colleagues: "You've got a fantastic headteacher like [name] sitting there and all the people I work with, and she's not NCSL accredited or trained, but the best experience or advice I ever get is talking to people like her" (Project 15). Heads recognise that the profession are policymakers: "most of the good things that have happened in the schools that I've worked in have started out with an idea somewhere, and then two or three people have sat down and improved the ideas" (Project 15).

Within CEPS there is an epistemic tradition that is known internationally as *Policy Sociology* (PS), where field members in England are located historically with researchers globally (see Ozga 1987; Byrne and Ozga 2008; Ozga 2021; Savage et al 2021), and with an emphasis on scrutinising reforms through social sciences theories and methodologies (for example, McPherson and Raab 1988; Smyth 1989; Ball 1990a; Halpin and Troyna 1994; Grace 1995; Blackmore 1999; Gewirtz 2002; Rivzi and Lingard 2010; Whitty et al 2016; Wilkins 2016; Smyth 2017) and a study of knowledge production (for example, Halpin and Troyna 1994). While *description* is recognised as important for criticality, on its own it can be a form of what Raab (1994) describes as 'mindless empiricism' (18) that is disconnected from analysis about power. This deficit is also shared with *entrepreneurialism* and *science* that 'support rather than interrogate policy' (Halpin 1994: 201), where one professor makes the point:

'I had very experienced researchers in the field tell me in good faith, and thinking that there is nothing wrong with this, that you have to realise that you mustn't write anything critical of official policy, you can hint at things and say things when you meet them as part of the feedback but you never include them in your writing.' (Project 15)

Such policy prescription is regarded as limited, and one professor describes school effectiveness research as "dislocated from moral purposes" (Project 15), not least because as Dale (1994) identifies, 'the self-imposed limitations of a problem-solving approach (that) severely curtail its ability to solve problems' (40). Consequently, as one professor states, the EEIR field have "backed themselves into a corner" whereby all the focus is on hierarchical and elitist forms of leadership, and while there are attempts to reposition away from the "mistrust of the profession", the concept of leadership remains "fairly empty" and it "flies in the face of quite a lot of the good research evidence about the significance of the teacher in the classroom as the key factor in making a difference to school performance" (Project 15). Concerns have been raised about *science* in particular, it is 'seductive in its concreteness, its apparently value-free and objective stance, and its direct relation to action', and so debates are 'what gets lost' (Grace 1991: 26). This critique is summed up by a professor who argues: "the problem with policy-driven research as opposed to policy-relevant research is the policy-driven research can in two years be of no interest to anybody, whereas policy-relevant research can, by focusing much more on processes, can still be of interest even when the particular policy has disappeared" (Project 15).

Such critiques are evident in sociological investigations into the school leadership field, whereby as one professor stated: "It's almost become a panacea for everything" where knowledge production for and by the NCSL has "strengthened the idea that you don't need to read about anything else in order to run a good school" (Project 15). Another professor goes into detail about the "impoverishment" of headship through "technicist" training, and asks the question: "do governments and official agencies generally want to stimulate in school leaders a critical stance?" And answers the question: "Of course they don't, because if people are educated in a critical stance then they are going to be more troublesome" (Project 15). Hence policy sociologists focus on the *intellectual development* of the professional whereby knowledge production is educative in regard to conceptualisation, design, analysis, and engagement, where it is argued that researchers such as Grace (1994) give more attention to '"complex hope" rather than the "simple hope" of the school improvement lobby' (Whitty 2002: 16). In doing so, it is recognised that policy actors need to develop a more educative disposition in order to be able to engage with field plurality and to think about how change is actually made unmanageable through descriptive, scientific, and entrepreneurial knowledge production, where a professor states: "we would like to inform practitioners and policymakers, but we are absolutely sure that nobody is going to listen, certainly not the policymakers, because the messages that come out of our work are very uncomfortable" (Project 15). Another professor identifies that "it is easier to go with the flow of policy rather than be a dissenter" (Project 15), but it is also acknowledged that when research is listened to by professionals there is evidence of productive understanding and long term engagement (Gunter 2013).

Ball (2021) notes that policy sociology research has developed from 'trying to make sense of how policy gets done' regarding 'who does policy and with what ideas' towards 'how policy forms the objects about which it speaks' (387). Approaches to doing this do vary, where one professor who states how his/her work on the neoliberal agenda is about: "trying to understand how it works itself out in relation to the daily lives and experiences of teachers" (Project 15). Such work not only focuses on policy ideas, texts, and actors, but also how the policy process creates and engages with problems that enable and sustain the private in the provision of and access to school places. In framing and seeking independent funding, researchers have interplayed data about practice with conceptual tools in order to bring new insights and explanations:

> 'What I try to do in my work is move in a creative but productive way between research and theory, between data and theory, to inform data with the interpretive frameworks offered by theoretical possibilities, but also to address, challenge theory with data … I don't think any social science practice is possible without interpretation, so I think objectivism or neutrality are kind of nonsense. Social scientists are part of the world, and we can only make sense of that world through particular frameworks that we bring to bear on it. … So sociology provides me with my intellectual tools for dealing with the world.' (Project 15)

What sociology allows the researcher to do is to think otherwise about everyday lives, and so expose how class, race, gender, and eugenics are integral to explaining how advantage and disadvantage work (for example, Chitty 2007), and how the power structures that preserve inequity need to be subject to scrutiny (Ball and Collet-Sabé 2021). In doing so the field is racked by 'fissiparous tendencies' (Ranson 1995: 442) regarding the idea and reality of contribution, whereby some would argue that their work makes visible the power structures at work, while others argue there is a need to engage in activism as well (see Troyna 1994). As one professor states:

> 'it's easy to stand back and critique and say, oh this is all wrong you should be doing it differently, it's much harder to … take seriously the perspectives of the people you're studying and to think what they could do differently, and it shouldn't be up to them to sort that out because that's the hardest thing to do, academics should be working on that as well.' (Project 15)

In summary, policy scholarship disputes the framing of headteacher 'wants', 'needs' and 'likes' within and for the ERC, and instead focuses on the educability of and by the professional through access to educational research within the social sciences. Speaking to the professional as an intellectual and working with the professional in accessing, thinking with, and adding to intellectual resources is vital, where different positions are taken regarding the types of actual and possible research contributions.

Summary

Investigating the relationship between the state, public policy and knowledge production in the production and preservation of the ERC demonstrates the importance of a political sociology of intellectual histories. The case example from EPKP *Theme 4: Knowledge Production* used in this chapter shows that the relationship between CEPS and policy is related to different positions taken about criticality. The dominance of entrepreneurial forms of criticality means that professional wants (what do I do?) and needs (what should I do?) are worked and reworked according to likes (what am I keen on doing?). This is vital for understanding how and why the legitimate, authorised, and intelligent policy violence regarding all of the illustrative cases from the EPKP projects in Chapters 5–8 is dominant, and hence why the physical and emotional violence that opened this chapter remains, intensifies, and is unlikely to be eradicated. Different forms of criticality that are located in scholarship that connects knowledges and activism are available, where ideas and strategy are focused on working for and securing social justice. However, it is not in the interests of oligarchic occupiers of the core vantage point to acknowledge the plurality of viewpoints, to engage in inclusive regimes of practice or to be involved in exchange relationships that reach out to those who are traditionally marginalised and othered. Policy violence is integral to oligarchic club sovereignty, where fabricated social mobility (Chapter 2), the vending of problem solving techniques (Chapter 3), and declarations of policy success, all require 'deserts' of failure (Chapter 4), and so entrepreneurialism thrives in the constant production of risk and responsibility.

An important outcome of the Sarah Everard and other cases is that the claimocracy has been subject to more public scrutiny. For example, the argument has been made that women are responsible for safety, and have been advised that if they feel that they are in danger then a woman can flag down a bus to ask for help. So, women are 'in a paradoxical situation whereby they have to change their behaviour to avoid the risk of harassment or violence, while also trying not to overreact to dangers they're often told do not exist or aren't common' (Bows 2021: NP). Such a brutal political-sociological culture is evident in the ERC, whereby blame is normalised through how parents are required to be aspirational and choose but are also told that the potential of their offspring is determined by their genes and so they need to know their place. The ERC as articulations of such lived experiences requires CEPS to rethink purposes and agendas, and it is to this that I now turn.

10

Conclusion: Intellectual activism

Introduction

On 28 November 2021, *The Sunday Telegraph* published a front page story under the headline: *'Woke' anti-Government speakers barred from Whitehall*. Malnick (2021), the journalist who broke the story, reveals that a leaked memo to civil servants states that they must do 'due diligence' on proposed speakers regarding their public statements (for example, social media), and that they must not issue invitations to those who have 'spoken against key government policies'. The aim is to remove 'woke and politicised' (NP) views and activities from policymaking processes. Such a public revelation of censorship raises questions about the relationship between the state, public policy, and knowledge production, and while education research in general, and the EPKP projects in particular, may demonstrate a plurality of ideas, evidence, and debates as resources for education policy, it is the case that oligarchic club sovereignty holds dominion. While the current UK government rails against what is labelled 'cancel culture', the impression is given that cancelling researchers and research is integral to claimocracy scoping and strategy (Malnick 2021), and so it seems that policy violence based on authority, legitimacy, and intelligence just became more publicly brutal. For CEPS this unfolding contextual setting matters, and it raises issues not only about policy actors who are in core and privileged vantage points, who espouse approved-of viewpoints and fabricate libertarian standpoints, who relate and exchange within and between official regimes, but it also requires that attention is given to the othered and marginal who have their ideas, evidence, and debates negated because independent data and analysis reveal how knowledge production actually works, and might work differently. Indeed, CEPS research and researchers, that includes the EPKP projects, have been labelled woke and cancelled, and this is why such research is vital.

I begin this final chapter with a summary of the gains made through writing this political sociology *of* and *about* the education reform claimocracy through the TPSF, and I then go on to examine how and why developing intellectual activism requires a political sociology *for* and *by* critical education policy studies. Such a political sociology focuses on the development of a CEPS 'little agoras' (Chapter 4), where eugenicist populism is confronted (Chapter 2), and productive intellectual resources and practices regarding education policy might be developed through engaging with Cox's (1981) approach to critical theory (Chapter 3).

A political sociology of and about CEPS

Claimocracies in public policy are vital for dominion security, where the inclusion–exclusion game continues to be fundamental to oligarchic club sovereignty: first, the occupation of the state through inherited and immutable superiority; second, concessions to elite interests within civil society to enter a mutual preservation project; and third, retraction of concessions to non-elite interests through downgrading and removal of in-common services. Modernising claims are vital to how the game is played because it is 'an empty term hiding the single sin of having nothing to say' (Finlayson 1998: 11), and so it can be filled with novel ways in which individuals, families, and communities are constituted and categorised within and by policy, and is sustained through fabrications that have believability, and hence longevity. As the EPKP projects show, governing through knowledge production enables the ERC to be integral to the denial but actuality of policy violence, where the unmodern is masked by a language of success, but in reality the vending of education policy problems and solutions is premised on failure (see Evans 2007).

The TPSF provides opportunities for understanding and explanation that is partially or fully missing from particular critical positions within CEPS. The intellectual history of the field shows evidence of research and debate about bodies and segregation of educational services (for example, Chitty 2007; Ball 2013; Youdell and Lindley 2019), but the majority of CEPS projects are conducted without due regard to the ruptures in ordinary lives caused by policy violence. For example, the personalisation of public services has dominated UK public policy for the past 50 years, whereby when asked about using the NHS, Thatcher stated at an election press conference in 1987: 'I, along with something like five million other people, insure to enable me to go into hospital on the day I want, at the time I want, and with a doctor I want', and then went on to say: 'It might be different if it were a very very complicated operation because, quite honestly, that is much much more expensive' (Thatcher 1987: NP). Such a position encapsulates the contradictions within modernisation projects to remove and prevent collective and shared services through individual choice, but at the same time recognise the need for social insurance because private insurance/resources may not be sufficient. In spite of the reality of even the very rich potentially requiring public services, it is the case that the promotion and actuality of personalisation dominates in public policy in general and in education policy in particular.

Eugenicist personalisation underpins education policy and is accepted in much CEPS research. Humans inherit fixed potential and so the problem is with nature. Personalisation focuses on who is and who is not educable and suitable to breed and lead. Measurement of bodies and intellectual aptitudes is about the diagnosis of 'mental deficiency' with the potential to identify 'the cleverest of the clever' (quoted in Chitty 2013: 360). Cyril Burt developed intelligence testing that is known in England as the 11+ examination that segregates children into academic grammar and vocational secondary modern schools, and where he had: 'a real determination to prevent the deterioration of the (white) race by ensuring that the "able" and the "gifted" were given the positions of authority in society that their "intelligence" clearly merited' (Chitty 2013: 357). Eugenicist personalisation was challenged (Jackson and Marsden 1962) but it continues to secure segregated provision and access (see Chapter 2) regarding class and race (Gillborn and Youdell 2000; Gillborn et al 2017).

The TPSF enables recognition of how and why two additional trends have entered and reworked eugenics in the modernisation agenda. The first trend is *service personalisation* whereby it is argued that humans can be better organised to release their potential, and so the problem is how to design pedagogy through 'tailor-made services' that are delivered by 'building the organisation of schooling around the needs, interests, and aptitudes of individual pupils' (Miliband 2006: 23–24). New Labour (1997–2010) encoded and delivered personalised learning to the profession (for example, Miliband 2004) through alliances with CEPS, including high-profile networked support (for example, OECD 2006), influential advocates (for example, Leadbetter 2006), and enabled through school improvement claims (for example, Hopkins 2007). Reports scoped the ideas (for example, Gilbert 2006), were translated into practical guides (for example, DCSF 2008), with professional endorsements (for example, Cresswell et al 2006), and were promoted by government organisations (for example, Hargreaves 2004). Reforms meant that teachers would become 'advocates, advisers, brokers, and ultimately, solution assemblers' in order 'to mediate the individual's relationship with the services they need' (Leadbeater 2004: 22). However, New Labour's personalisation agenda floundered because it did not confront segregation, where distinction was intensified through specialist schools policy (for example, language schools, science schools), and the ongoing deregulation of school place providers (for example, academies) (Chitty 2007; Courtney 2015). Consequently, tailoring was a decorative cover for assumed bodily needs, where *'eugenic modes of thought remain thoroughly ingrained within education policy and practice'* (Ball 2013: 91, original emphasis).

The second trend is *genetic personalisation*, where human potential can be better identified through knowledge of the genetic code: 'it is now well established that educational attainment is heritable and can be predicted from an individual's DNA' (Harden et al 2020: NP). The problem is therefore the lack of scientific knowledge about the nature of the individual and the failure to organise nurture on the basis of this knowledge. Asbury and Plomin (2014) argue that teachers should know about genes, because 'genes can in large part account for the differences between children in how well they can read' (23), and: 'if we are serious about figuring out how to raise mathematics achievement – and we should be – we need to begin by taking genes into account and by deciding whose mathematics achievement we want to raise' (55). Asbury and Plomin (2014) have entered CEPS territory in order to argue for investment in basic education: 'to provide whatever is required to give every child enough facility with words, numbers and computers to be able to live an independent life in the twenty-first century' (6). They then offer 'eleven policy ideas' for provision beyond the basic, where they emphasise that *personalizing education is the best way to realize the potential of individual children who are "naturally" different* (175, original emphasis). Therefore, it is argued that teacher training needs to include knowledge of 'the genetics of ability and achievement and the implications of individual differences for teaching practice' (175). Finally, the argument is made for the 'genetically sensitive school' where 'every child of every faith, every race, and every social background will want to be educated there' (178–179), and so this seemingly deals with the problem of segregated provision and access.

Scientists are questioning over-claiming, where Professor Ian Dreary at Edinburgh is quoted as saying: 'it is difficult to name even one gene that is reliably associated with normal intelligence in young, healthy adults' (Evans 2018: NP). Broader debates question 'sex differences' research (for example, Saini 2017), and the endurance of 'race science' (for example, Saini 2019). Craig Venter who worked on decoding the human genome is quoted as saying: 'there is no basis in scientific fact or in the human genetic code for the notion that skin colour will be predictive of intelligence' (Evans 2018: NP). Notably, Plomin's (2018) book *Blueprint* and wider project is subject to critique (for example, Dorling 2015; Gillborn 2016; Feinstein 2017; Ball 2018; Mithen 2018). For example, Dorling (2019) argues that 'the blueprint within all of us is related only tangentially to who we become' (48), in other words Plomin does not prove genetic underpinning to potential achievement. Indeed, Ball (2018) argues that Plomin is concerned with 'difference *between* individuals, not *to* individuals' (60, original emphasis) and this is questioned because 'the problem is that we don't all have a shared "given situation" – we each have a distinct life' (61). In other words, teachers and schools do matter:

> Even for your average western youngster, individual experience can make a huge difference. A kind deed, a sensitive teacher or, conversely, a nasty encounter or accident can be life-changing. Sure, these things

won't show up among population averages – but to say that they 'don't make a difference' is deeply unhelpful. (Ball 2018: 61)

The argument is that there is too much emphasis on what can be measured rather than what matters to a person in their life. Consequently, the 'genetically sensitive school' (Asbury and Plomin 2014: 178) as an inclusive school for all is a seductive and dangerous conceit because genes as a technology cannot be disconnected from the policy violence inflicted by the inclusion–exclusion game. Indeed, research into the interplay between genes and the environment (see Meloni 2019) shows that: 'we are *not* determined by the genome' and instead 'the molecular body is subject to subtle ongoing influence – including environment and experience – and change. Epigenetics means that biological and the social are not separate after all' (Youdell 2016: 54, original emphasis).

Engagement with this knowledge production in CEPS is limited, and following Arendt, there is a tendency to pre-suppose that what is the case actually is the case, and so in Baehr's (2002) terms we might 'tragically ignore' what is distinctive about a situation through 'received categories and intellectual reflexes' (826). The TPSF gives recognition to a plurality of intellectual histories and practices, and goes further by providing an explanation of and about how and why policy actors put disciplinary patterns and methodologies before understanding, and so impose theoretical applications on the world:

Vantage points

Policy actors have legitimacy, authority, and intelligence through oligarchic occupation of the core and privileged vantage points – hence eugenicist personalization is integral to dominion, and those who promote service personalization have either accepted segregation or have been marginalised or othered, and those who are currently asserting genetic personalization are in the process of being privileged.

Viewpoints

Policy actors present legitimate, authoritative, and intelligent oligarchic knowledgeable declarations from core and privileged vantage points as normative-functional – hence eugenicist personalization is common sense and speaks to those who can see that certain bodies actually do, and so must count as more important than others, and so service personalization is not worth the investment, but genetic personalization is worth listening to as it could enable the choice process of bodily needs to accurately fit with segregated provision.

Regimes of practice

Policy actors inter-connect their legitimacy, authority, and intelligence through viewpoints adopted by those who occupy core and privileged vantage points as state regimes interplayed with approved-of satellite regimes – hence eugenicist personalization is normalised through the beliefs and experiences of policy actors, where service personalization was a short term but ultimately failed concession, and where genetic personalization is an opportunity to bring scientific methodology and data to justify segregation.

Exchange relationships

Policy actors exercise legitimacy, authority, and intelligence through vantage points, viewpoints, and regimes of practice in ways that guarantee defendable legality through personal-cultural contractualism – hence eugenicist personalization is sustained, modified, and developed through interactions, where service personalization was in the ascendance for a time but the underlying defence of oligarchic club sovereignty has ensured it has been discredited, not least through how genetic personalization can be selectively engaged with to confirm beliefs.

Intellectual histories

Policy actors locate, develop, and sustain their legitimate, authoritative, and intelligent knowledge production in relation to vantage points, viewpoints, regimes, and exchange relationships through biographical agency, where the pre-eminence of entrepreneurialism enables ideas to be packaged, retailed, and enacted – hence eugenicist personalization is a given, and so products make segregation work better, where trials of service personalization have been helpful for some families but ultimately it is genetic personalization that has the potential to be commodified and vended in service of segregation.

This political sociology of and about CEPS is based on the EPKP projects and analysis as outlined in the book, and summarised through the personalisation case analysis, all have implications for research and researchers. Intellectual histories of CEPS ideas, biographies, and practices as scoped in Chapter 9 demonstrate that CEPS members are actively involved in knowledge production for, about, and within the ERC, and hence are involved in the design and delivery of policy violence. Investigating this, and developing a strategic agenda for eradicating the ERC, requires a political sociology for and by CEPS, and it is to this that I now turn.

A political sociology for and by CEPS

Thinking both politically and sociologically has generated a conceptualisation of the ERC as policy violence that requires addressing by the CEPS research community. Following Arendtian and Bourdieusian scholarship, policy violence is an absence of power, and yet as the intellectual histories of and about critical education policy research demonstrate, there are different positions taken – from collaboration through to resistance (Chapter 9). A political and sociological investigation for and by CEPS would examine how policy violence works to shape and settle research purposes, identities, and practices. Here I make a contribution to this demanding agenda through scoping the idea of CEPS little agoras (Chapter 4), where following Kennelly (2018, see Chapter 1) this enables a shift from the 'whatness' of doing and served by technical skills to be imposed by oligarchic club sovereignty, to the 'whoness' of intellectual activism as vital for educative and democratising renewal in the public realm.

The idea and reality of an agora is persistently threatened through the 'whatness' of the inclusion–exclusion game, where thinking about the EPKP project data through Bourdieu's tools demonstrates how the *illusio* generated through the ERC *doxa* works to explain what is at stake in the field, and how recognising struggles over capital investment into policy violence is crucial for understanding knowledge production. Arendt's metaphor of the table (see Chapter 3) is useful for developing explanations whereby as already shown (see Chapter 9) there are siloed tables in CEPS regarding how criticality is ontologically and epistemologically understood and practiced: policy description, for example, EMAL; policy science, for example, EEIR; policy entrepreneurialism, for example, PEP; and policy sociology, for example, PS (for example, compare these two special issues of journals, Reynolds 2014; Savage 2021). Eugenicist populist practices combined with apolitical and anti-political consensus-seeking tactics position and trap researchers into places at tables that reveal personal and professional biographies and dispositions, not least by inflecting notions of superior–inferior and poor–good quality research onto named researchers, projects, and universities. The CEPS research community engages in border exclusions in regard to appointments, research centres, project teams, through to reference citations (Gunter 2016; see Reay 2020), and this is also evident in reviews of knowledge production (for example, Angus 1994; Gunter 1997; Thrupp and Willmott 2003; Ozga 2013; Ball 2020), with public debates about purposes and practices (for example, Reynolds and Teddlie 2001; Slee and Weiner 2001; Teddlie and Reynolds 2001; Thrupp 2001). It is in the interests of oligarchic club sovereignty to colonise CEPS research and do policy violence to researchers through deploying a claimocracy that demands the construction and positioning of approved-of tables of useful research for users that in Arendtian terms creates a binary of assimilation and alienation.

For example, in examining the life of Rahel Varnhagen, Arendt (1974) identifies the *parvenu* who has had to forget who they are, and so live as a willing and seemingly in control but obedient fraud in order to be accepted. The EPKP projects are replete with data that demonstrate parvenu positioning where in the study of a CEO of a MAT, Hughes et al (2020) think about a professional career whereby the shift from teacher and headteacher in a public system to a CEO of a privatising system demonstrates 'Edwards was actually *a parvenu in waiting*', and 'through the emerging MAT system he positioned as a parvenu *abandonneur* in surrendering his values and beliefs situated in public education, ultimately becoming a parvenu *par excellence*' (282, original emphasis). Researchers as parvenu are evident through what Thrupp and Willmott (2003) characterise as 'textual apologists' who practice belonged compliance located in the actuality and potential of core and privileged vantage points, normative-functional viewpoints, state regimes, and personal-cultural contractual exchanges that reveal collaboration with and development of the ERC, along with the ridicule of primary researchers who are marginalised and usually are positioned as othered *pariahs* (see Gunter 2012). The forgetting required of parvenus is actually impossible, where Arendt argues that 'they must carry their identity with them through the world, even if that means they are an outsider' (Hill 2021: 75). Importantly this requires researchers to be 'conscious pariahs' as vitally necessary outcasts, but who should also question such categorisation through challenging segregationist-assimilationist formal borders (for example, membership of a learned society) and informal borders (for example, networks of who you know and who knows you).

If critical researchers 'self-consciously claim dissent as their distinctiveness' (Parker and Thomas 2011: 421), then the challenge for CEPS researchers is in how to engage with dissent about what that distinctiveness actually means for knowledge production and positioning within it. A focus on thinking (as distinct from relentless bid writing and data production to support contract renewal) means that in an Arendtian sense CEPS requires different tables, or little agoras. This is an outcome of the EPKP projects (Projects 24, 25), and requires social and political relational participation that is beyond me as a CEPS member, and explanations that are beyond the scope of a chapter. However, I can begin to examine what the agenda might be for policy actors who are researchers, and how this relates to the plurality of policy actors in the public realm agora.

Taking a 'whoness' approach has a number of possibilities for current and potential little agoras as sites for the formal and informal challenges to the ERC. Formal in the sense of how the public realm develops a new constitutional settlement for England and the UK as a whole, and informal through how everyday practice engages with knowledge production differently. This has been debated in CEPS where Ranson (1995) identifies that the task is not only to provide descriptions and argumentation about the situation in education, but also 'to theorise the conditions for a different form of polity and public policy' (443). Consequently, Arendtian forms of political relationality require attention, whereby the role of theory is not only to expose social injustice but to renew democracy through a '*practical theory*' (444, original emphasis), and so 'develop understanding of the values, purposes, conditions, and practice of public policy for a democratic learning society' (444). This commitment to standpoint knowledge is also evident in a second example, where Troyna (1994) argues that while policy sociology, and what he labels as 'critical social research', have similar questions, when a comparison is made it is the case that policy sociology does not 'harness that analysis to an explicit political commitment to change things' (72). Key dilemmas involved have been neatly summed up by Savage et al (2021) who in reviewing the current state of policy sociology are concerned about who determines what projects researchers actually do: 'we see great danger in research that relies on *eliteness* as a precondition for engagement, questioning whether researchers seeking to "critique" elite networks might instead be partaking in the *research of elites, by elites and for elites*' (11, original emphasis). In other words, CEPS researchers have some decisions to make about whether they see their purposes as parvenues who feed the ERC through entrepreneurial forms of criticality, or feed off the ERC as pariahs through providing criticality as descriptions, data, and/or scholarship, or replace the ERC as through intellectual activism by using criticality to provide alternatives to the ERC or even the idea of an ERC. Claims interplayed with facts and data is a feature of research design and outcomes, but a claimocracy (including a cocktail of facts, evidence, beliefs, lies, misrepresentations, myths, bullshit) is a dangerous confection of policy by deceit and conceit, and so exposing this *politically* and *sociologically* is an important site for CEPS action. There is more to do than this. The alternatives to the actuality and idea of the ERC are possible and desirable, and are located in borderless thinking and how this relates in Bourdieusian terms to reflexivity for and about positioning, and in Arendtian terms to action, natality, and plurality.

The actuality and validity of intellectual activism to both create and sustain little agoras within and for CEPS research requires attention, not least how this inter-relates with the rescue and recovery of a wider public realm agora. Following the work of Collins (2013) such intellectual activism is about ideas, people, and practices, and so it can be understood as 'the myriad ways that people place the power of their ideas in service to social justice' (ix). Accounts of the realities of doing this are evident in CEPS: first, by using research data and analysis to factually and conceptually expose policy violence whereby 'this form of truth-telling harnesses the power of ideas toward the specific goal of confronting existing power relations' (xii), and is evident in the EPKP projects (for example, Projects 15, 21) and the wider CEPS research (for example, Apple 2013) and professional (for example,

Winkley 2002) communities. Second, by aiming to 'speak the truth directly to the people' because communicating with and on behalf of oligarchic occupiers 'inadvertently bolsters the belief that elites are the only social actors who count' (Collins 2013: xiii), and this is evident in the EPKP projects (for example, Projects 11, 22) and the wider CEPS research (for example, Apple and Beane 1999) and professional (for example, Wrigley et al 2012) communities. Importantly, Smyth et al (2014) demonstrate how their work is not only about listening, talking, and respecting people who experience the brutality of policy violence, but also by 'working with schools, teachers, students, and communities in producing "local responses" to globally generated issues – which means crafting the spaces in which people who have been marginalised can prudently and cogently *speak back* in the struggle for more socially just policies' (151). This analysis and recognition of intellectual activism for and by CEPS is connected to Fay's (1977) presentation of an 'educative model' as distinct from an 'instrumental model' (201) regarding how and why CEPS researchers engage for and about research dissent. For little agoras to be productive there is a need to recognise that much of CEPS is dependent on the instrumental model of rule production and delivery, and so 'freedom ... results from knowing how to achieve what one wants', whereas educative models focus on 'freedom to be self-determining in the sense of being able to decide for oneself, on the basis of a lucid, critical self-awareness, the manner in which one wishes to live' (Fay 1977: 207). This requires 'thinking without a banister' (Arendt 2018), where the safe structures of disciplinary identities can no longer be seen as essential to hold onto in order to produce understandings, explanations, and action.

There are many truths that CEPS have to confront in order to take action as intellectual activists in little agoras. For example, the ERC may characterise teachers as deficit and this enables researchers to conform by providing the language and tactics for improvement and the effective delivery of policy (for example, Harris and Muijs 2005), or the ERC can be challenged and potentially replaced through how evidence can be used to demonstrate teachers as local policy makers (for example, Ozga 2000). However, both of these texts do not confront the provision of and access to segregated education services, and how policy violence works to invest in one set of ideas (such as EEIR) and denounce another set of ideas (such as PS). In other words researchers who sit at different tables actually engage in power structures that prevent truths being spoken (see Hall 1999). CEPS is implicated in some shape or form in the injustices that actual and would be policy actors suffer within and seek to rectify. In doing this Clarke (2020) argues that no one should fantasise a world

> in which everything would be wonderful if only we could return to some putative golden era of democratic education or if we could just

get rid of the elite class of neoliberal policymakers; alas, there was no such golden era while all of us, not just elite policy makers, are complicit in one way or another in the destructive logics of neoliberal education policy. (Clarke 2020: 164)

Confronting this is problematic for a myriad of reasons, as there could be ontological and epistemological reasons why CEPS members do not see this agenda. In addition, there could be status reasons why borders are protected, and this can be inflected with political ideology whereby those who do research have beliefs about the human condition and how this is or is not appropriately characterised by oligarchic occupiers. Nevertheless, I intend going forward by examining a significant 'truth' issue about the study of power regarding the location of CEPS in the social sciences.

Intellectual activism means that CEPS researchers have access to the social sciences as a methodological and conceptual resource to work with children, families, communities, and educational professionals. This is already evident through important projects and debates (see Furlong and Lawn 2011), where landmark texts have facilitated field reflexivity and agendas (for example, Young 1971), and where social science theorising has been used to design fieldwork and provide convincing explanations of data (for example, Deem et al 1995). However, CEPS has a challenging relationship with opening up access to the social sciences: first, that the social sciences are a power structure that can prevent the thinking that is pertinent to educational matters (see Becher 1989), where Arendt (1958) identified the limitations of sociology through the application of abstract rules (for example, behaviourism) that may manipulate rather enable understanding; and second, the social sciences have been colonised by oligarchic club sovereignty in order to harness research to its policy interests, where Bourdieu (1999) has identified that 'social science cannot by itself combat politicians' propensity to ensure their own success by gratifying superficial demand, all of which turns politics into a barely disguised form of marketing' (628). These judgements not only speak to the absence of thinking within and outside of the social sciences but also to how the social sciences are conceptualised as a resource and engaged with strategically and tactically in the public realm.

Notably, it is recognised that sociology has an important and reflexive contribution to make by those who see themselves as sociologists of education (see Savage 2021). However, concerns have been made public about the domination of sociology on understanding and theorising (Tapper 1997), where Raab (1994) states that the label 'education policy sociology' may prevail, but 'there is nothing exclusively "sociological" about education policy sociology' (23). Both Halpin (1994) and Dale (1994) alert the field to the potential traps of 'disciplinary parochialism' (or in Arendtian and Bourdieusian terms, struggles over pariah and parvenu capitals) by researchers who do not give recognition to how and why other forms of theorising are pertinent. For example, political studies seems to be a sub-field of policy sociology, providing a back drop for the contextual setting in which knowledge is produced (see Ozga 2021), and errors about the UK uncodified constitution are in evidence (for example, use of the phrase 'English government' when there is no English government, Clarke 2020; Ball 2021).

Importantly, CEPS researchers do recognise the consequences of sociological domination: 'historians, psychologists, economists, political scientists, anthropologists, evaluators, and those who deliberately transcend disciplinary boundaries may have much to contribute to our understanding of the sources, nature and effects of education policy' (Halpin 1994: 200), with recent evidence of the vibrancy of historical analysis (for example, Martin 2022), and the list has been added to in regard to the growing importance of 'nature and ecology' (Means and Slater 2021: 1). Crossing borders and being in conversation with ideas outside of sociology (and political studies) matters, and what constitutes an inter-disciplinary team has been challenged, whereby it has been recognised that the relationship with the natural sciences requires attention (for example, Youdell and Lindley 2019), not least because of the endurance of a 'eugenic logic' and the emergence of 'newgenics' (Wilson 2018: 149). Such collaborations draw on pluralist traditions regarding how biological knowledges and rationalities are engaged with and deployed (see Canter and Turner 2012; Gulson and Baker 2018). This work is already within research traditions in the social sciences (for example, Rose 2007; Kline 2010;) and education policy (for example, Chitty 2007; Ball 2013; Allen 2014), and continues in contemporary projects and analysis (for example, Gillborn 2016; Youdell 2016; Gulson and Baker 2018; Gunter 2018). The task is not only to learn from the natural sciences, but to also inform the natural sciences, not least by developing understandings of the policy process and the conduct of policy actors (in government, business, media, and civil society) in ways that inform how claims are read/misread and engaged with.

Such debates require a shift from examining disciplinary borders and identities towards understanding educational issues and the intellectual work necessary to investigate and explain them, and this raises questions about how professionals are conceptualised and engaged with as intellectual activists. A core issue is how the state is understood and engaged with through the policy process, where forms of policy description (for example, EMAL), science (for example, EEIR) and entrepreneurialism (for example, PEP) accept the state as the source of problem identification and solutions, and hence it is the site for influence and impact with gains regarding funding and recognition. Policy sociology recognises this (for example, Thrupp and Willmott 2003), and goes further by examining the impact of neoliberalism, and what Ball (2009a) characterises as 'new state forms and modalities (governance, networks and performance management)' (83, see also Ball 2007), where there is a focus on processes (conceptualisations of policy texts, cycles, and discourses, for example, Bowe et al 1992; Ball 1993a, and sources, scoping, and patterns, for example, Ozga and Dale 1991). Such studies show that there are two main positions: first, Ball (1994) and Ozga (2000) have focused on the plurality of policy actors who connect with but who are located externally to the state, and second, Dale (1989a, b) and Hatcher and Troyna (1994) have focused on networked interests within the capitalist state (see Rizvi and Lingard 2010).

Beginning with the decentring of the state enables the first position to be engaged with. There is evidence from a range of contributions that the state is conceptualised as a referee of pluralist interests, whereby professional practice is about the interpretation of policy texts (for example, Bowe et al 1992). This is what Taylor (2010) describes as 'society-centred' (15) enquiry, where Ball (2007) identifies a shift from the 'Keynesian National Welfare State' to the 'Schumpeterian Workfare State' (3), and so explanation is not located in the hierarchy of state institutions or the complexities of markets, but through 'heterarchies' as 'horizontal self-organisation among mutually interdependent actors' (Jessop 2000: 15, see Ball and Junemann 2012). Consequently, the state engages in 'the regulation of knowledge' (Grek and Ozga 2010: 271) and so coordinates by 'steering at a distance' (Ball 1993b: 65). What this means in relation to local, national, and globalised reform processes for professional practice is the importance of studying the micropolitics of the organisation (Ball 1987), with a focus on 'policy *translation* and *enactment*' (Ball 2015: 306, original emphasis).

The EPKP projects have been developed and located alongside the second position, and so policy scholarship projects from the mid 1990s, (for example, Dale 1992; Lingard 1993; Dale 1994; Gale 1994; Hatcher and Troyna 1994; Power 1995) are an important resource. Indeed, Hatcher and Troyna (1994) argue 'for an understanding of the policy process that, while acknowledging processes of institutional reinterpretation, gives much greater weight to the ability of the state to control outcomes than Ball and his colleagues do' (162). This control is about intervention, evaluation, and restructuring/reculturing by the state, and so demonstrates the legal imposition of a reform (for example, 1988 Education Reform Act, and the Local Management of Schools and Formula Funding), where a law is not a discourse but an actual change because 'state control has the upper hand' (Hatcher and Troyna 1994: 165). Ball (1994) answers back by claiming that he does 'not deny the power of the state, or its forcefulness' (172), but he rejects the implication that 'teachers are cultural and political dupes' (177) and so he is 'unhappy with the totalitarian vision of state and the disempowerment of "ordinary" social actors which that involves' (172). This has been restated by Ball (2009a), and it has been taken forward through challenging forms of 'methodological nationalist assumptions' (Seddon 2014: 10) and promoting a research position regarding the study of 'globalisation and transnationalism' (12).

The EPKP projects demonstrate that it is insufficient to chart the activity of policy actors in policy networks without recognising that their contractual and juridical rights and duties that provide legitimacy, authority, and intelligent interpretations are determined by the state. Ball (1994) counters such thinking by arguing that 'I get no sense whatever from H(atcher) and T(royna) of what the state cannot do' (179). Such an analysis is a product of policy sociology whereby Ball's (2009a, b) adoption of networked 'heterarchical' governance, and Ozga's (2009) claims about 'steering by data' (159), are based on a misrecognition of how oligarchic club re-positioning within existing and new structures uses sovereign power to deny political and sociological relational power through policy violence. Political sociology engages differently through how and why the state, in Ball's terms, *can do all* through the legitimacy and authority of the law, and within an uncodified constitution there remain important powers that are medieval (for example, Royal Prerogative) that allow intelligent interpretations. Hence while the state has been under attack (for example, Bobbitt 2002), with influential texts produced to justify ending the state's involvement in education services (for example, Tooley 2000), the EPKP projects show that oligarchic occupational capture and deployment of state legitimacy, authority, and intelligence has not actually changed, but the mode of governing has adapted in order to protect elite interests in their occupation and control of that governing (see Gunter et al 2016).

Political sociology addresses the sovereignty issue in ways that expose the limitations of policy sociology. This is evident in projects that focus on Europeanisation and globalisation: first, research that seeks to understand the conditions in which knowledge production takes place (for example, Lawn and Grek 2012); and second, where claims are made about research that 'means shedding or at least bracketing, the methodologically nationalist and statist assumptions' (Dale 2009: 37). As the EPKP projects demonstrate such concerns actually limit understanding of how education policy is located within and is a product of the nation state, and how policy actors may travel and indeed exclude themselves from certain states (for example, for tax purposes), but they are anchored (for business, residence, passport) by the nation state, where liberty is granted or curtailed through the judicial system. Policy actors may network in spaces and in the shadows, but those shadows are cast and manipulated by those who are in and enabled by the core vantage point. In the UK it is the idea and reality of sovereignty through the workings of Parliament, elections, and monarchical prerogative that matters in regard to who enters and controls public institutions (Gunter 2012, 2018), where globalised corporate media owners may live off shore but they actively use onshore oligarchic club control of sovereignty for their own purposes.

The study of policy actors, networks, and the nation state is vital, but beyond the mapping of interconnectivity, actual impact requires political studies to have parity with sociology. This has been recognised by Goodwin (2009) who in replying to Ball (2008b, see Ball 2009b) argues that identifying connections between policy actors is insufficient, and so such analysis requires an investigation into 'which networks and which actors matter in education governance' (686). The EPKP projects address Goodwin's (2009) legitimate concerns through giving recognition to the complex state and the implications for objective relationships regarding those who have ideas, methods, and credibility to inform, scope, and deliver on policy mandates. Whereas Byrne and Ozga (2008) identify that policy sociology is concerned with 'who defines policy?', and 'who sets the agenda and in whose interests?' (383), the EPKP projects are concerned with more than this: where do those definition making processes take place, and with what authority, legitimacy, and intelligence? Those who occupy roles and exercise influence in state institutions determine the borders and intersections with other hierarchically powerful actors in civil society. In addition, they frame purposes and practices regarding what is public and private (or hybrid), and so contract particular vantage points and viewpoints, and control not only regime purposes but also exchange relationships and practices.

Staying here and moving on…

The use of a TPSF through and with data from the EPKP projects has provided an approach to a political sociology of education that is pertinent to both of and about CEPS and for and by CEPS. Understanding and explaining the reform of public education services requires a shift from the sanctity of the discipline to actively using intellectual resources to support understandings of the issues and/or events that are in front of us. For example, news reports show the relationship between private capital accumulation and public austerity, where a shift from school budgets to crowdfunding for pedagogic supplies and salaries is evident in a range of national systems (for example, Dosa et al 2019). Reports from the US show that in December 2021 teachers in Sioux Falls, South Dakota, were invited onto an ice rink during a break in a hockey game to scramble for $5,000 in single dollar bills that had been laid out: 'footage of the competition that went viral on social media showed teachers stuffing notes down their jumpers and into hats while the audience cheered'. The money had 'been donated by CU Mortgage Direct to fund teaching supplies and classroom repairs', and while it was designed to be fun there was realisation that it was 'degrading and insulting' (Taylor 2021: NP). A TPSF analysis of this event would bring understandings and explanations of and about education policy, but would require an approach to CEPS research that is located in plurality, natality, and activist knowledge production from the social and natural sciences. Here I have made and demonstrated the case for giving parity to the political with the sociological in ways that are based on a 40-year researching life. Of itself such thinking helps CEPS to both stay here in order to examine field purposes and re-positioning in regard to policy violence, and also to provide a codification of research-based thinking about how CEPS actually moves on through making a contribution to a post-ERC public education service.

Thinking with Arendt and Bourdieu about power structures in knowledge production means that the starting point is with how researchers can take time to think about the shift from locating and/or being located in relation to policy violence towards the practice of intellectual activism. The ERC prevents thinking, and what the isolation of research-based thinking does is to 'remove us from this world of common sense' (Bartscherer 2021: 44). In Arendtian terms, countering the TINA within the ERC requires 'out of order' knowledge production, where thinking 'interrupts any doing, any ordinary activities, no matter what they happen to be. All thinking demands a stop-and-think' (Arendt 1978: 78), and so:

> Arendt shows us how to think the world anew, how to free ourselves from the tradition of Western political thought, how to hold ourselves accountable for our actions, how to think critically without succumbing to ideology. Only when we do this, she says, will we be able to love the world. (Hill 2021: 14)

Hence the tables at which we are sat have either facilitated collaboration with the ERC as what works or opposition to the ERC as misrecognised damage. There is merit in both positions regarding different types of activity that are directed at supporting educational professionals at times of major reforms (see Angus 1994). However, public education systems in western style democracies are now beyond a reform agenda, where oligarchic insurgency and restoration projects are crushing aspirations and dismantling public access. Each chapter in this book begins with an example of what is unfolding in England, where the EPKP projects show that policy violence should not be 'improved' or made 'effective' but should be exposed for what it is, and participatory power processes should be engaged with to demonstrate how alternatives are in evidence. Arendt (1994) realised with the burning of the Reichstag that 'from that moment on I felt responsible. That is, I was no longer of the opinion that one can simply be a bystander' (Arendt 1994: 5). Whether it is teachers who are literally scrambling for money, or parents campaigning against academisation, or foodbanks feeding children who are going hungry, the wider issue is that educational services are proactively and unnecessarily segregated, and this is the grand challenge that CEPS is located within.

I opened the book by engaging with the question articulated by Jenkins (2002): 'how does a social system in which a substantial section of the population are obviously disadvantaged and exploited survive without its rulers having to depend on physical coercion for the maintenance of order?' (119). Addressing this question through the TPSF has brought illumination about the CEPS field by interplaying Arendtian and Bourdieusian scholarship regarding the relationship between the ERC and policy violence. Suffering has been made evident, and following Bourdieu (1999) it is the case that making this public it vital for people to realise that they are not the cause of their own misfortune. And yet a danger could be 'naïve idealism' (Fay 1977: 207), where new ideas are insufficient for democratic renewal, where what matters are practices in research little agoras. As Fay (1977) argues, what knowledge does is to help people to 'understand their lives; hence they can now act on the basis of their informed reflection rather than being determined by conditions about which they had no control' (225). However, the educative model remains problematic, 'as long as it fails to provide some understanding of the ways in which those enlightened by the theory can overcome the opposition of those in power' (233). This is particularly problematic at a time when the UK government is seeking to criminalise Arendtian forms of action, plurality, and natality. The broader political culture in which ideas, evidence, and debate are located is facing censorship through the passage of the Police, Crime, Sentencing and Courts Bill through Parliament, where Monbiot (2021) states that the right to protest is under threat and tactics are being used to avoid democratic scrutiny, and when combined with other proposals (for example, voter ID, the limits to the Electoral Commission, and curbs to civil rights), then democracy is in danger. These are serious examples of the hostile context in which research communities (as well as the general public) are located within. An important shift is taking place from dismissing and ignoring researcher knowledge by what Hyman (2005) referred to as inconvenient and irritating policy enemies to the legal identification of named knowers who will be tried and punished as criminalised enemies (Monbiot 2021). Intellectual activism is in danger because CEPS is located in a context in which the wokeness and cancellation that opened this chapter are euphemisms for a direct attack on legitimate dissent through any form of criticality in knowledge production.

Appendix: EPKP projects

Project	Date	Project title	Funder	Role
26	1999–2022	*Supervision and completion of 38 doctoral projects.* Full list: helengunter.co.uk	Various, including two ESRC studentships: ES/J500094/1 and ES/GO39860/1	Supervisor
25	2019–2020	*The Education Policy Knowledgeable Polity (EPKP) project: a contribution to critical education policy scholarship*	DSocSc (part time), University of Manchester	Principal Investigator
24	2017	*Knowledgeable polities and the politics of public education*	Professorial Enhanced Research Leave (PERL), Faculty of Humanities, University of Manchester	Principal Investigator
23	2015–2018	*The new private educational sector in Chile: entrepreneurialism and competition*	ESRC (Newton Fund) ES/N000676/1	Co-Investigator
22	2014–2017	*Arendt and the politics of public education reform*	Sarah Fielden Honorary Professor of Education, The Manchester Institute of Education, University of Manchester	Principal Investigator
21	2013–2014	*Consultancy and knowledge production in education project*	British Academy / Leverhulme SG121698	Principal Investigator
20	2009–2010	*Distributed leadership and the social practices of school organisation in England*	ESRC RES-000-22-3610	Co-Investigator
19	2008–2009	*BME leadership and careers in schools*	National Association of School Masters and Union of Women Teachers, and National College for School Leadership	Co-Investigator
18	2008–2009	*Women Teachers' Careers: Phase 2: Gender in Leadership*	National Association of School Masters and Union of Women Teachers	Co-Investigator

Appendix

Project	Date	Project title	Funder	Role
17	2006–2007	Women Teachers' Careers: Phase 1	National Association of School Masters and Union of Women Teachers	Co-Investigator
16	2007–2008	Entrepreneurialism, leadership and organisational reform in the public sector: the case of an independent state school in the inner city	British Academy	Co-Investigator
15	2006–2007	Knowledge Production in Educational Leadership	ESRC RES-000-23-1192	Principal Investigator
14	2005–2006	Education and poverty: conceptualising the evidence base	Joseph Rowntree Foundation	Co-Investigator
13	2005–2006	Developing an archive of the UFA	National University of the First Age/ Department for Education and Skills	Principal Investigator
12	2005	Leaders of Learning: effective middle leadership in schools in New Zealand and England	International Research Associate Scheme, National College for School Leadership	Co-Principal Investigator
11	2004	Evaluation of the innovation project at Kingswood High School	Department for Education and Skills, Innovation Unit	Co-Principal Investigator
10	2002–2004	Evaluation of the National University of the First Age	National University of the First Age/ Department for Education and Skills	Principal Investigator
9	2002–2003	Challenging the orthodoxy of school leadership: towards new theoretical perspectives	ESRC Seminar Series	Co-Investigator
8	2002	ICT Test Bed Baseline Project	Department for Education and Skills	Co-Principal Investigator
7	2002–2003	Evaluation of the Transforming School Workforce Pathfinder Project	Department for Education and Skills	Co-Principal Investigator
6	2001–2002	Evaluation of the National University of the First Age	National University of the First Age/ Department for Education and Skills	Principal Investigator

Project	Date	Project title	Funder	Role
5	2001	*Evaluation of the Education Development Plan, Priority 4, Children at Risk of Underachieving*	Birmingham Local Education Authority Advisory and Support Service	Principal Investigator
4	1995–1999	*An intellectual history of the field of education management from 1960*	PhD (part time), Keele University	Principal Investigator
3	1995–1996	*Evaluation of the implementation of Successmaker at Her Majesty's Prison [Name]*	Millwharf Educational Services	Co-Investigator
2	1993–1996	*TALK Project (Teacher Appraisal at Leeds and Keele) research into teacher appraisal in the north of England*	Nuffield Foundation Social Sciences Small Grant Scheme	Principal Investigator
1	1987–1999	*Changing relationships between central government, LEA, and schools*	MSc Educational Management (part time)	Principal Investigator

References

Adams, R. (2021) 'Gavin Williamson wants to turn more state schools into academies', *The Guardian*, [online] 28 April, Available from: https://www.theguardian.com/education/2021/apr/28/gavin-williamson-wants-to-turn-more-state-schools-into-academies [Accessed 7 May 2021].

Adamson, F. and Galloway, M. (2019) 'Education privatisation in the United States: increasing saturation and segregation', *Education Policy Analysis Archives*, 27(129): 1–48.

Adonis, A. (2007) *Address to Headmasters' and Headmistresses' Annual Conference*, Bournemouth, [online] 2 October, Available from: www.dcsf.gov.uk/speeches/search_detail.dfm?ID=681 [Accessed 26 October 2009].

Adonis, A. (2008) 'Foreword', in: J. Astle and C. Ryan (eds) *Academies and the Future of State Education*, London: CentreForum, pp v–xi.

Adonis, A. (2012) *Education, Education, Education: Reforming England's Schools*, London: Biteback Publishing Ltd.

Allen, A. (2014) *Education in and Beyond the Age of Reason*, Basingstoke: Palgrave Macmillan.

Allen, R. and West, A. (2011) 'Why do faith secondary schools have advantaged intakes? The relative importance of neighbourhood characteristics, social background and religious identification amongst parents', *British Educational Research Journal*, 37(4): 691–712.

Amnesty International (2010) 'Steps to end segregation in education. Briefing to the Government of Slovakia', London: Amnesty International Publications.

Angus, L. (1993) 'The sociology of school effectiveness', *British Journal of Sociology of Education*, 14(3): 333–345.

Angus, L. (1994) 'Sociological analysis and education management: the social context of the self-managing school', *British Journal of Sociology of Education*, 15(1): 79–91.

Appadurai, A. (2017) 'Democracy fatigue', in: H. Geiselberger (ed) *The Great Regression*, Cambridge: Polity Press, pp 1–12.

Apple, M.W. (2006) 'Interrupting the right: on doing critical educational work in conservative times', in: G. Ladson-Billings and W.F. Tate (eds) *Education Research in the Public Interest*, New York, NY: Teachers College Press, pp 27–45.

Apple, M.W. (2013) *Can Education Change Society?* New York, NY: Routledge.

Apple, M.W. and Beane, J.A. (1999) *Democratic Schools*, Buckingham: Open University Press.

Apple, M.W., Ball, S.J., and Gandin, L.A. (eds) (2010) *The Routledge International Handbook of the Sociology of Education*, Abingdon: Routledge.

Arendt, H. (1958) *The Human Condition* (2nd edn), Chicago: The University of Chicago Press.

Arendt, H. (1963) *Eichmann in Jerusalem*, London: Penguin.

Arendt, H. (1970) *On Violence*, New York, NY: Harcourt Brace Jovanovich, Inc.

Arendt, H. (1972) *Crises of the Republic*, New York, NY: Harcourt Brace Jovanovich, Inc.

Arendt, H. (1974) *Rahel Varnhagen: The Life of a Jewish Woman*, New York, NY: Harcourt Brace Jovanovich Inc.

Arendt, H. (1977) *Between Past and Future*, New York, NY: Penguin Books.

Arendt, H. (1978) *The Life of the Mind*, Orlando, FL: Harcourt Inc.

Arendt, H. (1993) *Men in Dark Times*, San Diego: A Harvest Book, Harcourt Brace & Company.

Arendt, H. (1994) *Essays in Understanding*, New York, NY: Schocken Books.

Arendt, H. (2003) *Responsibility and Judgement*, New York, NY: Schocken Books.

Arendt, H. (2005) *The Promise of Politics*, New York, NY: Schocken Books.

Arendt, H. (2009) *The Origins of Totalitarianism* (1958, 2nd edn), Garsington: Benediction Books.

Arendt, H. (2013) *The Last Interview and Other Conversations*, Brooklyn, NY: Melville House.

Arendt, H. (2018) *Thinking Without a Banister: Essays in Understanding 1953–1975*, Edited with an introduction by Jerome Kohn, New York, NY: Schocken Books.

Arrowsmith, R. (2001) 'A right performance', in: D. Gleeson and C. Husbands (eds) *The Performing School*, London: RoutledgeFalmer, pp 33–43.

Asbury, K. and Plomin, R. (2014) *G is for Genes: The Impact of Genetics on Education and Achievement*, Chichester: John Wiley.

Asthana, A. and Mason, R. (2018) 'Ben Bradley under fire for urging jobless to have vasectomies', *The Guardian*, [online] 16 January, Available from: https://www.theguardian.com/politics/2018/jan/16/ben-bradley-under-fire-for-blogpost-urging-jobless-people-to-have-vasectomies [Accessed 17 January 2018].

Astle, J. and Ryan, C. (eds) (2008) *Academies and the Future of State Education*, London: CentreForum.

Bache, I. (2003) 'Governing through governance: education policy control under New Labour', *Political Studies*, 51: 300–314.

Bachrach, P. and Baratz, M.S. (1962) 'Two faces of power', *The American Political Science Review*, 56(4): 947–952.

Baehr, P. (2002) 'Identifying the unprecedented: Hannah Arendt, totalitarianism, and the critique of sociology', *American Sociological Review*, 67(6): 804–831.

Baker, K. (1987) 'Education Reform Bill, Order for Second Reading read', UK Parliament Hansard, [online] 1 December, Available from: https://api.parliament.uk/historic-hansard/commons/1987/dec/01/education-reform-bill-1 [Accessed 22 November 2021].

Baki, R. (2004) 'Gender-segregated education in Saudi Arabia: its impact on social norms and the Saudi Labor Market', *Education Policy Analysis Archives*, 12(2): 1–15.

Ball, P. (2018) 'Who do we think we are?', *Prospect*, November: 59–61.

Ball, S.J. (1987) *The Micropolitics of the School*, London: Routledge.

Ball, S.J. (1990a) *Politics and Policymaking in Education: Explorations in Policy Sociology*, London: Routledge.

Ball, S.J. (1990b) 'Management as a moral technology: a Luddite analysis', in: S.J. Ball (ed) *Foucault and Education*, London: Routledge, pp 153–166.

Ball, S.J. (1993a) 'What is policy? Texts, trajectories and toolboxes', *Discourse: Studies in the Cultural Politics of Education*, 13(2): 10–17.

Ball, S.J. (1993b) 'Culture, cost and control: self-management and entrepreneurial schooling in England and Wales', in: J. Smyth (ed) *A Socially Critical View of the Self-Managing School*, London: The Falmer Press, pp 63–82.

Ball, S.J. (1994) 'Some reflections on policy theory: a brief response to Hatcher and Troyna', *Journal of Education Policy*, 9(2): 171–182.

Ball, S.J. (2003) 'The teacher's soul and the terrors of performativity', *Journal of Education Policy*, 18(2): 215–228.

Ball, S.J. (2007) *Education PLC*, London: Routledge.

Ball, S.J. (2008a) *The Education Debate*, Bristol: Policy Press.

Ball, S.J. (2008b) 'New philanthropy, new networks and new governance in education', *Political Studies*, 56(4): 747–765.

Ball, S.J. (2009a) 'Privatising education, privatizing education policy, privatizing educational research: network governance and the "competition state"', *Journal of Education Policy*, 24(1): 83–99.

Ball, S.J. (2009b) 'Beyond networks? A brief response to "Which networks matter in education governance?"', *Political Studies*, 57(3): 688–691.

Ball, S.J. (2012) 'The *reluctant* state and the beginning of the end of state education', *Journal of Educational Administration and History*, 44(2): 89–103.

Ball, S.J. (2013) *Foucault, Power and Education*, Abingdon: Routledge.

Ball, S.J. (2015) 'What is policy? 21 years later: reflections on the possibilities of policy research', *Discourse: Studies in the Cultural Politics of Education*, 36(3): 306–313.

Ball, S.J. (2020) 'The errors of redemptive sociology or giving up on hope and despair', *British Journal of Sociology of Education*, 41(6): 870–880.

Ball, S.J. (2021) 'Response: policy? Policy research? How absurd?' *Critical Studies in Education*, 62(3): 387–393.

Ball, S.J. and Collet-Sabé, J. (2021) 'Against school: an epistemological critique', *Discourse: Studies in the Cultural Politics of Education*, [online] https://doi.org/10.1080/01596306.2021.1947780 [Accessed 27 June 2022].

Ball, S.J. and Junemann, C. (2012) *Networks, New Governance and Education*, Bristol: Policy Press.

Ball, S.J., Maguire, M., and Braun, A., with Hoskins, K. and Perryman, J. (2012) *How Schools Do Policy, Policy Enactments in Secondary Schools*, Abingdon: Routledge.
Barber, M. (1996) *The Learning Game: Arguments for a Learning Revolution*, London: Victor Gollancz.
Barber, M. (2007a) *Instruction to Deliver*, London: Politico's Publishing.
Barber, M. (2007b) *Three Paradigms of Public Sector Reform*, London: McKinsey & Company.
Barczewski, S. (2016) *Heroic Failure and the British*, New Haven: Yale University Press.
Barnes, M. and Prior, D. (2009) *Subversive Citizens*, Bristol: Policy Press.
Bartscherer, T. (2021) 'Thinking out of order', *The Philosopher*, 109(4): 44–49.
Bauman, Z. (1999) *In Search of Politics*, Cambridge: Polity Press.
Becher, T. (1989) *Academic Tribes and Territories*, Buckingham: SRHE and Open University Press.
Beckett, F. (2007) *The Great City Academy Fraud*, London: Continuum.
Beetham, D. (2016) 'Political legitimacy', in: E. Amenta, K. Nash, and A. Scott (eds) *The Wiley Blackwell Companion to Political Sociology*, Chichester: John Wiley and Sons Ltd, pp 120–129.
Bell, R. (2008) 'That joke isn't funny anymore', *Education Guardian*, 4 November, p 3.
Benhabib, S. (ed) (2010) *Politics in Dark Times*, Cambridge: Cambridge University Press.
Benito, R., Alegre, M.À., and Gonzàlez-Balletbò, I. (2014) 'School segregation and its effects on educational equality and efficiency in 16 OECD comprehensive school systems', *Comparative Education Review*, 58(1): 104–134.
Benn, C. and Chitty, C. (1997) *Thirty Years On*, London: Penguin Books.
Bernstein, R.J. (2013) *Violence Thinking Without Banisters*, Cambridge: Polity Press.
Bevir, M. and Rhodes, R.A.W. (2003) *Interpreting British Governance*, Abingdon: Routledge.
Bhimani, N. (2020) 'Some historical sources on intelligence testing, eugenics and children with special educational needs', UCL Special Collections [blog], 24 August, Available from: https://blogs.ucl.ac.uk/special-collections/2020/08/24/some-early-20th-century-sources-on-intelligence-testing/ [Accessed 2 February 2022].
Bhopal, K. (2018) *White Privilege*, Bristol: Policy Press.
Bienkov, A. (2020) 'Boris Johnson called gay men "tank-topped bumboys" and black people "piccaninnies" with "watermelon smiles"', *Business Insider*, [online] 9 June, Available from: https://www.businessinsider.com/boris-johnson-record-sexist-homophobic-and-racist-comments-bumboys-piccaninnies-2019-6?r=US&IR=T [Accessed 15 March 2021].

References

Blackmore, J. (1999) *Troubling Women*, Buckingham: OUP.

Blatchford, P., Bassett, P., Brown, P., Martine, C., Russell, A., and Webster, R. (2009) 'Deployment and impact of support staff in schools. Research Report No DCSF-RR154', London: DfES.

Blick, A. and Hennessy, P. (2019) *Good Chaps No More?*, London: The Constitution Society.

Blunkett, D. (2000a) 'Blunkett announces locations for first three academies', Press Notice, 15 September, London: DCSF.

Blunkett, D. (2000b) *National College for School Leadership*, London: DfEE.

Blunkett, D. (2001) *National College for School Leadership: Further Remit*, London: DfEE.

Bobbitt, P. (2002) *The Shield of Achilles*, London: Penguin.

Bonal, X. and Bellei, C. (eds) (2020a) *Understanding School Segregation*, London: Bloomsbury.

Bonal, X. and Bellei, C. (2020b) 'Introduction: the renaissance of school segregation in a context of globalisation', in: X. Bonal and C. Bellei (eds) *Understanding School Segregation*, London: Bloomsbury, pp 1–25.

Boterman, W.R. (2019) 'The role of geography in school segregation in the free parental choice context of Dutch cities', *Urban Studies*, 56(15): 3074–3094.

Bourdieu, P. (1988) *Homo Academicus*, Cambridge: Polity Press in association with Blackwell Publishers.

Bourdieu, P. (1989) 'Social space and symbolic power', *Sociological Theory*, 7(1): 14–25.

Bourdieu, P. (1990) *In Other Words: Essays Towards a Reflexive Sociology*, Translated by Matthew Adamson, Cambridge: Polity Press in association with Blackwell Publishers.

Bourdieu, P. (1992) *The Logic of Practice*, Cambridge: Polity Press.

Bourdieu, P. (1994) 'Rethinking the State: genesis and structure of the bureaucratic field', Translated by L.J.D. Wacquant and S. Farage, *Sociological Theory*, 12(1): 1–18.

Bourdieu, P. (1996) *The State Nobility*, Cambridge: Polity Press.

Bourdieu, P. (1998) *Acts of Resistance*, Cambridge: Polity Press.

Bourdieu, P. (1999) 'Postscript', in: Bourdieu, P. and Accardo, A., Balazs, G., Beaud, S., Bonvin, R., Bourdieu, E., Bourgois, P., Broccolichi, S., Champagne, P., Christin, R., Faguer, J., Garcia, S., Lenoir, R., Œuvrard, F., Pialoux, M., Pinto, L., Podalydès, D., Sayad, A., Soulié, C., and Wacquant, L., *The Weight of the World: Social Suffering in Contemporary Society*, Cambridge: Polity Press, pp 627–629.

Bourdieu, P. (2000) *Pascalian Meditations*, Cambridge: Polity Press.

Bourdieu, P. (2003) *Firing Back*, London: Verso.

Bourdieu, P. (2014) *On the State*, Cambridge: Polity Press.

Bourdieu, P. and Wacquant, L.J.D. (1992) *An Invitation to Reflexive Sociology*, Cambridge: Polity Press in association with Blackwell Publishers.

Bowe, R. and Ball, S.J., with Gold, A. (1992) *Reforming Education and Changing Schools: Case Studies in Policy Sociology*, London: Routledge.

Bowring, F. (2011) *Hannah Arendt: A Critical Introduction*, London: Pluto Press.

Bows, H. (2021) 'Sarah Everard: why women shouldn't have to risk trading their freedom for safety', The Conversation, [online], Available from: https://theconversation.com/sarah-everard-why-women-shouldnt-have-to-risk-trading-their-freedom-for-safety-157029 [Accessed 25 November 2021].

Boyson, R. (1975) *The Crisis in Education*, London: The Woburn Press.

Bradbury, L. and Gunter, H.M. (2006) 'Dialogic identities: the experiences of women who are headteachers and mothers in English primary schools', *School Leadership and Management*, 26(5): 489–504.

British Broadcasting Corporation (BBC) (1998a) 'Blair sends heads back to college', BBC [online], Available from: http://news.bbc.co.uk/1/hi/education/196779.stm [Accessed 24 September 2021].

British Broadcasting Corporation (BBC) (1998b) 'Failing schools face closure', BBC, [online], Available from: http://news.bbc.co.uk/1/hi/education/104314.stm [Accessed 28 September 2020].

British Broadcasting Corporation (BBC) (2007) 'Academies "popular with parents"', BBC, [online], Available from: http://news.bbc.co.uk/1/hi/education/6908306.stm [Accessed 2 July 2021].

British Broadcasting Corporation (BBC) (2020a) 'A-levels and GCSEs: how did the exam algorithm work?' BBC, [online], Available from: https://www.bbc.co.uk/news/explainers-53807730 [Accessed 14 April 2021].

British Broadcasting Corporation (BBC) (2020b) 'Windrush generation: who are they and why are they facing problems?' BBC, [online], Available from: https://www.bbc.co.uk/news/uk-43782241 [Accessed 2 August 2021].

Budge, D. (1996) 'A cosy world of trivial pursuits?' *Times Educational Supplement*, 28 June, p 14.

Burgess, S. and Wilson, D. (2005) 'Ethnic segregation in England's schools', *Transactions of the Institute of British Geographers*, 30(1): 20–36.

Burnham, P. (2001) 'New Labour and the politics of depoliticisation', *British Journal of Politics and International Relations*, 3(2): 127–149.

Bush, T., Bell, L., Bolam, R., Glatter, R., and Ribbins, P. (eds) (1999) *Educational Management: Redefining Theory, Policy and Practice*, London: PCP.

Butler, P. (2021) 'Rashford demands a "meal a day" for all school pupils in need', *The Guardian*, [online], 20 January, Available from: https://www.theguardian.com/education/2021/jan/20/rashford-demands-a-meal-a-day-for-all-school-pupils-in-need [Accessed 29 June 2021].

Butt, G. and Gunter, H.M. (eds) (2007) *Modernizing Schools: People, Learning and Organizations*, London: Continuum.

Byrne, D. and Ozga, J. (2008) 'BERA review 2006: education research and policy', *Research Papers in Education*, 23(4): 377–405.

Cain, M. and Gunter, H.M. (2012) 'An investigation into primary school leadership practice: introducing the PIVOT framework of leadership', *Management in Education*, 26(4): 187–191.

Caldwell, B.J. and Spinks, J.M. (1988) *The Self-Managing School*, London: Falmer Press.

Canter, D. and Turner, D. (2012) Special Issue: Biologising the Social Sciences: Challenging Darwinian and Neurscience Explanations, *Contemporary Social Science*, 7(2): 95–115.

Capano, G., Howlett, M., and Ramesh, M. (2015) 'Bringing governments back in: governance and governing in a comparative policy analysis', *Journal of Comparative Policy Analysis*, 17(4): 311–321.

Carrasco, A. and Gunter, H.M. (2019) 'The "private" in the privatization of schools: the case of Chile', *Educational Review*, 71(1): 67–80.

Charter Cities Institute (2022) 'What is a charter city?', [online] Available from: https://chartercitiesinstitute.org/intro/ [Accessed 11 May 2022].

Cheema, G.S. and Rondinelli, D.A. (eds) (2007) *Decentralizing Governance*, Washington, DC: Brookings Institution Press.

Chernilo, D. (2006) 'Social Theory's methodological nationalism, myth and reality', *European Journal of Social Theory*, 9(1): 5–22.

Chitty, C. (1997) 'Keith Joseph with Clyde Chitty', in: P. Ribbins and B. Sherratt (eds) *Radical Educational Policies and Conservative Secretaries of State*, London: Cassell, pp 78–86.

Chitty, C. (2007) *Eugenics, Race and Intelligence in Education*, London: Continuum.

Chitty, C. (2013) 'The educational legacy of Francis Galton', *History of Education*, 42(3): 350–364.

Clark, P. (1998) *Back from the Brink*, London: Metro Books.

Clarke, J. and Newman, J. (1997) *The Managerial State*, London: Sage.

Clarke, M. (2020) 'Eyes wide shut: the fantasies and disavowals of education policy', *Journal of Education Policy*, 35(2): 151–167.

Clemens, E.S. (2016) *What is Political Sociology?*, Cambridge: Polity.

Coldron, J., Cripps, C., and Shipton, L. (2010) 'Why are English secondary schools socially segregated?', *Journal of Education Policy*, 25(1): 19–35.

Coles, M.J. and Southworth, G. (eds) (2005) *Developing Leadership*, Maidenhead: Open University Press.

Collarbone, P. (2005) 'Touching tomorrow: remodelling in English schools', *The Australian Economic Review*, 38(1): 75–82.

Collins, J.C. (2001) *Good to great: Why some companies make the leap… and others don't*. New York, NY: Collins Business.

Collins, P.H. (2013) *On Intellectual Activism*, Philadelphia, PA: Temple University Press.

Confederation of School Trusts (2019) 'Future shape of the education system in England, a sector-led "white paper"', Nottingham: CST.

Confederation of School Trusts (2021) 'CST Consultation on the core responsibilities of CEOs', [online] Available from: https://cstuk.org.uk/policy-research/research/cst-consultation [Accessed 3 November 2021].

Conservative Party (1979) *Conservative Party Manifesto, 1979*, [online] Available from: https://www.margaretthatcher.org/document/110858 [Accessed 25 November 2021].

Coopers and Lybrand (1988) *Local Management of Schools, A Report to the Department of Education and Science*, London: HMSO.

Council of Europe Commissioner for Human Rights (2017) 'Fighting school segregation in Europe through inclusive education: a position paper', Strasbourg: Council of Europe.

Coughlan, S. (2015) 'Study reveals school segregation', BBC, [online] 6 July, Available from: https://www.bbc.co.uk/news/education-33409111 [Accessed 9 March 2021].

Courtney, S.J. (2015) 'Mapping school types in England', *Oxford Review of Education*, 41(6): 799–818.

Courtney, S.J. (2017) 'The courtier's empire: a case study of providers and provision', in: H.M. Gunter, D. Hall, and M. Apple (eds) *Corporate Elites and the Reform of Public Education*, Bristol: Policy Press, pp 177–189.

Courtney, S.J. and Gunter, H.M. (2015) '"Get off my bus!" School leaders, vision work and the elimination of teachers', *International Journal of Leadership in Education*, 18(4): 395–417.

Courtney, S.J. and Gunter, H.M. (2020) 'Corporatised fabrications: the methodological challenges of professional biographies at a time of neoliberalisation', in: J. Lynch, J. Rowlands, T. Gale, and S. Parker, (eds) *Practical Methodologies in Education Research*, London: Routledge, pp 27–47.

Cox, C.B. and Dyson, A.E. (eds) (1968) *Fight for Education*, London: The Critical Quarterly Society.

Cox, C.B. and Dyson, A.E. (eds) (1969) *The Crisis in Education*, London: The Critical Quarterly Society.

Cox, R.W. (1981) 'Social forces, states and world orders: beyond international relations theory', *Millennium: Journal of International Studies*, 10(2): 126–155.

Cresswell, L., Morrissey, P., and Soles, G. (2006) *Personalising the Curriculum at 14–19*. Nottingham: National College for School Leadership.

Croft, J., Sahlgren, G.H., and Howes, A. (2013) *School Vouchers for England*, London: Adam Smith Institute and Centre for Market Reform of Education.

Cruddas, L. (2019) School Trusts as New Civic Structures, [online], Available from: https://trust-journal.org.uk/past-editions/school-trusts-as-new-civic-structures/ [Accessed 14 May 2021].

Cummings, D. (2013) 'Some thoughts on education and political priorities', *The Guardian*, [online] 11 October, Available from: https://www.theguardian.com/politics/interactive/2013/oct/11/dominic-cummings-michael-gove-thoughts-education-pdf [Accessed 7 May 2020].

Cunliffe, R. (2021) 'The government can't say there's no money for education', *New Statesman*, 11–17 June 2021, pp 16–17.

Curtis, P. (2003) 'NUT makes strike threats over workload', *The Guardian*, [online] 3 September, Available from: https://www.theguardian.com/education/2003/sep/03/schools.uk1 [Accessed 16 September 2021].

Czerniawski, G. and Kidd, W. (eds) (2011) *The Handbook of Student Voice*, Bingley: Emerald.

Dale, R. (1989a) *The State and Education Policy*, Buckingham: Open University Press.

Dale, R. (1989b) 'The Thatcherite project in education: the case of the City Technology Colleges', *Critical Social Policy*, 9(27): 4–19.

Dale, R. (1992) 'Whither the state and education policy? Recent work in Australia and New Zealand', *British Journal of Sociology of Education*, 13(3): 387–395.

Dale, R. (1994) 'Applied education politics or political sociology of education? Contrasting approaches to the study of recent education reform in England and Wales', in: D. Halpin and B. Troyna (eds) *Researching Education Policy: Ethical and Methodological Issues*. London: The Falmer Press, pp 31–41.

Dale, R. (2009) 'Contexts, constraints and resources in the development of European Education space and European education policy', in: R. Dale and S. Robertson (eds) *Globalisation and Europeanisation in Education*, Oxford: Symposium Books, pp 23–43.

Davidson, J.D. and Rees-Mogg, W. (2020) *The Sovereign Individual*, New York, NY: Touchstone.

Davies, J.S. (2002) 'The governance of urban regeneration: a critique of the "governing without government" thesis', *Public Administration* 80(2): 301–322.

Davies, J.S. (2011) *Challenging Governance Theory: From Networks to Hegemony*, Bristol: Policy Press.

Day, C., Sammons, P., Hopkins, D., Harris, A., Leithwood, K., Gu, Q., Brown, E., Ahtaridou, E., and Kington, A. (2009) *The Impact of School Leadership on Pupil Outcomes*, London: DCSF/NCSL.

DCSF (2008) *Personalised Learning – A Practical Guide*, Nottingham: DCSF Publications.

Deem, R., Brehony, K., and Heath, S. (1995) *Active Citizenship and the Governing of Schools*, Buckingham: Open University Press.
Dennett, K. (2021) 'Eton of the north: prestigious school will fund three new sixth form colleges aimed at young people who live in deprived parts of the north of England', *Daily Mail*, [online] 26 June, Available from: https://www.dailymail.co.uk/news/article-9727755/Eton-fund-three-new-sixth-form-colleges-aimed-young-people-live-deprived-areas.html [Accessed 28 June 2021].
de Waal, A. (ed) (2015) *The Ins and Outs of Selective Secondary Schools*, London: Civitas.
DfE (2010) *The Case For School Freedom: National and International Evidence (Gove Mythbuster 2)*, London: DfE.
DfE (2011) *The National Strategies 1997–2011*, London: DfE.
DfE (2014a) *A World-Class Teaching Profession, Government Consultation*, London: DfE.
DfE (2014b) *The Equality Act 2010 and Schools*, London: DfE.
DfE (2015) '2010 to 2015 government policy: academies and free schools', Gov.UK, [online] 8 May, Available from: https://www.gov.uk/government/publications/2010-to-2015-government-policy-academies-and-free-schools/2010-to-2015-government-policy-academies-and-free-schools [Accessed 22 November 2021].
DfE (2016) *Educational Excellence Everywhere CM9230*, London: DfE.
DfE (2018) *Schools that Work for Everyone: Government Consultation Response*, London: DfE.
DfE (2020) *Schools Causing Concern*, London: DfE.
DfE (2021a) 'Schools, pupils and their characteristics', Gov.UK, [online], Available from: https://explore-education-statistics.service.gov.uk/find-statistics/school-pupils-and-their-characteristics [Accessed 11 March 2021].
DfE (2021b) *Building Strong Academy Trusts. Guidance for Academy Trusts and Prospective Converters*, London: DfE.
DfEE (1997) *Excellence in Schools*, Cm 3681, London: DfEE.
DfEE (1998) *Teachers: meeting the challenge of change*, Cm 4164, London: The Stationery Office.
DfEE (1999) *National College for School Leadership: A Prospectus*, London: DfES.
DfEE (2000a) 'Influence or irrelevance: can social science improve government?', Secretary of State's ESRC Speech, 2 February, London: DfEE.
DfEE (2000b) *City Academies, Schools to Make a Difference: A Prospectus for Sponsors and Other Partners*, London: DfEE.
DfES (2002) *Time for Standards: Reforming the School Workforce*, London: DfES.
DfES (2004) *Smoking Out Underachievement: Guidance and Advice to Help Secondary Schools Use Value Added Approaches with Data*, London: DfES.
DfES/PwC (2007) *Independent Study into School Leadership*, London: DfES.

Dickens, J. (2016) 'Try before you buy: the new way for multi-academy trusts to take over schools', Schools Week, [online] 25 November, Available from: https://schoolsweek.co.uk/try-before-you-buy-the-new-way-for-multi-academy-trusts-to-takeover-schools/ [Accessed 24 May 2021].

Dickens, J. (2021) '"Try before you buy" academy offer – what you need to know', Schools Week, [online] 28 April, Available from: https://schoolsweek.co.uk/try-before-you-buy-academy-offer-what-you-need-to-know/ [Accessed 24 May 2021].

Dittert, A. (2021) 'The politics of lies: Boris Johnson and the erosion of the rule of law', [online] 15 July, Available from: https://www.newstatesman.com/politics/uk/2021/07/politics-lies-boris-johnson-and-erosion-rule-law [Accessed 22 July 2021].

Donnor, J.K. (2016) 'Lies, myths, stock stories, and other tropes: understanding rice and white's policy preferences in education', *Urban Education*, 51(3): 343–360.

Dorling, D. (2011) *Injustice*, Bristol: Policy Press.

Dorling, D. (2014) *Inequality and the 1%*, London: Verso.

Dorling, D. (2015) 'G is for Genes', *International Journal of Epidemiology*, 44(1): 374–378.

Dorling, D. (2019) 'Good genes, bad choices', *Times Higher Education*, 10 January 2019, p 48.

Dosa, M., with Oxford and District Action on Child Poverty (2019) *The Costs of Education in an Age of Austerity: A Local Study*, London: CPAG.

du Gay, P. (2005) 'The values of bureaucracy: an introduction', in: P. du Gay (ed) *The Values of Bureaucracy*, Oxford: Oxford University Press, pp 1–13.

Dunleavy, P., Margetts, H., Bastow, S., and Tinkler, J. (2006) *Digital Era Governance*, Oxford: Oxford University Press.

Earl, L., Watson, N., Levin, B., Leithwood, K., Fullan M., and Torrance, N. (2003) *Final Report of the External Evaluation of England's National Literacy and Numeracy Strategies. Final Report. Watching and Learning 3*, London: Department for Education and Skills.

Earley, P., Evans, J., Collarbone, P., Gold, A., and Halpin, D. (2002) *Establishing the Current State of School Leadership in England: Research Report 336*, London: DfES.

Easterling, K. (2014) *Extrastatecraft*, London: Verso.

Easton, C. Wilson, R., and Sharp, C. (2005) *National Remodelling Team: Evaluation Study (Year 2): Final Report*, Slough: NFER.

Easton, C., Eames, A., Wilson, R., Walker, M., and Sharp, C. (2006) *Evaluation of The National Remodelling Team: Year 3*, Slough: NFER.

Editorial (2020) 'Challenging the structures of racism', *Soundings*, 5(Summer): 4–12.

Equality and Human Rights Commission (2021) 'Race Report Statistics', [online], Available from: https://www.equalityhumanrights.com/en/race-report-statistics [Accessed 15 March 2021].

Evans, G. (2007) *Educational Failure and Working Class White Children in Britain*, Basingstoke: Palgrave Macmillan.

Evans, G. (2018) 'The unwelcome revival of "race science"', *The Guardian*, [online] 2 March, Available from: https://www.theguardian.com/news/2018/mar/02/the-unwelcome-revival-of-race-science [Accessed 11 December 2018].

Evaristo, B. (2022) 'Pupils and prejudice', *The New Statesman*, 28 January – 3 February, pp 42–43.

Express and Star (2020) '2,300 children suspended from England's state schools each day', [online] 3 July, Available from: https://www.expressandstar.com/news/uk-news/2020/07/30/2300-children-suspended-from-englands-state-schools-each-day/ [Accessed 13 April 2021].

Fabes, R.A., Pahlke, E., Martin, C.L., and Hanish, L.D. (2013) 'Gender-segregated schooling and gender stereotyping', *Educational Studies*, 39(3): 315–319.

Fair Admissions Campaign (2021) 'Number of schools by type', [online], Available from: https://fairadmissions.org.uk/why-is-this-an-issue/number-of-schools-by-type/ [Accessed 11 March 2021].

Fairburn, C. (2019) 'Charitable status and independent schools', House of Commons Library Briefing Paper Number 05222, 17 October, London: House of Commons Library.

Fairclough, N. (2000) *New Labour, New Language?*, London: Routledge.

Fay, B. (1975) *Social Theory and Political Practice*, London: George Allen & Unwin Ltd.

Fay, B. (1977) 'How people change themselves: the relationship between critical theory and its audience', in: T. Ball (ed) *Political Theory and Praxis*, Minneapolis: University of Minnesota Press, pp 200–233.

Feinstein, L. (2017) 'On genetics and social mobility: why Toby Young's structural inequality argument is not science', Politics and Policy [Blog], Available from: https://blogs.lse.ac.uk/politicsandpolicy/on-genetics-and-social-mobility/ [Accessed 11 January 2018].

Ferguson, D. (2019) '"I cook, clean and fix": how cuts are forcing headteachers to take on extra roles', *The Guardian*, [online] 28 April, Available from: https://www.theguardian.com/education/2019/apr/28/school-budget-cuts-headteachers-cook-clean-fix-naht-conference [Accessed 23 November 2021].

Field, J.A. (1911) 'The progress of eugenics', *The Quarterly Journal of Economics*, 26(1): 1–67.

Fielding, M. (2006) 'Leadership, radical student engagement and the necessity of person-centred education', *International Journal of Leadership in Education*, 9(4): 299–313.

Fielding, M. and Moss, P. (2011) *Radical Education and the Common School*, Abingdon: Routledge.

Fine, C. (2010) *Delusions of Gender*, London: Icon Books Ltd.

Finlayson, A. (1998) 'Tony Blair and the jargon of modernisation', *Soundings*, 10: 11–27.

Fitzgerald, T. and Gunter, H.M. (2005) 'Trends in the administration and history of education: what counts? A reply to Roy Lowe', Invited paper, *Journal of Educational Administration and History*, 37(2): 127–136.

Fitzgerald, T. and Gunter, H.M., with Eaton, J. (2006) 'The missing link? Middle Leadership in Schools in New Zealand and England', *New Zealand Journal of Educational Leadership*, 21(1): 29–43.

Frankfurt, H. (1986) 'On bullshit', [online], Available from: http://www2.csudh.edu/ccauthen/576f12/frankfurt__harry_-_on_bullshit.pdf [Accessed 22 July 2021].

Friedman, M. (2002) *Capitalism and Freedom*, Chicago: University of Chicago Press.

Fullan, M. (2001) *Leading in a Culture of Change*, San Francisco, CA: Jossey-Bass.

Furlong, J. and Lawn, M. (eds) (2011) *Disciplines of Education*, Abingdon: Routledge.

Gale, T. (1994) 'Beyond caricature: exploring theories of educational policy production and implementation', *The Australian Educational Researcher*, 21(2): 1–12.

Galton, F. (1874) *English Men of Science: Their Nature and Nurture*, New York, NY: Appleton.

Gamsu, S. (2021) 'Why are some children worth more than others?' [online], Available from: https://www.common-wealth.co.uk/reports/why-are-some-children-worth-more-than-others [Accessed 15 June 2021].

Gandin, L. and Apple, M.W. (2012) 'Can critical democracy last? Porto Alegre and the struggle over "thick" democracy in education', *Journal of Education Policy*, 27(5): 621–639.

Garner, R. (2013) '100 academics savage Education Secretary Michael Gove for "conveyor-belt curriculum" for schools', [online], Available from: https://www.independent.co.uk/news/education/education-news/100-academics-savage-education-secretary-michael-gove-conveyor-belt-curriculum-schools-8541262.html [Accessed 2 August 2021].

Gayle, D. (2020) 'One-third of children in UK "have heard racist comments at school"', *The Guardian*, [online] 22 September, Available from: https://www.theguardian.com/education/2020/sep/22/one-third-of-children-in-uk-have-heard-racist-comments-at-school [Accessed 1 February 2022].

George, M. (2019) 'Academy use of unqualified teachers "widens inequality"', *TES Magazine* [online], Available from: https://www.tes.com/news/academy-use-unqualified-teachers-widens-inequality [Accessed 16 September 2021].

Gewirtz, S. (2002) *The Managerial School*, London: Routledge.

Giddens, A. (2000) *The Third Way and its Critics*, Cambridge: Polity Press.

Gilbert, C. (2006) *2020 Vision Report of the Teaching and Learning in 2020 Review Group*, London: DfES publications.

Gilbert, I. (2018) *The Working Class*, Bancyfelin: Independent Thinking Press.

Gillard, D. (2018) 'Education in England: a history', [online], Available from: http://www.educationengland.org.uk/history/chapter15.html [Accessed 28 April 2021].

Gillborn, D. (2016) 'Softly, softly: genetics, intelligence and the hidden racism of the new geneism', *Journal of Education Policy*, 31(4): 365–388.

Gillborn, D. and Youdell, D. (2000) *Rationing Education*, Buckingham: Open University Press.

Gillborn, D., Demack, S., Rollock, N., and Warmington, P. (2017) 'Moving the goalposts: education policy and 25 years of the Black/White achievement gap', *British Educational Research Journal*, 43(5): 848–874.

Goodwin, M. (2009) 'Which networks matter in education governance? A reply to Ball's "New philanthropy, new networks and new governance in education"', *Political Studies* 57(3): 680–687.

Gorard, S. (2016) 'The complex determinants of school intake characteristics and segregation, England 1989 to 2014', *Cambridge Journal of Education*, 46(1): 131–146.

Gorard, S. (2018) *Education Policy*, Bristol: Policy Press.

Gorard, S. and Siddiqui, N. (2018) 'Grammar Schools in England: a new analysis of social segregation and academic outcomes', *British Journal of Sociology of Education*, 39 (7): 909–924.

Gorard, S. and Smith, E. (2004) 'An international comparison of equity in education systems', *Comparative Education*, 40(1): 15–28.

Gorski, P.C. and Zenkov, K. (eds) (2014) *The Big Lies of School Reform*, New York, NY: Routledge.

Gov.UK (2021) 'Social Mobility Commission', [online], Available from: https://www.gov.uk/government/organisations/social-mobility-commission [Accessed 16 June 2021].

Gove, M. (2013a) 'The progressive betrayal. Michael Gove speech to the Social Market Foundation, 5th February 2013', [online], Available from: https://www.smf.co.uk/michael-gove-speaks-at-the-smf/ [Accessed 2 August 2021].

Gove, M. (2013b) 'I refuse to surrender to the Marxist teachers hell-bent on destroying our schools: Education Secretary berates "the new enemies of promise" for opposing his plans', *Daily Mail*, [online] 23 March, Available from: https://www.dailymail.co.uk/debate/article-2298146/I-refuse-surrender-Marxist-teachers-hell-bent-destroying-schools-Education-Secretary-berates-new-enemies-promise-opposing-plans.html [Accessed 2 August 2021].

Grace, G. (1991) 'Welfare Labourism versus the New Right: the struggle in New Zealand's education policy', *International Studies in the Sociology of Education*, 1(1–2): 25–42.

Grace, G. (1994) 'Urban education and the culture of contentment: the politics, culture and economics of inner-city schooling', in: N. Stromquist (ed) *Education in Urban Areas: Cross-National Dimensions*, Westport, CT: Praeger, pp 45–59.

Grace, G. (1995) *School Leadership: Beyond Educational Management*, London: The Falmer Press.

Gramsci, A. (1971) *Selections from Prison Notebooks*, Edited and translated by Quintin Hoare and Geoffrey Nowell Smith, London: Lawrence and Wishart.

Grant, H. and Michael, C. (2019) 'Too poor to play: children in social housing blocked from communal playground', *The Guardian*, [online] 25 March, Available from: https://www.theguardian.com/cities/2019/mar/25/too-poor-to-play-children-in-social-housing-blocked-from-communal-playground [Accessed 9 March 2021].

Green, F. and Kynaston, D. (2019) *Engines of Privilege*, London: Bloomsbury.

Gregory, A. (2019) 'Tory candidate suggests people using food banks can't "manage their budget" properly', *Independent*, [online] 8 December, Available from: https://www.independent.co.uk/news/uk/politics/tory-candidate-food-banks-poor-families-budget-darren-henry-broxtowe-a9238076.html [Accessed 7 February 2022].

Grek, S. (2013) 'Expert moves: international comparative testing and the rise of expertocracy', *Journal of Education Policy*, 28(5): 695–709.

Grek, S. and Ozga, J. (2010) 'Re-inventing public education: the new role of knowledge in education policymaking', *Public Policy and Administration*, 25(3): 271–288.

Gulson, K.N. and Baker, B.M. (2018) 'New biological rationalities in education', *Discourse: Studies in the Cultural Politics of Education*, 39(2): 159–168.

Gunter, H.M. (1990) 'Changing relationships between central government, LEA, and schools', Dissertation for MSc Educational Management, Council for National Academic Awards (CNAA).

Gunter, H.M. (1997) *Rethinking Education: The Consequences of Jurassic Management*, London: Cassell.

Gunter, H.M. (1999) 'An intellectual history of the field of education management from 1960', Unpublished PhD thesis, Keele University, UK.

Gunter, H.M. (2002) 'Teacher appraisal 1988–1998: a case study', *School Leadership and Management*, 22(1): 61–72.

Gunter, H.M. (2004) 'Labels and labelling in the field of educational leadership', *Discourse*, 25(1): 21–42.

Gunter, H.M. (2008) 'Policy and workforce reform in England', *Educational Management Administration and Leadership*, 36(2): 253–270.
Gunter, H.M. (ed) (2011) *The State and Education Policy: the Academies Programme*, London: Continuum.
Gunter, H.M. (2012) *Leadership and the Reform of Education*, Bristol: The Policy Press.
Gunter, H.M. (2013) 'On not researching school leadership: the contribution of S.J. Ball', *London Review of Education*, 11(3): 218–228.
Gunter, H.M. (2014) *Educational Leadership and Hannah Arendt*, Abingdon: Routledge.
Gunter, H.M. (2016) *An Intellectual History of School Leadership Practice and Research*, London: Bloomsbury Press.
Gunter, H.M. (2017) 'Corporate consultancy practices in education services in England', in: H.M. Gunter, D. Hall, and M. Apple (eds) *Corporate Elites and the Reform of Public Education*, Bristol: Policy Press, pp 149–163.
Gunter, H.M. (2018) *The Politics of Public Education: Reform Ideas and Issues*, Bristol: Policy Press.
Gunter, H.M. (2019) 'Depoliticisation and education policy', in: J. Wilkinson, R. Niesche, and S. Eacott (eds) *Challenges for Public Education*, London: Routledge, pp 87–100.
Gunter, H.M. (2020a) 'The Education Policy Knowledgeable Polity (EPKP) project: a contribution to critical education policy scholarship', Unpublished Doctor of Social Science thesis, The University of Manchester, UK.
Gunter, H.M. (2020b) 'Consultancy in the UK government: modernising privatism', in: C. van den Berg, M. Howlett, H.M. Gunter, M. Howard, A. Migone, and F. Pemer (eds) *Policy Consultancy in Comparative Perspective: Patterns, Nuances and Implications for the Contractor State*, Cambridge: Cambridge University Press, pp 20–51.
Gunter, H.M. (2020c) 'Thinking politically with Arendt: depoliticised privatism and education policy', in: W. Veck and H.M. Gunter (eds) *Hannah Arendt on Educational Thinking and Practice in Dark Times: Education for a World in Crisis*, London: Bloomsbury, pp 79–166.
Gunter, H.M. (2020d) 'A short history of criticality in the field of educational administration', In R. Papa (ed), *[Oxford] Encyclopedia of Educational Administration*, New York, NY: Oxford University Press, pp 1–20.
Gunter, H.M. (2020e) 'Forgetting our intellectual histories and the implications for educational professionals', in: L. Moos, E. Nihfors, and J.M. Paulsen (eds) *Re-Centering the Critical in Nordic School Leadership Research: Fundamental But Often Forgotten Perspectives*, Cham, Switzerland: Springer, pp 37–52.
Gunter, H.M. (2021) 'Eugenics and personalisation in educational services', *Forum*, 63(1): 91–97.

Gunter, H.M. (2022) 'An intellectual history of the political in the EMAL field', *Educational Management Administration and History*, 50(2): 252–268.

Gunter, H.M. and Courtney, S.J. (2021) 'Socio-economic class and educational leadership', in: S.J. Courtney, H.M. Gunter, R. Niesche, and T. Trujillo (eds) *Understanding Educational Leadership: Critical Perspectives and Approaches*, London: Bloomsbury, pp 295–308.

Gunter, H.M. and Forrester, G. (2008) 'New Labour and school leadership 1997–2007', *British Journal of Educational Studies*, 55(2): 144–162.

Gunter, H.M. and Forrester, G. (2009) 'Institutionalised governance: the case of the National College for School Leadership', *International Journal of Public Administration*, 32(5): 349–369.

Gunter, H.M. and Forrester, G. (2010) 'Education Reform and School Leadership', in: S. Brookes and K. Grint (eds) *The Public Sector Leadership Challenge*, London: Palgrave, pp 54–69.

Gunter, H.M. and McGinity, R. (2014) 'The Politics of the Academies Programme: natality and plurality in education policymaking', *Research Papers in Education*, 29(3): 300–314.

Gunter, H.M. and Mills, C. (2016) 'Knowledge Production and the rise of consultocracy in education policymaking in England', in: A. Verger, C. Lubienski, and G. Steiner-Khamsi (eds) *World Yearbook of Education 2016: The Global Education Industry*, London: Routledge, pp 125–141.

Gunter, H.M. and Mills, C. (2017) *Consultants and Consultancy: The Case of Education*, Cham, Switzerland: Springer.

Gunter, H.M. and Thomson, P. (2004) *Kingswood High School: Baseline Report 2004*, Report to the DfES Innovation Unit, London.

Gunter, H.M. and Thomson, P. (2006) 'Stories from the field of commissioned research', Paper presented to the British Educational Research Association Conference, University of Warwick, September 2006.

Gunter, H.M. and Thomson, P. (2009) 'The makeover: a new logic in leadership development in England?', *Educational Review*, 61(4): 469–483.

Gunter, H.M., Hall, D., and Apple, M. (eds) (2017) *Corporate Elites and the Reform of Public Education*, Bristol: Policy Press.

Gunter, H.M., Courtney, S.J., Hall, D., and McGinity, R. (2018) 'School principals in neoliberal times: a case of luxury leadership?', in: A.J. Means and K.J. Saltman (eds) *Handbook of Global Education Reform*, New York, NY: Wiley-Blackwell, pp 113–130.

Gunter, H.M., Grimaldi, E., Hall, D., and Serpieri, R. (eds) (2016) *New Public Management and the Reform of Education: European Lessons for Policy and Practice*, London: Routledge.

Gunter, H.M., Rayner, S., Butt, G., Fielding, A., Lance, A., and Thomas, H. (2007) 'Transforming the school workforce: perspectives on school reform in England', *Journal of Educational Change*, 8(1): 25–39.

Gutiérrez, G., Jerrim, J., and Torres, R. (2020) 'School segregation across the world: has any progress been made in reducing the separation of the rich from the poor?', *The Journal of Economic Inequality*, 18: 157–179.

Hailsham, Lord. (1976) *Elective Dictatorship*, The Richard Dimbleby Lecture. London: BBC.

Hall, D., Gunter, H.M., and Bragg, J. (2012) 'Leadership, new public management and the re-modeling and regulation of teacher identities', *International Journal of Leadership in Education*, 16(2): 173–190.

Hall, V. (1999) 'Gender and education management: duel or dialogue?', in: T. Bush, L. Bell, R. Bolam, R. Glatter, and P. Ribbins (eds) *Educational Management: Redefining Theory, Policy and Practice*. London: PCP, pp 155–165.

Hall, V. and Southworth, G. (1997) 'Headship', *School Leadership and Management*, 17(2): 151–170.

Hallam, S. and Parsons, S. (2013) 'Prevalence of streaming in UK primary schools: evidence from the Millennium Cohort Study', *British Educational Research Journal*, 39(3): 514–544.

Hallinger, P. and Heck, R.H. (1998) 'Exploring the principal's contribution to school effectiveness: 1980–1995', *School Effectiveness and School Improvement*, 9(2): 157–191.

Halpin, D. (1994) 'Practice and prospects in education policy research', in: D. Halpin and B. Troyna (eds) *Researching Education Policy: Ethical and Methodological Issues*, London: The Falmer Press, pp 198–206.

Halpin, D. and Troyna, B. (Eds.) (1994) *Researching Education Policy: Ethical and Methodological Issues*. London: The Falmer Press.

Harden, K.P., Domingue, B.W., Belsky, D.W., Boardman, J.D., Crosnoe, R., Malanchini, M., Nivard, M., Trucker-Drob, E.M., and Harris, K.M. (2020) 'Genetic associations with mathematics tracking and persistence in secondary school', *NPJ Science of Learning*, 5(1) https://doi.org/10.1038/s41539-020-0060-2

Harding, A. (2000) 'Regime formation in Manchester and Edinburgh', in: G. Stoker (ed) *The New Politics of British Local Governance*, Basingstoke: MacMillan, pp 54–71.

Harding, E. (2015) 'Failing headteachers will be sacked if they can't turn schools around, says Education Secretary Nicky Morgan', *Daily Mail*, [online], Available from: https://www.dailymail.co.uk/news/article-3085681/I-want-sack-failing-heads-says-Morgan-Education-Secretary-promises-raft-tough-new-measures-announcement-Election.html [Accessed 28 September 2020].

Harding, L. (2021) ' "Hyper-creepy": Gavin Williamson mocked over One Britain, One Nation Song', *The Guardian*, [online] 23 June, Available from: https://www.theguardian.com/uk-news/2021/jun/23/uk-education-secretary-mocked-for-one-britain-one-nation-day-song [Accessed 1 February 2022].

Hargreaves, D.H. (2004) *Personalising Learning – 2. Student Voice and Assessment for Learning*, London: Specialist Schools Trust.

Hargreaves, D.H. and Hopkins, D. (1991) *The Empowered School: The Management and Practice of Development Planning*, London: Cassell.

Harris, J. (2021) 'Britain's overgrown Eton schoolboys have turned the country into their playground', *The Guardian*, [online] 2 May, Available from: https://www.theguardian.com/commentisfree/2021/may/02/westminster-eton-schoolboys-boris-johnson-david-cameron [Accessed 5 May 2021].

Harris, A. and Muijs, D. (2005) *Improving Schools Through Teacher Leadership*, Maidenhead: Open University Press.

Harvey, D. (2007) *A Brief History of Neoliberalism*, Oxford: Oxford University Press.

Hatcher, R. (2005) 'The distribution of leadership and power in schools', *British Journal of Sociology of Education*, 26(2): 253–267.

Hatcher, R. and Troyna, B. (1994) 'The "policy cycle": a Ball by Ball account', *Journal of Education Policy*, 9(2): 155–170.

Havel, V. (2018) *The Power of the Powerless*, London: Vintage.

Hayek, F.A. (2001) *The Road to Serfdom*, Abingdon: Routledge.

Hazell, W. (2020) 'Number of children in home education rockets by 119% in some parts of England', *iNews*, [online], Available from: https://inews.co.uk/news/children-in-home-education-rocket-england-405854 [Accessed 13 April 2021].

Helsby, G. (1999) *Changing Teachers' Work*, Buckingham: Open University Press.

Henry, J. (2018) 'Private schools "abuse charity status" by giving discounts to richer families', *The Guardian*, [online] 3 June, Available from: https://www.theguardian.com/education/2018/jun/03/private-schools-abuse-charity-status-by-giving-discounts-to-richer-families [Accessed 28 June 2021].

Herrnstein, R.J. and Murray, C. (1994) *The Bell Curve: Intelligence and Class Structure in American Life*, New York, NY: Free Press.

Hill, C. (2020) *The World Turned Upside Down: Radical Ideas During the English Revolution*, London: Penguin.

Hill, S. (2021) *Hannah Arendt*, London: Reaktion Books Ltd.

Hindess, B. (1997) 'A society governed by contract?', in: G. Davis, B. Sullivan, and A. Yeatman (eds) *The New Contractualism?*, Melbourne: Macmillan Education, pp 14–26.

Hodge, G. (ed) (2006) *Privatisation and Market Development*, Cheltenham: Edward Elgar.

Hogan, A., Sellar, S., and Lingard, B. (2016) 'Commercialising comparison: Pearson puts the TLC in soft capitalism', *Journal of Education Policy*, 31(3): 243–258.

Hopkins, D. (2001) *'Think Tank' Report to Governing Council*, Nottingham: NCSL.

Hopkins, D. (2007) *Every School a Great School*, Maidenhead: OUP.

Horgan, G. (2009) '"That child is smart because he's rich": the impact of poverty on young children's experiences of school', *International Journal of Inclusive Education*, 13(4): 359–376.

Howlett, M. (2012) 'The lessons of failure: learning and blame avoidance in public policy-making', *International Political Science Review*, 33(5): 539–555.

Huber, S., Moorman, H., and Pont, B. (2007) *School Leadership for Systemic Improvement in England. A Case Study Report for the OECD Activity Improving School Leadership*, Paris: OECD.

Hughes, B.C. (2019) 'Investigating the CEO of a MAT: examining practices and positions on "the street"', *Educational Management Administration and Leadership*, 48(3): 478–495.

Hughes, B.C. (2020) 'Investigating the realist networks of the Chief Executive Officer of a multi-academy trust', *Educational Review*. https://doi.org/10.1080/00131911.2020.1721436

Hughes, B., Gunter, H.M., and Courtney, S.J. (2020) 'Researching professional biographies of educational professionals in *new* dark times', *British Journal of Educational Studies*, 68(3): 275–293.

Hutchings, M., Seeds, K., Coleman, N., Harding, C., Mansaray, A., Maylor, U., Minty, S, and Pickering, E. (2009) *Aspects of School Workforce Remodelling*, Research Report No DCSF-RR153, London: DCSF.

Hyman, P. (2005) *One Out Of Ten, From Downing Street Vision to Classroom Reality*, London: Vintage.

Jackson, B. and Marsden, D. (1962) *Education and the Working Class*, London: Routledge and Keegen Paul Ltd.

Jackson, D.S. (2000) 'The school improvement journey: perspectives on leadership', *School Leadership and Management*. 20(1): 61–78.

Jenkins, R. (2002) *Pierre Bourdieu*, London: Routledge.

Jenkins, S.P., Micklewright, J., and Schnepf, S.V. (2006) 'Social segregation in secondary schools: how does England compare with other countries? IZA Discussion Paper No. 1959', Bonn: IZA Institute for the Study of Labor.

Jessop, B. (2000) 'Governance failure', in: G. Stoker (ed) *The New Politics of British Local Governance*, Basingstoke: Macmillan Press Ltd, pp 11–32.

Johnson, A. (2007) *National College for School Leadership (NCSL) Priorities: 2007–2008*, London: DfES.

Jones, O. (2012) *Chavs: The Demonization of the Working Class*, London: Verso.

Jones, O. (2014) *The Establishment*, London: Allen Lane.

Joseph, K. (1974) *Speech at the Grand Hotel, Birmingham, Saturday 19th October 1974*, [online], Available from: https://www.margaretthatcher.org/document/101830 [Accessed 8 June 2020].

Joseph, K. (1984) 'Speech by the Rt Hon Sir Keith Joseph, Secretary of State for Education and Science at the North of England Education Conference, Sheffield, on Friday 6th January 1984', *Oxford Review of Education*, 10(2): 137–146.

Jowit, J. (2013) 'Strivers v shirkers: the language of the welfare debate', *The Guardian*, [online] 8 January, Available from: https://www.theguardian.com/politics/2013/jan/08/strivers-shirkers-language-welfare [Accessed 4 November 2021].

Kakutani, M. (2018) *The Death of Truth*, London: William Collins.

Kaufmann, E. and Cantle, T. (2016) 'Is segregation on the increase in the UK?', [online], Available from: https://www.opendemocracy.net/en/is-segregation-on-increase-in-uk/ [Accessed 9 March 2021].

Kavanagh, D. (1987) *Thatcherism and British Politics: The End of Consensus?* Oxford: Oxford Paperbacks.

Keay, D. (1987) 'Margaret Thatcher', Interview for *Woman's Own*, [online], Available from: https://www.margaretthatcher.org/document/106689 [Accessed 9 September 2021].

Kelly, R. (2004) *National College for School Leadership Priorities: 2005–06*, London: DfES.

Kelly, R. (2005) *National College for School Leadership (NCSL) Priorities: 2006–07*, London: DfES.

Kennelly, J. (2018) 'Envisioning democracy: participatory filmmaking with homeless youth', *Canadian Review of Sociology*, 55(2): 190–210.

Kevles, D.J. (1999) 'Eugenics and human rights', *BMJ*, 319(14 August): 435–438.

Kickert, W. (1995) 'Steering at a distance: a new paradigm of public governance in Dutch Higher Education', *Governance: An International Journal of Policy and Administration*, 8(1): 135–157.

Kickert, W., Klijn, E-H., and Koppenjan, J.F.M. (eds) (1997) *Managing Complex Networks*, London: Sage.

Kincheloe, J.L., Steinberg, S.R., and Gresson III, A.D. (eds) (1996) *Measured Lies, the Bell Curve Examined*, New York, NY: St Martin's Press.

King, D. and Le Galès, P. (2016) 'State', in: E. Amenta, K. Nash, and A. Scott (eds) *The Wiley Blackwell Companion to Political Sociology*, Chichester: John Wiley and Sons Ltd, pp 107–119.

Kliewer, C. and Drake, S. (1998) 'Disability, eugenics and the current ideology of segregation: a modern moral tale', *Disability & Society*, 13(1): 95–111.

Kline, W. (2010) *Bodies of Knowledge*. Chicago, IL: The University of Chicago Press.

Kornhall, P. and Bender, G. (2019) *School Segregation in Sweden: Evidence From The Local Level. NESET Ad Hoc Report*, Brussels: NESET.

Kulz, C. (2011) '"Structure frees"; the production and intersection of race and class in a London secondary academy', in: C. Alexander and M. James (eds) *New Directions, New Voices, Emerging Research on Race and Ethnicity*, London: The Runnymede Trust, pp 28–30.

Kulz, C. (2017) 'Heroic heads, mobility mythologies and the power of ambiguity', *British Journal of Sociology of Education*, 38(2): 85–104.

Kwarteng, K., Patel, P., Raab, D., Skidmore, C., and Truss, E. (2012) *Britannia Unchanged*, Basingstoke: Palgrave Macmillan.

Lawlor, S. (1988) *Opting Out: A Guide to Why and How*, London: Centre for Policy Studies.

Lawn, M. and Grek, S. (2012) *Europeanizing Education: Governing a New Policy Space*, Oxford: Symposium Books Ltd.

Leadbeater, C. (2004) *Learning About Personalization: How Can We Put the Learner at the Heart of the Education System?*, Nottingham: DfES.

Leadbeater, C. (2006) 'The future of public services: personalized learning', in: OECD (ed) *Personalising Education*, Paris: OECD, pp 101–114.

Leithwood, K., Day, C., Sammons, P., Harris, A., and Hopkins, D. (2006) *Seven Strong Claims About Successful School Leadership*, Nottingham: NCSL.

Levačić, R. and Marsh, A. (2007) 'Secondary modern schools: are their pupils disadvantaged?', *British Educational Research Journal*, 33(2): 1469–1518.

Levine, P. and Bashford, A. (2010) 'Introduction: Eugenics and the modern world', in: A. Bashford and P. Levine (eds) *The Oxford Handbook of the History of Eugenics*, Oxford: Oxford University Press, pp 3–24.

Levitsky, S. and Ziblatt, D. (2019) *How Democracies Die*, London: Penguin Books.

Lightfoot, L. (2020) *Outstanding primary schools fail Ofsted inspections under sudden rule change*. https://www.theguardian.com/education/2020/feb/04/outstanding-primary-schools-fail-ofsted-inspections-under-sudden-rule-switch [Accessed 7th July 2022].

Lingard, B. (1993) 'The changing state of policy production in education: some Australian reflections on the state of policy sociology', *International Studies in the Sociology of Education*, 3(1): 25–47.

Lingard, B., Hayes, D., Mills, M., and Christie, P. (2003) *Leading Learning*, Maidenhead: OUP.

Longfield, A. (2020) *Childhood in the Time of Covid*, London: Children's Commissioner for England, [online], Available from: https://www.childrenscommissioner.gov.uk/report/childhood-in-the-time-of-covid/ [Accessed 7 April 2021].

Lowe, R. (1979) 'Eugenicists, doctors and the quest for national efficiency: an educational crusade, 1900–1939', *History of Education*, 8(4): 293–306.

Lucey, H. and Reay, D. (2002) 'A market in waste: psychic and structural dimensions of school-choice policy in the UK and children's narratives on "demonized" schools', *Discourse: Studies in the Cultural Politics of Education*, 23(3): 253–266.

Lukes, S. (1974) *Power*, London: The Macmillan Press Ltd.

Lupton, R. and Hayes, D. (2021) *Great Mistakes in Education Policy: And How to Avoid Them in the Future*, Bristol: Policy Press.

MacGilchrist, B., Myers, K., and Reed, J. (1997) *The Intelligent School*, London: PCP.

Macpherson, C.B. (2011) *The Political Theory of Possessive Individualism*, Oxford: Oxford University Press.

Malnick, E. (2021) '"Woke" anti-Government speakers barred from Whitehall', *The Telegraph*, [online], Available from: https://www.telegraph.co.uk/politics/2021/11/27/woke-speakers-critical-boris-johnson-banned-whitehall/ [Accessed 1 December 2021].

Mann, M. (1986) *The Sources of Social Power, Volume 1*, Cambridge: Cambridge University Press.

Mansell, W. (2017) 'Sixty "orphan" schools shunned by academy sponsors', *The Guardian*, [online] 7 February, Available from: https://www.theguardian.com/education/2017/feb/07/failing-schools-academy-sponsor-ofsted [Accessed 23 November 2021].

Mansell, W. (2021a) 'Hereditary principle kicking in at Harris Federation', [online], Available from: https://www.educationuncovered.co.uk/diary/diary/150121/hereditary-principle-kicking-in-at-harris-federation.thtml [Accessed 24 March 2021].

Mansell, W. (2021b) 'Multi-academy trust moved children between schools "without consulting parents"', [online], Available from: https://www.educationuncovered.co.uk/news/150816/multiacademy-trust-moves-children-between-schools-without-consulting-parents.thtml [Accessed 14 May 2021].

Marinetto, M. (2003) 'Governing beyond the centre: a critique of the anglo-governance school', *Political Studies*, 51: 592–608.

Marquand, D. (1981) 'Club government – the crisis of the Labour Party in the national perspective', *Government and Opposition*, 16(1): 19–36.

Marquand, D. (2004) *Decline of the Public*, Cambridge: Polity Press.

Mason, R. (2020) 'Boris Johnson adviser quits over race and eugenics controversy', *The Guardian*, [online] 17 February, Available from: https://www.theguardian.com/politics/2020/feb/17/boris-johnson-adviser-quits-over-race-and-eugenics-writings [Accessed 16 March 2021].

Massucato, M. (2013) *The Entrepreneurial State*, London: Anthem Press.

Martin, J. (2022) *Gender and Education in England since 1870*, Cham: Palgrave Macmillan.

May, T. (2016) 'Full text: Theresa May's speech on grammar schools', *New Statesman*, [online], Available from: https://www.newstatesman.com/politics/education/2016/09/full-text-theresa-mays-speech-grammar-schools [Accessed 17 June 2021].

McBain, S. (2021) 'The reckoning. Girls say a sexual assault epidemic is gripping British schools. Is anyone listening', *The New Statesman*, 8–14 October, pp 20–25.

McConnell, A. (2015) 'What is policy failure? A primer to help navigate the maze', *Public Policy and Administration*, 30(3–4): 221–242.

McGinity, R. (2013) 'Modernisation through personalized public services: an investigation into localized school policymaking', Unpublished PhD, University of Manchester, UK.

McGinity, R. and Gunter, H.M. (2012) 'Living improvement 2: a case study of a secondary school in England', *Improving Schools*, 15(3): 228–244.

McGinity, R. and Gunter, H.M. (2017) 'New practices and old hierarchies: academy conversion in a successful English Secondary School', in: P. Thomson (ed) *Educational Leadership and Pierre Bourdieu*, London: Routledge, pp 98–111.

McNamara, O., Howson, J., Gunter, H.M., and Fryers, A. (2009) *The Leadership Aspirations and Careers of Black and Ethnic Minority Teachers*, Birmingham: NASUWT.

McNamara, O., Howson, J., Gunter, H.M. and Fryers, A. (2010) *No Job For a Woman: The Impact of Gender in School Leadership*, Birmingham: NASUWT.

McPherson, A. and Raab, C.D. (1988) *Governing Education: A Sociology of Policy Since 1945*, Edinburgh: Edinburgh University Press.

Means, A.J. and Slater, G.B. (2021) 'World, planet, territory: toward a geo-logic in the critical sociology of education', *British Journal of Sociology of Education*, 42(5–6): 633–650.

Meatto, K. (2019) 'Still separate, still unequal: teaching about school segregation and eduational inequality', *New York Times*, [online], Available from: https://www.nytimes.com/2019/05/02/learning/lesson-plans/still-separate-still-unequal-teaching-about-school-segregation-and-educational-inequality.html [Accessed 9 March 2021].

Meloni, M. (2019) *Impressionable Biologies*, New York, NY: Routledge.

Meyers, C.V. and Murphy, J. (2007) 'Turning around failing schools: an analysis', *Journal of School Leadership*, 17(September): 631–659.

Miliband, D. (2003) '*Challenges For School Leadership*', Speech to the SHA Conference On Leadership, London, 1 July, DCSF, [online], Available from: www.dcsf.gov.uk/speeches/search_detail.cfm?ID=81 [Accessed 20 November 2009].

Miliband, D. (2004) '*Speech on the Future of Teaching*', Cambridge, 3 November, [online], Available from: https://www.ukpol.co.uk/david-miliband-2004-speech-on-the-future-of-teaching/ [Accessed 22 November 2021].

Miliband, D. (2006) '*Choice and voice in personalized learning*', in OECD (ed) *Personalising Education*, Paris: OECD, pp 21–30.

Miliband, R. (1973) *The State in Capitalist Society*, London: Quartet Books.

References

Miller, C. and Evans, S. (2019) 'England's worst schools REVEALED – is YOUR child's school on the list?', *Mirror*, [online] 24 January, Available from: https://www.mirror.co.uk/news/uk-news/breaking-englands-worst-schools-revealed-13899939 [Accessed 28 September 2020].

Miller, P. and Rose, N. (2008) *Governing the Present*, Cambridge: Polity.

Milliken, M., Bates, J., and Smith, A. (2021) 'Teaching across the divide: perceived barriers to the movement of teachers across the traditional sectors in Northern Ireland', *British Journal of Educational Studies*, 69(2): 133–154.

Mithen, S. (2018) 'Blueprint by Robert Plomin review – how DNA dictates who we are', *The Guardian*, [online] 24 October, Available from: https://www.theguardian.com/books/2018/oct/24/blueprint-by-robert-plomin-review [Accessed 20 April 2020].

Monbiot, G. (2021) 'Jailed for 51 weeks for protesting? Britain is becoming a police state by stealth', *The Guardian*, [online] 1 December, Available from: https://www.theguardian.com/commentisfree/2021/dec/01/imprisoned-51-weeks-protesting-britain-police-state [Accessed 1 December 2021].

Moran, M. (2003) *The British Regulatory State*, Oxford: Oxford University Press.

Morris, E. (2002) 'Full text of Estelle Morris's speech to the Labour Party conference', *The Guardian*, [online] 2 October, Available from: https://www.theguardian.com/politics/2002/oct/02/labourconference.labour5 [Accessed 12 May 2021].

Muller, J.Z. (2018) *The Tyranny of Metrics*, Princeton, NJ: Princeton University Press.

Müller, J-W. (2017) *What is Populism?*, London: Penguin Books.

Munby, S. (2019) *Imperfect Leadership*, Bancyfelin: Crown House Publishing Ltd.

Murray, C. (2020) *Human Diversity*, New York, NY: Twelve.

NCSL (Undated) *2002-03 Prospectus*, Nottingham: NCSL.

NCSL (2001) *Leadership Development Framework*, Nottingham: NCSL.

NCSL (2006) *Annual Review of Research 2004–2005*, Nottingham: NCSL.

Neave, G. (1988) 'On the cultivation of quality, efficiency and enterprise: an overview of recent trends in higher education in Western Europe 1986–1988', *European Journal of Education*, 23(1/2): 7–23.

Nichols, T. (2017) *The Death of Expertise*, New York, NY: Oxford University Press.

Nixon, J. (2001) 'Imagining ourselves into being: conversing with Hannah Arendt', *Pedagogy Culture and Society*, 9(2): 221–236.

OBON (2022) *Shout out Britain, OBON Day Anthem 2021*, [online], Available from: https://www.onebritainonenation.com/assets/pdf/song-anthem-words.pdf [Accessed 1 February 2022].

Oborne, P. (2021) *The Assault on Truth*, London: Simon & Schuster.

O'Brien, J. (2020) *How Not To Be Wrong*, London: WH Allen.

Office for National Statistics (2021) 'Health state life expectancies by national deprivation deciles, England and Wales: 2015 to 2017', [online], Available from: https://www.ons.gov.uk/peoplepopulationandcommunity/healthan dsocialcare/healthinequalities/bulletins/healthstatelifeexpectanciesbyin dexofmultipledeprivationimd/2015to2017 [Accessed 15 March 2021].

Ofsted (1999) 'Teacher well-being at work in schools and further education providers', [online], Available from: https://assets.publishing.service.gov. uk/government/uploads/system/uploads/attachment_data/file/936253/ Teacher_well-being_report_110719F.pdf [Accessed 16 February 2022].

Ofsted (2002) *Leadership and Management Training for Headteachers. Report by HMI, April 2002, HMI 457*, London: Ofsted.

Ofsted (2005) *Remodelling the School Workforce*, HMI 2596, London: OfSTED.

Olusoga, D. (2016) *Black and British: A Forgotten History*, London: Picador.

OECD (ed) (2006) *Personalising Education*, Paris: OECD.

OECD (2011) *School autonomy and accountability: Are they related to school performance?* Paris: OECD.

OECD (2012) *Equity and Quality in Education: Supporting Disadvantaged Students and Schools*, Paris: OECD.

Osborne, H. (2014) 'Poor doors: the segregation of London's inner-city flat dwellers', *The Guardian*, [online] 25 July, Available from: https://www.theg uardian.com/society/2014/jul/25/poor-doors-segregation-london-flats [Accessed 9 March 2021].

Ostrom, E. (2015) *Governing the Commons*, Cambridge: Cambridge University Press.

Ozga, J. (1987) 'Studying education policy through the lives of the policymakers: an attempt to close the macro-micro gap', in S. Walker and L. Barton (eds) *Changing Policies, Changing Teachers: New Directions for Schooling?*, Milton Keynes: OUP, pp 138–150.

Ozga, J. (2000) *Policy Research in Educational Settings*, Buckingham: OUP.

Ozga, J. (2009) 'Governing education through data in England: from regulation to self-evaluation', *Journal of Education Policy*, 24(2): 149–162.

Ozga, J. (2013) 'Leadership and the reform of education', *British Journal of Sociology of Education*, 34(2): 290–294.

Ozga, J. (2021) 'Problematising policy: the development of (critical) policy sociology', *Critical Studies in Education*, 62(3): 290–305.

Ozga, J. and Dale, R. (1991) *Module 1: Introducing Education Policy: Principles and Perspectives*, Milton Keynes: Open University Press.

Ozga, J., Dahler-Larsen, P., Segerholm, C., and Simola, H. (eds) (2011) *Fabricating Quality in Education*, Abingdon: Routledge.

Parker, M. and Thomas, R. (2011) 'What is a critical journal?', *Organization*, 18(4): 419–427.

Parry, G. (1976) *Political Elites*, London: George Allen & Unwin.

Pearton, M. (1982) *The Knowledgeable State, Diplomacy, War and Technology since 1830*, London: Burnett Books.

Peck, S. (2020) 'Are single-sex schools finished?', *The Telegraph*, [online] 24 March, Available from: https://www.telegraph.co.uk/education-and-careers/2020/03/24/single-sex-schools-finished/ [Accessed 11 March 2021].

Pells, R. (2017) 'Theresa May says "you can have all the evidence, but headteachers told me grammar schools are good", education researcher claims', *The Independent*, [online], Available from: https://www.independent.co.uk/news/education/education-news/theresa-may-grammar-school-research-evidence-general-election-twitter-karen-wespieser-nfer-maidenhead-duck-derby-a7750026.html [Accessed 17 June 2021].

Peters, M.A. (2017) 'From state responsibility for education and welfare to self-responsibilisation in the market', *Discourse: Studies in the Cultural Politics of Education*, 38(1): 138–145.

Phipps, C. (2016) 'British newspapers react to judges Brexit ruling: 'Enemies of the people', *The Guardian*, [online], Available from: https://www.theguardian.com/politics/2016/nov/04/enemies-of-the-people-british-newspapers-react-judges-brexit-ruling [Accessed 7th July 2022].

Plomin, R. (2018) *Blueprint*, London: Allen Lane.

Pollitt, C. (2007) 'New Labour's re-disorganization', *Public Management Review*, 9(4): 529–543.

Power, S. (1995) 'The detail and the bigger picture: the use of state-centred theory in explaining education policy and practice', *International Studies in Sociology of Education*, 5(1): 77–92.

PricewaterhouseCoopers (2001) *Teacher Workload Study*, London: DfES.

PricewaterhouseCoopers (2008) *Academies Evaluation: Fifth Annual Report*, London: Department for Children, Schools and Families.

Prieto-Latorre, C., Marcenaro-Gutierrez, O.D., and Vignoles, A. (2021) 'School segregation in public and semi-private primary schools in Andalusia', *British Journal of Educational Studies*, 69(2): 175–196.

Prime Minister and the Minister for the Cabinet Office (1999) *Modernising Government*, Cm 4310, London: HM Stationery Office.

Raab, C. (1994) 'Where we are now: reflections on the sociology of education policy', in: D. Halpin and B. Troyna (eds) *Researching Education Policy: Ethical and Methodological Issues*, London: The Falmer Press, pp 17–30.

Raab, D. (2009) *The Assault on Liberty*, London: 4th Estate.

Raffo, C., Dyson, A., Gunter, H.M, Hall, D., Jones, L., and Kalambouka, A. (eds) (2010) *Education and Poverty in Affluent Countries*, London: Routledge.

Ranson, S. (1984) 'Towards a tertiary tripartism: new codes of social control and the 17 plus', in: P. Broadfoot (ed) *Selection, Certification, and Control: Social Issues in Educational Assessment*, Lewes: Falmer Press, pp 221–244.

Ranson, S. (1995) 'Theorising education policy', *Journal of Education Policy*, 10(4): 427–448.

Ranson, S. (2003) 'Public accountability in the age of neo-liberal governance', *Journal of Education Policy*, 18(5): 459–480.

Ravitch, D. (2014) *Reign of Error*, New York, NY: Vintage Books.

Rawnsley, A. (2021) 'The Queen had a lucky escape from Boris Johnson's "sod it" attitude to Covid', *The Guardian*, [online] 25 July, Available from: https://www.theguardian.com/commentisfree/2021/jul/25/queen-had-lucky-escape-boris-johnson-sod-it-attitude-to-covid [Accessed 25 July 2021].

Rawolle, S., Rowlands, J., and Blackmore, J. (2017) 'The implications of contractualism for the responsibilisation of higher education', *Discourse: Studies in the Cultural Politics of Education*, 38(1): 109–122.

Rayner, S.M. and Gunter, H.M. (2020) 'Resistance, professional agency and the reform of education in England', *London Review of Education*. 18 (2), 265-280.

Rayner, S.M., Courtney, S.J., and Gunter, H.M. (2017) 'Theorising systemic change: learning from the academisation project in England', *Journal of Education Policy*, 33(1): 143–162.

Reay, D. (2020) 'Sociology of education: a personal reflection on politics, power and pragmatism', *British Journal of Sociology of Education*, 41(6): 817–829.

Reay, D., David, M.E., and Ball, S.J. (2005) *Degrees of Choice*, Stoke-on-Trent: Trentham Books.

Revell, P. (2003) 'Thrashing out the details', *The Guardian*, [online] 13 May, Available from: https://www.theguardian.com/education/workload/story/0,,954407,00.html [Accessed 16 September 2021].

Reynolds, D. (2007) 'It doesn't add up', *The Guardian*, [online] 16 May, Available from: https://www.theguardian.com/education/2007/may/16/schools.uk2 [Accessed 18 November 2021].

Reynolds, D. (2014) 'Editorial', *School Effectiveness and School Improvement: An International Journal of Research, Policy and Practice*, 25(2): 195–196.

Reynolds, D. and Teddlie, C. (2001) 'Reflection on the critics, and beyond them', *School Effectiveness and School Improvement*, 12(1): 99–114.

Reynolds, D., Sammons, P., Stoll, L., Barber, M. and Hillman, J. (1996) School effectiveness and school improvement in the United Kingdom. *School Effectiveness and School Improvement*. 7(2): 133–158.

Rhodes, R.A.W. (1994) 'The hollowing out of the state: the changing nature of the public service in Britain', *The Political Quarterly*, 65(2): 138–151.

Rhodes, R.A.W. (1996) 'The new governance: governing without government', *Political Studies*, XLIV: 652–667.

Ribbins, P. (1997a) 'Kenneth Baker with Peter Ribbins', in: P. Ribbins and B. Sherratt (eds) *Radical Educational Policies and Conservative Secretaries of State*, London: Continuum, pp 87–116.

Ribbins, P. (ed) (1997b) *Leaders and Leadership in the School, College and University*, London: Cassell.

Ribbins, P. and Sherratt, B. (1997) *Radical Educational Policies and Conservative Secretaries of State*, London: Continuum.

Ribbins, P., Bates, R., and Gunter, H.M. (2003) 'Reviewing research in education in Australia and the UK: evaluating the evaluations', *Journal of Educational Administration*, 41(4): 423–444.

Richardson, K. (2017) *Genes, Brains, and Human Potential*, New York: Columbia University Press.

Rizvi, F. and Lingard, B. (2010) *Globalizing Education Policy*, London: Routledge.

Rooks, N. (2017) *Cutting School: The Segrenomics of American Education*, New York, NY: The New Press.

Roscoe, T. (2020) 'Arendt's "thoughtfulness" and Bourdieu's "reflexivity": differences, similarities and consequences, Part 2', [online], Available from: https://clefthabitus.com/2020/02/05/arendts-thoughtfulness-bourdieus-reflexivity-differences-similarities-consequences-part-2/ [Accessed 16 June 2021].

Rose, N. (2007) *The Politics of Life Itself*. Princeton, NJ: Princeton University Press.

Ross, A. and Hutchings, M. (2003) *Attracting, Developing, and Retaining Effective Teachers in the United Kingdom of Great Britain and Northern Ireland*, OECD Background Report, Paris: OECD.

Rothstein, R. (2017) *The Color of Law*, New York, NY: Liveright Publishing Corporation.

Rudduck, J. and McIntyre, D. (eds) (1999) *Educational Research: The Challenge Facing Us*, London: Paul Chapman.

Rush, M. and Althoff, P. (1971) *An Introduction to Political Sociology*, London: Thomas Nelson and Sons Ltd.

Rushton, S. (2020) 'Calls to change Eton's charity 80% tax break as state schools suffer depths of austerity', *iNews*, [online], Available from: https://inews.co.uk/news/education/calls-to-change-etons-charity-80-tax-break-as-state-schools-suffer-depths-of-austerity-285190 [Accessed 28 June 2021].

Russell, J. (2002) 'Pay as you learn', *The Guardian*, [online] 8 April, Available from: https://www.theguardian.com/education/2002/apr/08/schools.uk [Accessed 2 November 2021].

Rutherford, A. (2020) *How to Argue With a Racist*, London: Weidenfeld and Nicolson.

Rutherford, A. (2022) *Control: The Dark History and Troubling Present of Eugenics*, London: Weidenfeld & Nicolson.

Sahoo, S. and Klasen, S. (2018) 'Gender segregation in education and its implications for labour market outcomes: evidence from India', IZA Discussion Paper No. 11660, Bonn: IZA Institute of Labor Economics.

Saini, A. (2017) *Inferior*, London: 4th Estate.

Saini, A. (2019) *Superior*, London: 4th Estate.

Saltman, K.J. (2010) *The Gift of Education*, New York, NY: Palgrave MacMillan.

Sammons, P. (1999) *School Effectiveness. Coming of Age in the Twenty First Century*, Lisse: Swets and Zeitlinger.

Sammons, P., Hillman, J., and Mortimore, P. (1995) *Key Characteristics of Effective Schools: A Review of School Effectiveness Research*, London: OfSTED.

Savage, G.C. (2021) 'The evolving state of policy sociology', *Critical Studies in Education*, 62(3): 275–289.

Savage, G.C., Gerrard, J., Gale, T., and Molla, T. (2021) 'The politics of critical policy sociology: mobilities, moorings and elite networks', *Critical Studies in Education*, 62(3): 306–321.

Savage, M. (2017) 'Call to fine schools that illegally exclude poorly performing pupils', *The Guardian*, [online] 17 December, Available from: https://www.theguardian.com/education/2017/dec/17/call-to-fine-schools-that-illegally-exclude-poorly-performing-pupils?CMP=share_btn_link [Accessed 20 December 2017].

School Teachers' Review Body (2002) *Special Review of Approaches to Reducing Teacher Workload*, Norwich: The Stationery Office Limited.

Scope (2021) 'Disability facts and figures', [online], Available from: https://www.scope.org.uk/media/disability-facts-figures/ [Accessed 15 March 2021].

Scott, J.C. (1998) *Seeing Like a State*, New Haven: Yale University Press.

Seddon, T. (2014) 'Renewing sociology of education? Knowledge spaces, situated enactments and sociological practice in a world on the move', *European Educational Research Journal*, 13(1): 9–25.

Sennett, R. (1999) *The Corrosion of Character*, New York, NY: W.W. Norton.

Sexton, S. (1994) 'Radical education reform', *The Journal of Education*, 176(2): 1–5.

Shain, F. (2011) *The New Folk Devils*, Stoke-on-Trent: Trentham Books.

Shamir, R. (2008) 'The age of responsibilisation: on market-embedded morality', *Economy and Society*, 37(1): 1–19.

Shepherd, J. and Curtis, P. (2009) 'Middle-class pupils have better genes, says Chris Woodhead', *The Guardian*, [online] 11 May, Available from: https://www.theguardian.com/education/2009/may/11/education-policy-class-bias [Accessed 7 April 2021].

Simon, B. (1955) *The Common Secondary School*, London: Lawrence and Wishart Ltd.

Sims, S. (2020) *Briefing Note School Absences and Pupil Achievement*, London: Centre for Education Policy and Equalising Opportunities, UCL.

Skipp, A. and Hopwood, V. (2019) *Deployment of Teaching Assistants in Schools*, London: DfE.

Slee, R. and Weiner, G. (2001) 'Education reform and reconstruction as a challenge to research genres: reconsidering school effectiveness research and inclusive schooling', *School Effectiveness and Improvement*, 12(1): 83–98.

Smithers, A. and Robinson, P. (2003) *Factors Affecting Teachers' Decisions to Leave the Profession*, Liverpool: Centre for Education and Employment Research.

Smithers, A. and Robinson, P. (2004) *Teacher Turnover, Wastage and Destinations*, Liverpool: Centre for Education and Employment Research.

Smyth, J. (ed.) (1989) *Critical Perspectives on Educational Leadership*, London: Falmer Press.

Smyth, J. (2017) *The Toxic University, Zombie Leadership, Academic Rock Starts and Neoliberal Ideology*, London: Palgrave Macmillan.

Smyth, J., Down, B., McInerney, P., and Hattam, R. (2014) *Doing Critical Educational Research*, New York, NY: Peter Lang.

Social Mobility Commission (2020) 'Monitoring social mobility', [online], Available from: https://assets.publishing.service.gov.uk/government/uploads/system/uploads/attachment_data/file/891155/Monitoring_report_2013-2020_-Web_version.pdf [Accessed 16 June 2021].

SSAT (Specialist Schools and Academies Trust) (2007) *City Technology Colleges: Conception and Legacy*, London: SSAT.

Star Academies (2021) 'Star Academies signs partnership agreement with Eton College', [online], Available from: https://staracademies.org/news-story/star-academies-signs-partnership-agreement-with-eton-college/ [Accessed 28 June 2021].

Stevens, J., Brown, J., Knibbs, S., and Smith, J. (2005) *Follow-Up Research into the State of School Leadership in England. Research Report 633*, London: DfES/Mori.

Stewart, H. (2003) 'Storm out of blue skies', *Times Educational Supplement*, 5 December.

Stewart, H. (2019) 'Boris Johnson claimed children of working mothers "more likely to mug you"', *The Guardian*, [online] 4 December, Available from: https://www.theguardian.com/politics/2019/dec/04/boris-johnson-claimed-children-of-working-mothers-more-likely-to-mug-you [Accessed 27 April 2021].

Stoker, G. (2006) *Why Politics Matters*, Basingstoke: PalgraveMacmillan.

Stoll, L. and Fink, D. (1996) *Changing Our Schools: Linking School Effectiveness and School Improvement*, Buckingham: Open University Press.

Stone, J. (2021) 'Priti Patel says fans have right to boo England team for "gesture politics" of taking the knee', [online], Available from: https://www.independent.co.uk/news/uk/politics/priti-patel-taking-knee-boo-england-b1865409.html [Accessed 2 August 2021].

Street, P. (2005) *Segregated Schools*, New York, NY: Routledge.

Stringer, C. (2021) 'Strikes at Peacehaven Heights and Telscombe Cliffs "likely"', *The Argus*, [online], Available from: https://www.theargus.co.uk/news/19073355.strikes-peacehaven-heights-telscombe-cliffs-likely/ [Accessed 7 May 2021].

Stubbs, M. (2003) *A Head of the Class*, London: John Murray.

Sumroy, A.L. (2022) '"We're not robots!": the interaction of co-operativism and neoliberalism for students at a Co-op academy', *British Journal of Sociology of Education*, [online], Available from: https://www.tandfonline.com/doi/pdf/10.1080/01425692.2021.2018649?needAccess=true

Tapper, T. (1997) *Fee-Paying Schools and Educational Change in Britain*, London: The Woburn Press.

Taylor, C. (2009) *A Good School for Every Child*, Abingdon: Routledge.

Taylor, E. (2021) '"No fear": privilege and the navigation of hierarchy at an elite boys' school in England', *British Journal of Sociology of Education*. DOI: 10.1080/01425692.2021.1953374

Taylor, G. (2010) *The New Political Sociology*, New York, NY: PalgraveMacmillan.

Taylor, J. (2021) 'South Dakota teachers scramble for dollar bills in "demeaning" game', *The Guardian*, [online] 13 December, Available from: https://www.theguardian.com/us-news/2021/dec/13/teachers-scramble-dollar-bills-south-dakota-dash-for-cash [Accessed 10 January 2022].

Teddlie, C. and Reynolds, D. (2001) 'Countering the critics: responses to recent criticisms of school effectiveness research', *School Effectiveness and School Improvement*, 12(1): 41–81.

Tett, G. (2021) 'Goldman Sachs', *Prospect*, November 2021, 9.

Thatcher, M. (1987) *General Election Press Conference (Health and Social Security)* [online], Available from: https://www.margaretthatcher.org/document/106866 [Accessed 29 November 2021].

The Equality Trust (2021) 'The scale of economic inequality in the UK', [online], Available from: https://www.equalitytrust.org.uk/scale-economic-inequality-uk [Accessed 15 March 2021].

The Trussell Trust (2021) '24th November 2021, More than 5,100 food parcels given to people facing crisis across the UK every day in the past six months, says the Trussell Trust', [online], Available from: https://www.trusselltrust.org/2021/11/24/more-than-5100-food-parcels-given-to-people-facing-crisis-across-the-uk-every-day-in-past-six-months-says-the-trussell-trust/ [Accessed 7 February 2022].

Thomas, H., Brown, C., Butt, G., Gunter, H.M.., Lance, A., and Rayner, S. (2002) *Baseline Evaluation of the TSW Pathfinder Project*, Report to the DfES.

Thomas, H., Butt, G., Fielding, A., Gunter, H.M., Lance, A., and Rayner, S. (2004) *The TSW Pathfinder Project: Final Report*, Report to the DfES.

Thomson, P. (2005) 'Bringing Bourdieu to policy sociology: codification, misrecognition and exchange value in the UK context', *Journal of Education Policy*, 20(6): 741–758.

Thompson, P. (2013) 'Why Michael Gove's invocation of Gramsci misses the point of his work', *The Guardian*, [online] 6 February, Available from: https://www.theguardian.com/commentisfree/2013/feb/06/michael-gove-gramsci-misses-point [Accessed 2 August 2021].

Thomson, P. (2020) *School Scandals*, Bristol: Policy Press.

Thomson, P. and Gunter, H.M. (2006) 'From "consulting pupils" to "pupils as researchers": a situated case narrative', *British Educational Research Journal*, 32(6): 839–856.

Thrupp, M. (2001) 'Sociological and political concerns about school effectiveness research: time for a new agenda', *School Effectiveness and School Improvement*, 12(1): 7–40.

Thrupp, M. and Willmott, R. (2003) *Education Management in Managerialist Times*, Maidenhead: OUP.

Todd, S. (2021) *Snakes and Ladders, The Great British Social Mobility Myth*, London: Chatto and Windus.

Tomlinson, S. (1997) 'Sociological perspectives on failing schools', *International Studies in Sociology of Education*, 7(1): 81–98.

Tomlinson, S. (2005) *Education in a Post-welfare Society*, Maidenhead: Open University Press.

Tooley, J. (2000) *Reclaiming Education*, London: Continuum.

Tooley, J. with Darby, D. (1998) *Educational Research: A Critique. A Survey of Published Educational Research*, London: OfSTED.

Topper, K. (2011) 'Arendt and Bourdieu between word and deed', *Political Theory*, 39(3): 352–377.

Troyna, B. (1994) 'Critical social research and education policy', *British Journal of Educational Studies*, 42(1): 70–84.

TTA (1998) *National Standards for Qualified Teacher Status, Subject Leaders, Special Educational Needs Co-ordinators, Headteachers*, London: TTA.

van den Berg, C., Howlett, M., Gunter, H.M. Howard, M., Migone, A., and Pemer, F. (2020) *Policy Consultancy in Comparative Perspective: Patterns, Nuances and Implications for the Contractor State*, Cambridge: Cambridge University Press.

van Zanten, A., Ball, S.J., and Darchy-Koechlin, B. (eds) (2015) *Elites, Privilege and Excellence, The National and Global Redefinition of Educational Advantage*, Abingdon: Routledge.

Veck, W. and Gunter, H.M. (Eds.) (2020) *Hannah Arendt on Educational Thinking and Practice in Dark Times: Education for a World in Crisis*. London: Bloomsbury.

Wacquant, L.J.D. (1989) 'Towards a reflexive sociology: a workshop with Pierre Bourdieu', *Sociological Theory*, 7(1): 26–63.

Wacquant, L.J.D. (1996) 'Foreword', in: Bourdieu, P., *The State Nobility*, Cambridge: Polity Press, pp ix–xxii.

Wakefield, J. (2021) 'Covid-19: the challenges of home-schooling', BBC, [online], Available from: https://www.bbc.co.uk/news/technology-55573803 [Accessed 11 March 2021].

Wall, T. and Osborne, H. (2018) '"Poor doors" are still creating wealth divide in new housing', *The Guardian*, [online] 25 November, Available from: https://www.theguardian.com/society/2018/nov/25/poor-doors-developers-segregate-rich-from-poor-london-housing-blocks [Accessed 9 March 2021].

Walsh, P. (2016) *Arendt Contra Sociology*, Abingdon: Routledge.

Watt, N. (2013) 'Boris Johnson invokes Thatcher spirit with greed is good speech', *The Guardian*, [online] 27 November, Available from: https://www.theguardian.com/politics/2013/nov/27/boris-johnson-thatcher-greed-good [Accessed 16 March 2021].

Weale, S. (2020) 'Marcus Rashford clashes with Tory MPs over free school meals', *The Guardian*, [online] 21 October, Available from: https://www.theguardian.com/education/2020/oct/21/marcus-rashford-clashes-with-tory-mps-over-free-school-meals [Accessed 29 June 2021].

Webb, R. and Vulliamy, G. (2006) 'The impact of New Labour's education policy on teachers and teaching at Key Stage 2', *Forum*, 48(2): 145–157.

Wedge, P. and Prosser, H. (1973) *Born to Fail?*, London: Arrow Books Limited.

Weekes-Bernard, D. (2007) *School Choice and Ethnic Segregation*, London: The Runnymede Trust.

West, A. (2014) 'Academies in England and independent schools (*fristående skolor*) in Sweden: policy, privatisation, access and segregation', *Research Papers in Education*, 29(3): 330–350.

Whittaker, F. (2019) 'Ministers turn to big business for help running schools', [online], Available from: https://schoolsweek.co.uk/ministers-turn-to-big-business-for-help-running-schools/ [Accessed 14 May 2021].

Whittaker, F. (2020) 'We must change the "fat cat" narrative of anti-academies groups, says CST', [online], Available from: https://schoolsweek.co.uk/we-must-change-the-fat-cat-narrative-of-anti-academies-groups-says-cst/ [Accessed 14 May 2021].

Whittaker R. (2017) 'Goodbye NCTL: hello Teaching Regulation Agency', [online], Available from: https://schoolsweek.co.uk/goodbye-nctl-hello-teaching-regulation-agency/ [Accessed 28 September 2021].

Whitty, G. (2002) *Making Sense of Education Policy*, London: Paul Chapman Press.

Whitty, G., Power, S., and Halpin, D. (1998) *Devolution and Choice in Education*, Buckingham: Open University Press.

Whitty, G. with Anders, J., Hayton, A., Tang, S., and Wisby, E. (2016) *Research and Policy in Education*, London: UCL Institute of Education Press.

Wilby, P (2011) 'Are university technical colleges the next big thing?', *The Guardian*, [online] 1 March, Available from: https://www.theguardian.com/education/2011/mar/01/university-technical-colleges-kenneth-baker [Accessed 23 November 2021].

Wilby, P. (2021) 'Public schools and the public', *New Statesman*, 19–25 March: 50–51.

Wilkins, A. (2016) *Modernising School Governance*, Abingdon: Routledge.

Wilkinson, R. and Pickett, K. (2009) *The Spirit Level*, London: Allen Lane.

Wilson, H. (1963) '*Labour's plan for science*', Speech at the Annual Conference, Scarborough, 1 October, London: Victoria House Printing Company.

Wilson, R.A. (2018) *The Eugenic Mind Project*, Cambridge, MA: Massachusetts Institute of Technology.

Wilson, R., Easton, C., Smith, P., and Sharp, C. (2005) *National Remodelling Team: Evaluation and Impact Study (Year 1), Final Report*, Slough: NFER.

Winkley, D. (2002) *Handsworth Revolution*, London: Giles de la Mare Publishers.

Wiseman, A.W. (2008) 'A culture of (in)equality? A cross-national study of gender parity and gender segregation in national school systems', *Research in Comparative and International Education*, 3(2): 179–201.

Women's Equality Party (2021) 'Why us, why now', [online], Available from: https://www.womensequality.org.uk/why-we [Accessed 15 March 2021].

Wood, M. and Flinders, M. (2014) 'Rethinking depoliticisation: beyond the governmental', *Policy & Politics*, 42(2): 151–170.

Woods, P., Woods, G. and Gunter, H.M. (2007) 'Academy schools and entrepreneurialism in education', *Journal of Education Policy*, 22(2): 263–285.

Wren-Lewis, S. (2018) *The Lies We Were Told*, Bristol: Bristol University Press.

Wright Mills, C. (1977) *The Power Elite*, Oxford: Oxford University Press.

Wrigley, T., Thomson, P., and Lingard, B. (eds) (2012) *Changing Schools: Alternative Ways to Make a World of Difference*, Abingdon: Routledge.

Yeatman, A. (1994) 'Interpreting Contemporary Contractualism', An Inaugural Lecture, School of Behavioural Sciences, Macquarie University, pp 1–12.

Youdell, D. (2016) 'A biosocial education future?', *Research in Education*, 96(1): 52–61.

Youdell, D. and Lindley, M.R. (2019) *Biosocial Education*, Abingdon: Routledge.

Young, M.F.D. (1971) *Knowledge and Control*, London: Collier-Macmillan Publishers.

Young, T. (2015) 'The fall of meritocracy', *Quadrant*, [online], Available from: https://quadrant.org.au/magazine/2015/09/fall-meritocracy/ [Accessed 20 April 2020].

Index

Note: References to tables appear in **bold**.

A

Adams, R. 51
Adonis, A. 30, 75, 124, 131
Allen, R. 7
Arendt, H. 12–14, 15
  action 13, 14, 24, 25, 151, 152
  dark times 12
  lying 5, 15
  natality 13, 14, 31–2, 47, 50, 64–5, 83, 153, 160, 161
  pariah 101, 152, 153, 155
  parvenu 152, 153, 155
  Pentagon Papers 15
  plurality 31–2, 47, 50, 64–5, 83, 109, 153, 159, 161
  public realm 13, 14, 33, 34, 41, 49, 64, 74, 83, 86, 151, 152, 153, 155
  social sciences 12
  table metaphor 48, 151, 160
  thinking without banister 154
  violence 34, 48, 49, 64–65
Asbury, K. 22, 148, 149
Astle, J. 130

B

Bache, I. 39
Bachrach, P. 11
Baehr, P. 149
Baker, K. 53–55
Ball, P. 148–149
Ball, S.J. 91, 101, 142, 143, 156–158
Barber, M. 45, 70, 85, 108, 115
Barczewski, S. 57
Barnes, M. 26
Bauman, Z. 64
Beckett, F. 101
Beetham, D. 65
Bell, R. 128
Benhabib, S. 12
Benn, C. 29
Bernstein, R.J. 12
Bevir, M. 38
Bienkov, A. 22
Blick, A. 8, 29, 40, 117
Blunkett, D. 75, 99, 104, 105, 106
Bobbitt, P. 99
Bonal, X. 7, 8
Bourdieu, P.
  capitals 14, 34, 64, 107, 125
  constitutive naming 14
  doxa 14, 48
  field 151, 155, 160
  game 47, 51, 64, 79, 146, 151
  habitus 14, 107, 114, 139, 142, 151
  hyperbolic doubt 49
  illusio 14, 47, 64, 102, 151
  power 12
  public participation 13, 34
  social sciences 155
  state metaphor 39–40
  symbolic capital 14
  symbolic violence 33
  violence 33–34
Bowe, R. 58, 59
Bowring, F. 13, 64
Bows, H. 144
Brighouse, T. 108
Budge, D. 87
Burnham, P. 39
Burt, C. 147
Butler, P. 82
Butt, G. 91
Byrne, D. 159

C

Caldwell, B.J. 56
Carney, M. 9
change 4–5, 90, 91, 93–94, **120**, 122, 123, 134–135
Charter Cities Institute 38
Cheema, G.S. 39
Chernilo, D. 8
Chitty, C. 19, 29, 42, 52, 147
Clarke, J. 53
Clarke, M. 154–155
Clemens, E.S. 11
Coldron, J. 28
Collarbone, P. 88, 90, 94, 100, 108
Collins, P.H. 153, 154
Coopers and Lybrand 3, 55, 99
Coughlan, S. 1
Courtney, S.J. 5, 44, 45, 61, 63, 74, 147
COVID-19 19, 35, 72, 82
Cox, C.B. 30, 43
Cox, R.W. 47–48, 146
Critical Education Policy Studies (CEPS) 15–16, 128–144, 145, 160–161
  examples of research groups
    Educational Effectiveness and Improvement Research (EEIR) 134–135, 141–142
    Educational Administration (EA) 132

200

Educational Management, Administration and Leadership (EMAL) 132–133
Policy Entrepreneurs and Popularisers (PEP) 138
Policy Research Regime (PRR) 101–102
Policy Sociology (PS) 101, 141, 142–143, 153
research positioning in 129–144
policy description 130–133
policy entrepreneurialism **130**, 136–139
policy scholarship **130**, 140–143
policy science **130**, 133–135
Cruddas, L. 44
Cunliffe, R. 90
Curtis, P. 29, 94

D

Daily Telegraph 73
Dale, R. 55, 58, 59, 141, 155, 157
Davidson, J.D. 10, 38
democracy 26, 38, 51, 54, 69, 111, 121, 153, 161
choice 24
citizenship 14
consent 45, 49, 92, 116, 117, 118
democratisation 39, 41, 120
elective dictatorship 8
institutions 39, 49
parental citizenship choice 14
parental consumer choice 121
participation 13
public interest 73
Dennett, K. 113
Dickens, J. 69
Donnor, J.K. 7
Dorling, D. 9, 29, 35, 148
Draghi, M. 9
Dreary, I. 148
du Gay, P. 37
du Quesnay, H. 108
Dunleavy, P. 39

E

Easterling, K. 38
Education Policy Knowledgeable Polity (EPKP) framework
club
hierarchy 15, 30–31, 39, 44, 77, 80, 125
oligarchy 9, 36–37, 39, 43–44, 45, 51, 71, 72
oligarchic club sovereignty 2, 9–11, 25, 26–27, 33, 36, 40, 41, 49, 52, 129
sovereignty 24–26, 49, 158
governing 35–50, 158
agora 64, 65, 145, 151, 152, 153–154, 161

governance 55–56
government 156
governmentality 38
knowledge production 15, 35, 36–50, **115**, 146
modernizing education 19–34
civil/civic sovereignty 25–26
corporate sovereignty 25, 26
enlightenment sovereignty 25, 26
medieval sovereignty 24–25
trade sovereignty 25
policy mortality 51–65
institutionalised governance 55–56, 111
failure 2, 15, 22, 33, 47, 52, 56–57, 79, 93, 125
failing schools 57–58, 69, 80
knowledgeable state 52–56, 110
political sociology 11–16, 156, 158, 159
of and about CEPS 146–150
for and by CEPS 151–159
political studies 156, 159
sociology 155, 156
social sciences 12, 43, 155, 156
Education Policy Knowledgeable Polity projects 2, 11–16
Academies Programme Projects 79, 128
Consultants and consultancy projects 55, 58, 61, 71, 73, 100–101, 108, 133, 136–139
details of individual projects 162–164
Distributed leadership and the Social Practices of School Organisation in England Project 132
Kingswood High School projects 122–126
Knowledge Production in Educational Leadership project 102, 104
Students as Researchers Project 122–123
Transforming the School Workforce Pathfinder Project 88–95
Theme 1: system design 59–60, 74–80
Theme 2: the workforce 60–61, 87–95
Theme 3: policy actors 61–62, 98–102, 112
Theme 4: knowledge production 62–63, 84–85
Education Reform Claimocracy (ERC) 2–6
academisation 124, 129–130
attack on LA system 51
attack on teaching profession 87
biopolitical distinctiveness 41
blame 144
capital investment 64
claimocracy 2
education research 45–46
EPKP projects 12
eugenicist populism 19, 28–29, 35
exchange relationships 119, 120

failing schools 57–58
fictions 5
functional problem-solving 47
lying 5
media 57, 73, 101
mimicry 5
NLPR 108
oligarchic club sovereignty 9, 10, 11, 33–34
simplifications 4, 5
soundbites 4
spin 4
system design 74–80
There Is No Alternative (TINA) 160
vantage points 73–74, 123
whatness 13, 14
Equality Trust 20
eugenics and genetics 14
  biopolitical distinctiveness 41
  discrimination 20, 23
  disposability of people 40
  genetically sensitive schools 149
  in education policy 29–31
  in Education Reform Claimocracy 19, 28–9, 35
  epigenetics 22, 149
eugenicist populism 2, 6, 13, 14, 19, 21–23, 24, 52, 73, 121
Evans, G. 146
Evans, G. 148
Everard, S. 128, 144
examinations in England
  A levels 35, 90, 122
  BTEC 79
  GCSEs 79, 122
Express and Star 28

F

Fabes, R.A. 7
Fairburn, C. 113
Fairclough, N. 4
Fay, B. 154, 161
Ferguson, D. 95
Field, J.A. 21
Fielding, M. 109
Finlayson, A. 25
Fitzgerald, T. 122
Foucault, M. 38
Frankfurt, H. 5
Friedman, M. 37
Fullan, M. 134–135

G

Galton, F. 1, 21
Gamsu, S. 30
Garner, R. 86
George, M. 90
Gibbons, M. 108
Gillborn, D. 147

Goodwin, M. 114–115, 159
Goody, J. 86
Gorard, S. 28
Gorski, P.C. 5, 6
Gove, M. 86
Grace, G. 142
Gramsci, A. 1, 4, 86
Grant, H. 1
Green, F. 30
Greenhalgh, R. 108
Gregory, A. 83
Grek, S. 157
Gunter, H.M. viii, ix, 1, 5, 9, 12, 24, 25, 26, 27, 29, 30, 37, 40, 41, 44–45, 47, 49, 51, 53, 55, 57, 58, 59, 60, 61, 62, 69, 70, 71, 72, 73, 74, 83, **84**, 87, 89, 91, 93, 95, **98**, 99, 100, 102, 103, 109, 110, 114, **115**, 119, 121, 122, 123, 124, 125, 129, **130**, 132, 136, 138, 140, 142, 151, 152, 156, 158, 162
  (*see also* Critical Education Policy Studies; Education Policy Knowledgeable Polity projects; Thinking Politically-Sociologically Framework)

H

Hailsham, Lord 8
Halfon, R. 90
Hall, V. 104
Hallam, S. 7
Hallinger, P. 104
Halpin, D. 101, 155, 156
Harden, K.P. 147
Harding, E. 57, 97, 98
Hargreaves, D.H. 85
Harris, J. 9, 10
Harvey, D. 52
Hatcher, R. 157
Havel, V. 5–6
Hayek, F.A. 37
Hazell, W. 27
Henry, D. 83
Henry, J. 113
Hill, S. 152, 160
Hindess, B. 117
Hogan, A. 56
Hopkins, D. 108, 109
Horgan, G. 33
Howlett, M. 58
Hughes, B.C. 45, 100, 152
Hyman, P. 73, 161

I

Independent 86

J

Jackson, B. 29, 147
Jackson, D. 108

Index

Jenkins, R. 13, 161
Jessop, B. 157
Johnson, A. 106
Johnson, B. 10, 22, 28, 30, 73
Johnson, R. 30
Jones, O. 9, 30
Joseph, K. 28, 41–42

K

Kakutani, M. 6
Kaufmann, E. 1
Kavanagh, D. 8
Keay, D. 82
Kelly, R. 105, 106
Kennelly, J. 12, 13, 14, 151
Kevles, D.J. 1
Kickert, W. 39
Kincheloe, J.L. 5
King, D. 8
Kwarteng, K. 38

L

leadership 29, 60, 102–103, 131, 141, 142
Leithwood, K. 85
Levačić, R. 8
Levine, P. 21
Levitsky, S. 38
Lightfoot, L. 58
Longfield, A. 19
Lowe, R. 21
Lucey, H. 33
Lupton, R. 58

M

MacGilchrist, B. 85
Mackay, T. 108
Macpherson, C.B. 64
Mail Online 86
Malnick, E. 145
Mann, M. 10–11
Mansell, W. 31, 44
Marinetto, M. 39
Marquand, D. 9, 21, 26, 36
Mason, R. 22
May, T. 33, 34
McBain, S. 128, 129
McConnell, A. 58
McGinity, R. 69, 74, 122, 123, 124, 125
McNamara, O. 27
Means, A.J. 156
Meatto, K. 1
Meyers, C.V. 57
Miliband, D. 147
Miller, C. 57
Miller, P. 38
Milliken, M. 27
Mitchell, H. 108
Monbiot, G. 161
Moran, M. 10, 26, 39, 53, 87

Müller, J-W. 21
Muller, J.Z. 47
Munby, S. 116

N

Neave, G. 53
Nichols, T. 74
Nixon, J. 12, 64, 65

O

O'Brien, J. 41
OECD 7
Olusoga, D. 23
"One Britain One Nation" (OBON) 97
Osborne, H. 1, 6
Ostrom, E. 25
Ozga, J. 101, 157, 158, 159

P

Parker, M. 140, 152
Pearton, M. 52
Peck, S. 28
Pells, R. 34
personalisation 146–149
  eugenicist personalisation 147
  genetic personalisation 147–149
  service personalisation 147
Pill, H. 9
Plomin, R. 148
policy violence 2, 15, 151, 160
  authorized 46, 47–48, 49, 78, 92, 106–107, 125
  legitimised 15, 20, 33, 76, 89, 90, 104, 105, 123
  intelligent 52, 63, 79, 93, 150
politics 26, 38, 58, 59, 64, 97, 121, 155, 157
  depoliticization 40–41, 43, 48, 75, 92, 99, 110
  depoliticised corporatisation 40, 44–45, 55
  depoliticised governing 15
  depoliticised populism 41, 45, 55
  depoliticised privatism 40, 44, 55
  politicisation 37
  repolitizisation 95, 99
Pollitt, C. 40
Portwood, N. 108
PricewaterhouseCoopers (PwC) 130

R

Raab, D. 141, 155
Ranson, S. 11, 47, 48, 143, 152–153
Rashford, M. 82, 83
Ravitch, D. 5
Rawnsley, A. 10
Rayner, Sir D. 27
Rayner, S.M. 59, 61, 69, 74
Reay, D. 28, 33, 140

Rees-Mogg, W. 10, 38
Revell, P. 94
Reynolds, D. 72, 134
Ribbins, P. 53–54
Rooks, N. 7
Ross, A. 88
Rothstein, R. 7
Rubin, R. 9
Rush, M. 11
Rushton, S. 113
Russell, J. 140
Rutherford, A. 23

S

Salt, T. 108
Saltman, K.J. 41
Sammons, P. 84
Sara, S. 128
Savage, M. 153
school workforce 89
  headteachers 4, 29, 60–61, 72, 73, 88, 90, 102–103, 131, 137, 141
  performance management 41
  professional knowledge 63
  professionalism 60
  remodelling 89, 91, 92
  student-teacher relationships 9–10
  Teach First (TF) 90
  Teaching Assistants (TAs) 90, 91, 93
  teaching profession 87–95
  trade unions 72, 94
  workforce 60–61, 87–95
  workload 88, 90–91, 92–93
schools
  academisation 51, 69, 79, 81, 124–125, 129–130
  Birch Tree school 118, 132
  City Academies 75
  City Technical Colleges (CTCs) 30, 53, 55
  comprehensive schools 27–28, 54–55, 75, 76, 86
  Confederation of School Trusts (CTS) 44
  Eton College 113, 126
  Fair Admissions Campaign 28
  faith schools 27, 33, 80
  free schools 51, 90
  grammar schools 27, 28, 33, 34, 55
  grant mainlined status (GMT) 30, 53–4, 71
  Harris Federation 31
  home education 27
  Kingswood High School (KHS) 122–126
  Local Authority maintained schools 51, 69, 70
  Local Management of Schools (LMS) 3
  Metropolitan City Academy (MCA) 75–80
  Multi-Academy Trusts (MATs) 31, 43, 44, 51, 69, 70, 80
  Peacehaven Heights Primary School 51
  private/fee paying schools private schools 9–10, 27, 30, 33, 35, 74, 86, 113
  public education 11, 35, 42–43, 45, 74
  pupil referral units 27
  Regional School Commissioner (RSC) 43
  secondary modern schools 27
  school places 44–45, 75
  Self-Evaluation Framework (SEF) 62
  special schools 27
  Specialist Schools and Academies Trust (SSAT) 31, 71, 101
  Star Academies MAT 113, 126
  studio schools 51
  system design 59–60, 74–80
  Telscombe Cliffs Primary School 51
  University Technical Colleges (UTC) 55
Scope 20
Scott, J.C. 4
Seddon, T. 158
segregation
  austerity 5, 94
  cohesion 118
  de facto 7, 77
  de jure 7
  disability 20
  domestic abuse 20
  parental/household income and wealth 19, 20
  food banks 82, 83
  free school meals 82–83
  gender 23, 128, 144
  housing 1
  individualism 24
  inequality 9, 20, 21, 22
  life expectancy (LE) 21
  permanent exclusions 28
  race inequality 20
  racism 28, 97
  rape 20, 128
  sexism/sexual abuse 128
  social mobility 31–32, 81
  unemployment 20
segregated education 6, 11, 27, 35
  ability 147
  class 7
  gender 7
  poverty 19, 20, 82
  race 7
  schools, between 28, 33
  schools, within 27
Sennett, R. 91
Shain, F. 28
Shepherd, J. 29

Singh, K. 97
Skipp, A. 94
Smith, D. 101
Smyth, J. 91, 154
Southworth, G. 108
Stewart, H. 28, 88, 90
Stoker, G. 25
Stone, J. 97
Street, P. 7
Stringer, C. 51
Sunak, R. 8–9
Sunday Telegraph 145

T

Tapper, T. 155
Taylor, E. 9–10
Taylor, G. 157
Taylor, J. 159
Taylor, Sir C. 71, 85, 100–101
Tett, G. 8
Thinking Politically-Sociologically Framework (TPSF) 15–16, 65
  exchange relationships and contractualism 114–119, 150
    cultural **115**, 117–119, 121
    employment **115**, 116
    personal 115–116, 121
    project **115**, 116–117
    socio-political **115**, 117
  intellectual histories 129, 146
    activism 153–155, 160, 161
    description 130–133, 156
    entrepreneurialism **130**, 136–139, 156
    scholarship **130**, 140–143
    science **130**, 133–135
  regimes of practice 98–102, 114, 150
    satellite **98**, 117, 119
      School Leadership Satellite Regime (SLSR) 100, 101, 108
    star **98**, 101–102, 117
      Policy Research Regime (PRR) 101–102
    state **98**, 99–100, 115, 116–117, 118–119
      Conservative Privatisation Regime (CPR) 99, 100, 106
      New Labour Performance Regime (NLPR) 99–100, 101–102, 103, 104, 106, 107, 108, 116
  vantage points 69–80, 109, 149
    core 70, 73, 76, 77, 83, 123, 129, 149
    marginal 71–72, 85–86, 124
    othered 72, 73, 85–86, 86, 101
    privileged 71, 73, 76, 77, 79, 80, 83, 138, 149
  viewpoints 83–95, 109, 149
    approaches

    critical **84**, 85
    interpretive 84
    positivist 84
    critical social justice **84**, 85, 94, 95
    functional science 84, **84**
    narrative description **84**, 85
    normative functionalism 83, 85, 93, 94, 97
    normative instrumentalism **84**, 85
    standpoints 86
Thomas, H. 87, 89, 91, 92, 93, 94
Thompson, P. 86
Thomson, P. 14, 122
Thrupp, M. 152
Todd, S. 32, 41
Tomlinson, S. 53, 57, 99
Tooley, J. 72
Topper, K. 12, 13, 33
Troyna, B. 153, 157
Trussell Trust 82

U

UK Government
  civil service 40
  DCSF (Department for Children, Schools and Families) 147
  DfE (Department for Education) 6, 20, 27, 30, 51, 53, 57, 88, 124, 129, 130, 140
  DfEE (Department for Education and Employment) 3–4, 6, 75, 87, 88, 102, 103, 104–5, 107, 109, 140
  DfES (Department for Education and Skills) 56, 57, 88–90, 91, 104, 106, 107, 111
  Efficiency Unit 27
  Equality and Human Rights Commission 20
  Innovation Unit 122
  Local Authorities 70
  National College for Leadership of Schools and Children's Services (NCLSCS) 106
  National College for School Leadership (NCSL) 63, 103–112, 116, 132
  National College for Teaching and Leadership (NCTL) 106
  National Remodelling Team (NRT) 94
  Office for National Statistics 20–21
  Ofsted 58, 59, 73, 84, 126
  public services 11, 25, 37, 146
  System Partnership Unit 113
  Whitehall 56, 70, 71, 104, 107
  Workforce Agreement Monitoring Group (WAMG) 94
UK Government policies
  Building Schools for the Future (BSF) 77
  Education Acts 53

Education Reform Act (ERA) 1988 3, 87
Every Child Counts 72
Higher Standards, Better Schools for All 29
"Mythbuster" (DfES) 129
National Agreement 94
Police, Crime, Sentencing and Courts Bill 161
Reducing the Bureaucratic Burden on Teachers (DfES 2002) 89
teachers: meeting the challenges of change (DfEE 1998) 4, 109
Time for Standards (DfES 2002) 88, 94
Workforce Reform (DfES) 90
UK Governments
  Blair government 99
  Blair, T. 6–8, 70, 73, 103, 104 (*see also* New Labour)
  Brown, G. 72
  Brown government 99
  Conservative-Brexit government 99
  Conservative-led Coalition 99, 129
  Conservative Party 121
  Major government 99
  New Labour 3, 130
  New Right 45
  Thatcher government 37, 99
  Thatcher, M. 121, 146
  Thatcherism 26, 101
universities 70, 116
US 7, 15, 74, 159

V

van den Berg, C. 53
van Zanten, A. 1
Varnhagen, R. 152

W

Wacquant, L.J.D. 12, 46
Wakefield, J. 19
Wall, T. 1
Walsh, P. 12, 14
Watt, N. 22
Weale, S. 83
Wedge, P. 22
Whittaker, R. 44, 106
Whitty, G. 100, 101, 142
Wilby, P. 30
Wilkinson, R. 9, 19
Williamson, G. 51, 97
Wilshaw, M. 73
Wilson, H. 29
Wilson, R. 94
Wilson, R.A. 21, 22, 23, 86, 156
Women's Equality Party 20
Wood, M. 40
Woodhead, C. 28–29
Woods, P. 44
Wren-Lewis, S. 5, 74

Y

Yeatman, A. 118
Youdell, D. 147, 149

www.ingramcontent.com/pod-product-compliance
Lightning Source LLC
Chambersburg PA
CBHW051543020426
42333CB00016B/2067